The Essentials of Husserl

Studies in Transcendental Phenomenology

V. C. Thomas

Pondicherry University

and

Centre for Phenomenological Studies, India

Series in Philosophy

VERNON PRESS

www.vernonpress.com

In the Americas:
Vernon Press
1000 N West Street, Suite 1200
Wilmington, Delaware, 19801
United States

In the rest of the world:
Vernon Press
C/Sancti Espiritu 17,
Malaga, 29006
Spain

Series in Philosophy

Library of Congress Control Number: 2020931406

ISBN: 978-1-64889-868-6

Also available: 978-1-62273-913-4 [Hardback], 978-1-64889-612-5 [PDF, E-Book]

Cover design by Vernon Press. Cover image from Wikimedia / Public domain.

Dedicated to Lucy, Anisha and Ashish
For what they are to me

Table of contents

List of Figures and Tables   *ix*

Acknowledgements   *xi*

Preface   *xiii*

Chapter 1   **Introduction**   1

     1.1 References   7

Chapter 2   **Phenomenology: A Study of Self and Beyond**   9

     2.1 What is Phenomenology?   9

     2.2 The Phenomenology of Self   17

     2.3 Beyond the Self   18

     2.4 References   20

     2.5 Further reading   21

Chapter 3   **Consciousness and Intentionality:
The Perspective of Husserl**   23

     3.1 Man, World and Intentionality   23

     3.2 Brentano's Notion of Intentionality 28

     3.3 The Basic Features of Husserl's Intentionality
Theory   30

     3.4 Characteristics of Intentionality   33

     3.5 Temporality of Intentionality   35

     3.6 Human Body in the Context of Intentionality 35

     3.7 Discussion on Mohanty's Theses 3, 15, 20 and 1 37

     3.8 References   38

Chapter 4   **Husserl's Investigation of Meaning**   41

     4.1 The Question of Meaning: Preliminaries 41

     4.2 Meanings and Monologue (Non-Linguistic
Expressions)   45

     4.3 Ideality of Meanings   47

	4.4 Meaning and Reference	49
	4.5 Platonic Theory of Meaning-Ontology and Ideality	53
	4.6 Meaning and Essence	55
	4.7 References	60
Chapter 5	**Natural Attitude, Epoché and Reductions**	**63**
	5.1 Natural Attitude	63
	5.2 Suspension of Natural Attitude	64
	5.3 Epoché	65
	5.4 Phenomenological Reductions	68
	5.5 Concluding Remarks	74
	5.6 References	76
Chapter 6	**Husserl's Treatment of Noesis and Noema: Conflict and Convergence**	**77**
	6.1 Introduction	77
	6.2 The Conflict: Gurwitsch and Føllesdal on the Notion of *Noema*	83
	6.3 Føllesdal's Treatment of *Noema*	85
	6.4 Possible Convergence of the views of Gurwitsch and Føllesdal	93
	6.5 References	100
Chapter 7	**Husserl's Examination of Lived Body**	**103**
	7.1 Introduction	103
	7.2 History of Husserl's Study of Body	104
	7.3 The Distinction Between *Leib* and *Körper*	105
	7.4 Three Ways of Studying Human Body	107
	7.5 Problems of Primacy of Touch	111
	7.6 Lived Body: The In-Between	111
	7.7 The Lived Body and Intentionality	112
	7.8 Interiority and Exteriority of the Body	113
	7.9 Lived Body and Perception	113
	7.10 Lived Body, Intersubjectivity and Empathy	114
	7.11 The Body of Others	115

7.12 Consequences of not having a Lived Body   116

7.13 Conclusions   116

7.14 References   118

Chapter 8   **Life world: A Conceptual Overview**   123

8.1 Introduction   123

8.2 From the World of Science to Life world   127

8.3 References   132

Chapter 9   **Husserl's Notion of The Other and
                Intersubjectivity**   135

9.1 Introduction   135

9.2 Part 1: The treatment of intersubjectivity in CM
    (V Meditation)   136

9.3 The Other and Myself (CM 55)   140

9.4 The Treatment of Intersubjectivity after CM   142

9.5 Conclusions   146

9.6 References   151

Chapter 10   **Husserl's Understanding of Lived Time** 153

10.1 Introduction   153

10.2 Husserl's Study of Time-Consciousness
     at Different Periods   156

10.3 Basic Notions in the Study of Time-Consciousness   159

10.4 Conclusions   175

10.5 References   177

10.6 Further reading   178

Chapter 11   **Conclusions**   181

Chapter 12   **Appendix**   191

12.1 On Presuppositionlessness in Phenomenology   191

12.2 References   193

Bibliography   195

Index   205

List of Figures and Tables

List of Figures

Figure 2.1 Relationship between the ego, consciousness and object   13

Figure 10.1 Relation among Retention, Protention and Prime impression   160

Figure 10.2 Primal Impression and its Horizons   161

Figure 10.3 Relation between Retention and Double Intentionality. The arrow represents the flow of a river, while its contents, X, Y, A, B, C, etc., represent the objects floating in it   165

Figure 10.4 The temporal nature of Protention, Primal impression and Retention   169

List of Tables

Table 6.1 Part and whole, explaining the relation between *Sinn* and *Bedeutung*   87

Table 8.1 Comparison of the world of Science and Life world   130

Table 10.1 Categorization of various sections of Husserliana X (1966): On the Phenomenology of the Consciousness of Internal Time (1893-1917)   157

Acknowledgements

I would like to express my most sincere thanks and heartfelt gratitude to Dr James Kurian, Head, Department of Philosophy, Madras Christian College, Chennai, who supplied me with all the necessary books for my study and reflection. I shall ever remain grateful to him for his kindness and generosity.

I would also like to express my sincere thanks to Dr E. P. Mathew, SJ, Department of Philosophy, Loyola College, Chennai for his constant support, inspiration, continued interest and encouragement in my work.

I would also like to thank Professor N. N. Natarajan, former Head, Department of English, Pondicherry University for proposing several valuable corrections in my work.

Centre for Phenomenological Studies conducted a one-month long course on Husserl's Phenomenology at Sri Aurobindo Centre for Advanced Research (SACAR), Pondicherry in October 2017. Twenty philosophy research scholars and teachers from different parts of India participated in the programme. I had opportunities to deliver lectures and participate in various discussions with them. I gained a lot from their critical observations and evaluatory comments. I am grateful to each one of them for their contributions to improve my understanding of the nuances of the various notions of Husserl that also helped sharpen my knowledge of phenomenology. I thank the authorities of SACAR for accommodating us during the programme.

V. C. Thomas

Preface

This book, *The Essentials of Husserl: Studies in Transcendental Phenomenology*, consists of ten well-studied and intensely researched essays, apart from an introduction and a brief appendix. After having studied the various phases of Husserl's phenomenology, namely, the realist, the static, the transcendental, the genetic, as well as the writings of the post-*Crisis*[1] (*of European Sciences*) period, I have selected topics considered to be representative of each period, for this book. Surely one can argue that other topics are important as well. I do not deny it. However, the importance of the topics selected here is undeniable as well.

Phenomenology: A Study of Self and Beyond (**Chapter 2**) focuses on the fundamental aspects of phenomenology as a study of modes of self, irrespective of its different phases. *Consciousness and Intentionality: The Perspective of Husserl* (**Chapter 3**) is the fulcrum upon which phenomenology rotates, considering the same to be a study of our conscious experiences. I am of the firm belief that *Husserl's Investigation of Meaning* (**Chapter 4**) is a very important topic in *Logical Investigations*. Although there is cosmetic change in Husserl's understanding of meaning from time to time, the sum and substance of his understanding of meaning remains almost the same throughout his phenomenology. One thing is for sure: phenomenology is a search for meaning, not for the meaning of words and expressions (these can be found in lexicographical works) but a search for the most personal and subjective kind of meanings. *Natural Attitude, Epoché and Reductions* (**Chapter 5**) and *Husserl's Treatment of Noesis and Noema: Conflict and Convergence* (**Chapter 6**) are the cruxes of the transcendental phases represented by *Ideas I*. It is this phase that distinguishes Husserl's phenomenology from all other phenomenologists, be it Heidegger, Jaspers, Sartre or Merleau-Ponty.

Husserl's Examination of Lived-body (**Chapter 7**), based on *Ideas II*, is a link indicating a transition from transcendental to genetic phenomenology. Husserl's phenomenology, which finds its culmination in genetic phenomenology, is represented here by *Life world: A Conceptual Overview* (**Chapter 8**) and is based primarily on the *Crisis of European Sciences and Transcendental Phenomenology*. *Husserl's Notion of the Other and Intersubjectivity* (**Chapter 9**) is based mainly on *Cartesian Meditations*. *Husserl's Understanding of Lived Time* (**Chapter 10**) is based on the various

---

[1] *Crisis* refers to Husserl's book *Crisis of European Sciences and Transcendental Phenomenology* and *Post Crisis* refers to Husserl's writings after the book Crisis.

volumes of *Husserliana*, specifically *volumes VIII, X* and *XXXIII*. Since Husserl's study on time commenced in 1893, long before his phenomenological career, and continued even during his post-*Crisis* period, this book covers not just the various phases of Husserl's phenomenology but his entire career as well. Special attention has been rendered to Husserl's 1904-05 lectures on time consciousness, edited by Heidegger in 1928 and published entitled, *On the Phenomenology of Consciousness of Internal Time*. In addition, short discussions on time consciousness based on *Bernau Manuscripts* and *C-Manuscripts* (*Husserliana volumes VIII* and *XXXIII*) have been included. The latter includes Husserl's contributions to time analysis during his pre-phenomenological, realist and transcendental phases. In my opinion, Husserl's study of time, spread across the different phases of his phenomenology, unifies the various phases of his philosophy. The *Appendix* (**Chapter 12**) concerns Husserl's contention that phenomenology is a presuppositionless science, which is a widely misunderstood concept amongst several authors and commentators. This brief note is the result of my personal studies and inquiries.

I have utilized several examples and simple diagrams to illustrate the nuances of phenomenology to my readers, and especially for the benefit of students. Through these, I strive to put forth my views and thoughts in a simple and straightforward manner.

Chapter 1

Introduction

The principal theme in *Phenomenology: A Study of Self and Beyond* (Chapter 2) is a discussion on the various aspects of phenomenology, including the origin and development of the term itself. I attempt to describe it with an example since nowhere does Husserl define the term phenomenology. While Euclid used the term '*Phainomena*' to characterize heavenly or astronomical bodies, philosophers such as Friedrich Oetinger, Johann Lambert, Earnest Mach and others also attempted to describe the same. There is no evidence to show that Husserl was aware of the contributions of Lambert and Oetinger, but he was well acquainted with and very much appreciative of the part played by Mach. Kant and Hegel were two great philosophers who contributed immensely to the growth of the term 'phenomenology'. While Hegel's contribution can be considered all too important, it was Husserl's teacher, Franz Brentano, who was his immediate source of inspiration.

The second part of the chapter focuses on the notion of the term, 'self'. Though the word 'self' may not appear explicitly in Husserl's realist (static) phenomenological phase, he accepts a kind of Humean understanding of self. But his transcendental phenomenological phase is devoted entirely to the study of transcendental ego in all its richness and variations. In the genetic phenomenological phase, his concern is not just the self or the transcendental ego, which is more or less identified with the human being, but several other things connected with the human. And I refer to the term 'beyond-self' to address his concern for humans and other things connected with the human. This concern for things connected with the human did not appear in his philosophy all of a sudden. A careful study of *Basic Problems of Phenomenology* (Husserl, 2006g) (Husserl's 1909-10 winter semester lectures) indicates that these concerns were in Husserl's mind right from the beginning of his philosophical career. However, he worked them out carefully, patiently and systematically throughout his life.

Consciousness and Intentionality: The Perspective of Husserl (Chapter 3) is devoted to Husserl's perspectives on consciousness and intentionality. All conscious states are intentional, but it can be pointed out that certain physiological acts like nausea and dizziness cannot be said to be intentional, though they are somehow conscious. Is intentionality the same as consciousness? I disagree with their identification. Consciousness has reference to an object, regardless of whether it is real or imaginary. Husserl derived the dictum that consciousness was always in reference to the consciousness of an object from his teacher Brentano, though his understanding of this principle was significantly different from the latter. While Brentano's understanding is akin to an object-theory of intentionality, Husserl leans toward a meaning-theory of intentionality. Intentionality is the primary characteristic of consciousness. It is devoid of not just a causal relationship but also any reference to the Freudian notions of consciousness, sub-consciousness and unconsciousness. The fundamental role of consciousness lies in discovering and establishing meanings. Certain aspects of the well-known Husserlian distinctions among act, content and object are also dealt with in this chapter. In the context of meaning, a brief discussion on *noema* describing the relation between object and meaning is also dealt with, though a full-fledged discussion is reserved for Chapter 5. The rest of the chapter focusses on the static and dynamic aspects of intentionality, with reference to *Logical Investigations* (Husserl, 1977s, 1977t) and *Ideas I* (Husserl, 1976d). The fundamentals of intentionality such as the ability to refer to an object, intentionality as the self-transcending phenomenon, intentionality and constitution, horizons and temporality of intentionality, intentionality and the human body, etc., are also dealt with. To conclude, theses by Prof. J. N. Mohanty, delivered in a lecture in 1996 at Bryn Mawr College, Philadelphia, USA are discussed (Mohanty, 2002b).

Husserl's Investigation of Meaning (Chapter 4) draws attention to the fact that Husserl focuses primarily on meaning in *Logical Investigations* (Husserl, 1977s) followed by several discussions on the same after *Crisis of European Sciences* (Husserl, 1970e). Throughout his journey in phenomenology, Husserl is committed to the question of meaning, not in the lexicographical sense, but rather in the personal sense, posing the question: what does it mean to *me*? Though meaning is usually signified by an expression, in the phenomenological sense, Husserl points out that meanings are ideal entities constituted in our interpretative acts and in our acts of understanding.

We can have different expressions with different meanings referring to one and the same object. In contrast, we can also have multiple acts referring to the same object, which, according to Husserl's identical or ideal meaning, are called universals. In the context of non-linguistical expressions and monologues, Husserl points out that meanings can be expressed outwardly, and articulated words can be dispensed with in the form of monologues or soliloquy, which are not communicative speech in the sense of speaking with others; rather it is a kind of confirmative speech with oneself. We thus transition from communicative speech to confirmative speech, a device in Husserl's subsequent philosophising for inner voice, namely, self-presence. This implies a kind of prefiguration of phenomenological reduction. We move on to touch upon meaning and reference and the Frege-Husserl controversy (Frege, 1960), during which Husserl corrected his own position in *Philosophy of Arithmetic* (Husserl, 2003) while reviewing Schröder's work. The question of the existence of a Platonic element in Husserl's Theory of Meaning is dealt with, along with a discussion on the Aristotelian notion of essence and the Husserlian notion of meaning. The chapter concludes with an analysis of Husserl's position on meaning-intention and meaning-fulfilment, and an exploration of Husserl's treatment of meaning in genetic phenomenology.

The principal theme of *Natural Attitude, Epoché and Phenomenological Reductions: Transcendental Phenomenological Method of Husserl* (Chapter 5) articulates and elucidates 1) natural attitude, 2) epoché, and 3) phenomenological reductions. The discussion on natural attitude includes its definition and basic aspects, how to suspend it, and finally, how to establish the superiority and supremacy of consciousness. Natural attitude is an epistemological problem. It is a negative expression, compelling us to avoid commitment to existence. Epoché is a methodological device enabling us to abstain from accenting the ontological status of the perceived object. This implies that I do not pay attention to the existence of the object perceived since I am concerned phenomenologically with its essence. In other words, in my search for essence, existence becomes irrelevant. After epoché is performed, we arrive at the essence or meaning of the object and at the transcendental ego, which is the source of all meanings, the irreducible foundation from which all reductions arise and all meanings originate. Finally, we reach the phenomenological reduction, the crux of Husserl's transcendental phenomenology, which raises the question, how many reductions are there in Husserl? He starts with one reduction in his *The Idea of Phenomenology* (Husserl, 1999) and concludes by stating that there are eight in *The Crisis of European Sciences and Transcendental Phenomenology* (Husserl, 1970e). Despite such inconsistencies, from a phenomenological point of view, Husserl upholds and defends four reductions: eidetic, psychological and transcendental reductions, mentioned in *Ideas I*, and finally, reduction by way of the ontology of Life world, according to *Crisis of European Sciences* (Husserl, 1970e). To conclude, Husserl should have paid a lot more attention while discussing these reductions, they being such a crucial issue in phenomenology and a source of contention between Husserl and his disciples. However, Husserl held on to the validity of his positions on his reductions until the very end.

The first part of *Noema and Noesis: Conflict and Convergence* (Chapter 6) is a detailed inquiry into Husserl's definition of *noema*. Though Husserl developed the notion of *noema* only in *Ideas I*, its seed was already sprouting in *Logical Investigations*, whence he had an intuition of the same while describing the notions of the content of intended objects, intentional and real content. I, myself, am the real content (*noesis*). The relationships between the essence and *noema*, *noema* and *noesis* and *noema* and transcendent object are also explored in this chapter. The second part of the chapter focuses on the conflict between Aron Gurwitsch and Dagfinn Føllesdal on *noema*. These two remain great milestones in the discussion of *noema*, and a deeper exploration reveals that they seem to be on two sides of the same coin. Gurwitsch's is a notion of perceptual *noema*, i.e., the perceived meaning. Though this notion is not found in *Logical Investigations*, it can be observed in its rudimentary form, especially when Husserl makes a distinction between quality and matter. But Husserl discusses the notion of *noema* in every possible manner in *Ideas I*. One thing is for sure: Gurwitsch's notion of perceptual *noema* goes far beyond the notion of sense perception, and it refers to meanings. The twelve theses of Føllesdal with regard to *noema* based on *Ideas III* are also analysed. In fact, this is the only major source of reference for Føllesdal, though he occasionally referred to *Ideas I*, which in turn is the sole source for Gurwitsch. Apart from Gurwitsch and Føllesdal, scholars like David Smith, Roland MacIntyre, William McKenna, Lenore Langsdrof, Mary Jeanne Larabee and several others have explored the notion of *noema* very seriously, though none surpassed Gurwitsch and Føllesdal. Apart from these, several first-generation disciples of Husserl like Alfred Schütz, Joseph J. Kochelmans and many others also examined the notion of *noema*. Critical analyses of these two scholars' works on *noema* prove that there is little difference between their works, akin to the description of two different sides of the same coin, both of which are essential to paint a complete picture of *noema*.

There is hardly any discussion of the human body in traditional philosophy, and even when the latter was discussed in philosophical contexts, it was held to be an objective, material and physical thing existing in space and time. In *Husserl's Examination of Lived Body* (Chapter 7), we explore Husserl's notion of the lived body, which differed in a very fundamental and foundational manner from traditional philosophy. Its significance grows even now, the distinction between *Körper*, the worldly, physical and objective body, and *Leib*, the living human body. He further added a revolutionary statement that *Leib* was a priori necessary condition to have *Körper*. Husserl's study of body varied at different periods. He started his discussion on body in 1907 in his lectures, *Thing and Space*, and continued the same during his winter semester lectures of 1910-11, *Basic Problems of Philosophy*, *Ideas II* and *Ideas III*, *Nature and Spirit*, *Phenomenological Psychology*, *Cartesian Mediations* (Husserl, 2006g), *Problems of Inter-subjectivity*, *Life world* and in several other manuscripts. *Leib* has several characteristics, such as organ and field of freedom, organ of perception, zero point of orientation. Husserl's contention that lived body is inserted between the material world and the subjective sphere of consciousness is worth noting. Husserl discusses, not only one's own body, but also the lived body of the other, and this is made possible by means of his concept of empathetic transfer. The importance Husserl confers to the primacy of touch is also studied very carefully. This poses a hypothetical question: what happens to me if I do not have a lived body? The answer to such a question is this: I shall definitely fall into solipsism. In conclusion, a few points essential to the understanding of lived body are discussed.

Husserl on Life world: A Conceptual Overview is the central theme of discussion in Chapter 8. This is a very crucial notion in later Husserlian literatures, especially in *The Crisis of European Sciences and Transcendental Phenomenology*. What does it consist of? Who were its architects? What does it mean? The crisis originated when western philosophy began to move away from concrete and positive realities of everyday experience towards abstract generalisations and objectively valid statements that provide knowledge. In other words, the everyday experiences of the real objective world, the bedrock of phenomenology, were pushed to the background, and instead, the exact and objectively valid knowledge of abstract constructions were brought to the forefront and treated as the most important concerns of daily life. The most eminent scholar who brought out this transformation was Galileo Galilei. Husserl, being a trained mathematician, realized the danger of grasping the universe in mathematical, geometrical terms and abstract frameworks. This is the crisis, not only of European sciences, but rather of any science whatsoever. It consists precisely in this transformation from the concrete to the abstract, from singular to the general. What might then the solution be? The solution consists in retracing one's roots and restart philosophising from the very foundations of one's life. This origin of philosophical speculation is called Life world, the world of the positive and concrete. The world of science is a superstructure built upon it, without which the former is not self-conscious, as claimed correctly by Husserl. Does it mean, therefore, that science, scientists and scientific theories are excluded from the purview of Life world? It appears to be so early on, but Husserl brings them into the purview of Life world in the later part of the discussion. Here, one might accuse Husserl of being unfaithful to his original insight, but a deeper analysis reveals that this is a requirement for expanding the horizon of phenomenology. Furthermore, Husserl defends his contentions with valid reasons and cogent justifications.

Chapter 9 speaks of *Husserl's Notion of the Other and Intersubjectivity*. Several scholars consider the fact that Husserl hardly speaks of the other as one of his fundamental weaknesses. This might be true for those familiar only with *Logical Investigations* and *Ideas I* (Husserl's static phenomenology phase). This paints an incomplete picture in the understanding of Husserl's phenomenology since his directions transformed completely in *Ideas II* and *Ideas III* (genetic phenomenology phase) (Husserl, 1980b, 1989c). This crystalizes further when one probes Husserl's 1909-1910 Winter semester lectures published entitled, *The Basic Problems of Phenomenology*, wherein Husserl speaks of the ontology of individuality of I-monads, the plurality of I, monads found through empathy, empathy and other I, the plurality of egos, and the empathy and inter-subjectivity. Later, in *Cartesian Meditations, The Crisis of European Sciences and Transcendental Phenomenology*, and in the post-*Crisis* period, he speaks extensively about the other. Ultimately, we need to understand that the *V Meditation* in *Cartesian Meditations* is exclusively devoted to the notion of the other. The distinctions between perception and apperception, presentation and appresentation are crucial to the discussion on the notion of the other. Husserl continued to work on the notion of the other until the last days of his philosophical career. Post-*Cartesian Meditations* discusses the notions of horizontal intentionality, open subjectivity, etc. There is no contradiction between Husserl's transcendental phase and genetic phase with regard to the notion of the other. I do not claim that Husserl solved the problem of the other absolutely, all he does is pave a sure and certain path, not just towards understanding the issues connected with the notion of the other, but also a possible solution to the same.

Chapter 10 focuses on *Husserl's Understanding of Lived Time*. Husserl analysed the issue of time from 1893, long before his phenomenological insight, starting with *Logical Investigations*. In fact, temporality is the only notion that Husserl studied throughout his life at different times. His lectures on time consciousness in the winter semester of 1904-1905 were edited first by Edith Stein and later on by Heidegger, and it was published under the title, *On the Phenomenology of the Consciousness and Internal Time* (Husserl, 1991b), followed by *Bernau Manuscripts* (Husserl, 2001d) in 1917-18, and finally, *C-Manuscripts* (Husserl, 1999) in 1920-36. According to Husserl, the question of time provides unity to all phenomenological notions in general, and that a phenomenological elucidation of time consciousness cannot be undertaken without looking into the constitution of temporal objects. Husserl, being completely convinced about the validity of his initial insights on time, never changed it, rather, developed and enriched it, eventually appending increasingly important phenomenologically notes and significant thrusts to it, some of which are discussed here. Temporality is grounded in the intentionality of consciousness, and the latter being temporal, infuses everything associated with it to be temporal. It is essential to distinguish temporal objects from the three temporal moments of inner time structures, viz., primal impression, retention and protention. Lived time is subjective, whose characteristics are its spreadoutness and flowing nature. Amongst the three temporal moments, primal impression, i.e., the now phase, enjoys a certain privileged position. It is the absolute point of reference for our conscious life. It is only in relation to the now phase that the past and future appear. Retention or fresh or primary memory is the consciousness of the immediate past or the just past. Finally, protention is intuition directed towards what is yet-to-come, it is an openness to the immediate future. Husserl speaks of three different modes of the same time consciousness, the first being the consciousness of the object, the intentional consciousness that constitutes objective time. The second is subjective time constituted in our experiences, namely, lived time, which is the temporality of subjectivity, the source of which is absolute time consciousness. It constitutes, not just subjective time, but also itself. In other words, absolute time consciousness arises due to the self-temporalisation of the transcendental ego, and according to the same, I am my experiences, i.e., there is an identity between myself and my experiences, cemented by self-temporalisation.

Chapter 11 is an *Appendix on Presuppositionlessness in Phenomenology*. Husserl's claim that phenomenology is a presuppositionless science has disturbed me immensely since the commencement of my studies in phenomenology for various reasons. Articles and books by eminent scholars only served to confuse me further. Finally, after a search of almost two decades, I have managed to understand the core of this idea, which is elucidated in this chapter.

1.1 References

Frege, G. (1960). On Sense and Reference. In M. Black & P. Geach (Eds.), *Translations from the Philosophical Writings of Gottlob Frege* (pp. 56–78). Oxford: Basil Blackwell.

Husserl, E. (1970). *The Crisis of European Sciences and Transcendental Phenomenology* (D. Carr, Trans.). Northwestern University Press.

Husserl, E. (1976). *Ideas: General Introduction to Pure Phenomenology and to a Phenomenological Philosophy* (W. R. B. Gibson, Trans.). Humanities Press.

Husserl, E. (1977a). *Logical Investigations, Volume 1* (J. N. Findlay, Trans.). Routledge & Kegan Paul.

Husserl, E. (1977b). *Logical Investigations, Volume 2* (J. N. Findlay, Trans.). Routledge & Kegan Paul.

Husserl, E. (1980a). *Ideas Pertaining to a Pure Phenomenology and to a Phenomenological Philosophy: Second Book: Studies in the Phenomenology of Constitution (Husserliana: Edmund Husserl-Collected Works, Vol. 3)* (R. Rojcewicz & A. Schuwer, Trans.). Martinus Nijhoff Publishers.

Husserl, E. (1980b). *Phenomenology and the Foundations of the Sciences: Third book: Ideas Pertaining to a Pure Phenomenology and to a Phenomenological Philosophy* (T. E. Klein & W. E. Pohl, Trans.). Martinus Nijhoff Publishers, The Hague.

Husserl, E. (1991). *On the Phenomenology of the Consciousness of Internal Time (1893-1917): Husserliana: Edmund Husserl-Collected Works, Volume 4* (J. B. Brough, Trans.). Springer Netherlands.

Husserl, E. (1999). *The Idea of Phenomenology: Husserliana: Edmund Husserl-Collected Works, Volume 8* (L. Hardy & R. Bernet, Trans.). Kluwer Academic Publishers.

Husserl, E. (2001). *Die Bernauer Manuskripte Über Das Zeitbewusstsein, Husserliana: Edmund Husserl-Gesammelte Werke Band XXXIII* (R. Bernet & D. Lohmar, Trans.). Springer Science+Business Media, B.V.

Husserl, E. (2003). *Philosophy of Arithmetic* (R. Bernet, Ed.; D. Willard, Trans.). Springer Netherlands.

Husserl, E. (2006). *The Basic Problems of Phenomenology* (F. Ingo & G. H. James, Trans.). Springer Netherlands.

Mohanty, J. N. (2002). Intentionality of Intentions: 20 Theses. In B. Gupta (Ed.), *Explorations in Philosophy: Western Philosophy* (pp. 123–124). Oxford University Press.

Chapter 2

Phenomenology: A Study of Self
and Beyond

2.1 What is Phenomenology?

Phenomenology is probably the most dynamic and creative subset of philosophy today, generating endless new ideas and fresh modes of thinking. Its applications are diverse; it is used in social sciences (psychology, sociology, history, education), natural sciences, contemporary western philosophy (existentialism, deconstruction and post-modernism), literature (novels, short stories, dramas, poetry), gender studies, nursing studies, management and so on. It is also applied in medicine extensively, especially in psychiatry and dentistry. Several scholars point out that it is now applied to almost three dozen disciplines, and there is a surge in the number of scholars in several fields that wish to specialize in a phenomenological approach to their subject. The primary reason for this surge is that phenomenology is, at its core, not so much a theory or a system of philosophy, but rather a style or a method of philosophizing.

Unfortunately, phenomenology is often misunderstood by many, since it does not have a singular core popular conception. Several scholars who raise relevant questions on phenomenology do not disturb the intellectual curiosity and cognitive imagination of their readers and listeners. Another reason could be that the language of phenomenology is difficult, and though phenomenologists often try to give new meanings and creative definitions to the terms and expressions they frequently use in their writings, their language has different shades of meaning, with grey areas of significance. But of late, phenomenology has influenced such a significant number of disciplines and very many eminent scholars that it cannot be left in the lurch, in obscurity or perplexity.

When we talk of phenomenology, the first question that arises is: whose phenomenology is it anyhow, and of what phase, of Husserl, Heidegger, Sartre, Merleau-Ponty or of somebody else's? Husserl has at least three phases in his phenomenology, Heidegger has two, Sartre has at least three, if not four. However, all these philosophers accept at least two basic dictums of phenomenology, the first being, return to things (themselves), and the second that consciousness is the consciousness of something. Added to these, each phenomenologist has different claims exclusive to himself. For example,

Husserl made unshared claims with regard to epoché, (phenomenological) reduction and transcendental ego, which none of his disciples accepted; in fact, they rejected Husserl's transcendental philosophical claims. They worked out details of Husserl's phenomenology with varying degrees of emphases, variation of themes and different ranges of commitment. Similarly, Heidegger made unique claims regarding hermeneutic phenomenology and Being, while Sartre made exclusive claims regarding descriptive phenomenology and bad faith. But all of them had a genuine concern for the above-mentioned two principles laid down by Husserl. In other words, we can find a kind of familial resemblance in their works.

Husserl declared phenomenology to be an absolute discipline achieved by elaborate methods, the genuine positive outcome of the philosophical efforts of centuries. It is an unending search for the most originary given, since it is the only foundation beyond doubt that is intuitively certain. Phenomenology stands first and foremost as a method of philosophizing (Husserl, 1981). It does not commit itself to any metaphysics. In the words of Spiegelberg, it is not a system, but rather a movement in philosophy since the beginning of the 20th century.

Phenomenology is a descriptive science. The moment we talk about description, the issues raised are, what is the difference between description and explanation, description and interpretation and description and theory? Description deals with facts whereas theories deal with construction, speculation and abstraction, in other words, some sort of metaphysics. Phenomenology is a rigorous science. It may be noted that for the first time in the history of philosophy, Husserl made an important distinction between exact and rigorous sciences. It does not borrow any presuppositions from theories; no phenomenon is constructed or deducted from theories or statements. A phenomenon means that it is to be taken simply in its modes of givenness to the subject, excluding all further beliefs, opinion, theories and presuppositions.

Phenomenological studies begin with the concrete description of lived experiences. Often, first-person accounts are set down in everyday language, avoiding abstract generalizations. The phenomenologist then proceeds by reflecting on and analyzing these descriptions. The best examples of such descriptions can be found in *Confessions by St. Augustine* and in *My Experiments with Truth* by Mahatma Gandhi. Descriptive phenomenology aims to reveal essential general meaning structures of phenomena. Such a phenomenologist stays true to what is given to him, and restricts himself to making assertions supported by intuitive validation. Husserl's phenomenology is a descriptive, eidetic science of one's own transcendental subjectivity, leading to transcendental intersubjectivity. In fact, phenomenological descriptions apply only to subjective experiences. Husserl's phenomenology is an enterprise committed to transcendental idealism. In *Logical Investigations* (Husserl, 1977s), Husserl described pre-transcendental philosophy as a kind of realism, consciously employing anti-metaphysical and anti-transcendental methods, describing phenomena in their givenness. Later on, Husserl gave up this stand, but never his stance on phenomenology being a descriptive science. Phenomenology, as transcendentalism, asserts that the world must be construed as constituted in transcendental subjectivity or consciousness. This subjectivity, this transcendental ego, is the absolute, towards which every worldly entity is relative.

The aim of phenomenological research is to describe the phenomenon as accurately as possible, refraining from any pre-given framework, but remaining true to facts, i.e., understanding the phenomenon from the perspective of lived experiences. Phenomenology seeks to provide a description of constituents of consciousness, i.e., the structure of phenomenon apprehended, and the structure of the acts apprehending them. It is due to this concern for structure that phenomenology is known as the structural description of the consciousness of things. To describe is to neither reduce nor to speculate, nor to hypothesise, nor to conjecture. Description aims at philosophizing without presuppositions, preconceptions, prejudices or prejudgements. In his attempt to overcome all forms of relativism, historicism and *Weltanschauung* philosophies, Husserl searched for the notion of non-linguistic, non-formal, non-nomological, non-psychological, non-speculative givenness, finally introducing phenomenological reduction to achieve his goal.

Husserl set out to establish phenomenology as a new discipline in philosophy, and as a science of consciousness. As the latter, phenomenology characterizes a given form of consciousness from the person's own subjective perspective. For example, imagine a physician studying a patient's pain. He studies somebody else's pain. It is an objectivist's study. In contrast, when I study pain on my right hand, that would be a phenomenological study. Phenomenology focuses primarily and exclusively on subjective experiences; it is concerned with a meaningful structure of experience, one that is subjective and strictly personal. It is the significant content of conscious experiences. Meaning distinguishes our experiences, making them noteworthy. Lexicographical meanings lead to logic and semantics, but phenomenology is not concerned with these. Meanings, according to Husserl, are ideal entities. Phenomenology studies experiences and their contents, viz., meanings, and not objects represented by them. Thus, we ascend from the first order experiences of things to a higher order of reflection of experiences and their meanings. In other words, in phenomenology, Husserl attends to consciousness as experienced, stating that the basic character of consciousness is the consciousness of something, i.e., it is intentional. In phenomenology, meaning of an experience is incompatible with the object (of experience). Phenomenologically, our consciousness is projected towards the object through meanings.

Phenomenology is a transcendental science, and it is this concern with meaning that makes it so. True, natural and empirical sciences are also meaningful, but their concern for meaning originate from empirical observations and generalizations, whereas phenomenology asks the question: how is it meaningful to *me*, and not just, what is meaning? Phenomenology seeks meanings rooted in lived experience. It is also a rigorous eidetic science of consciousness. It is important to note here that Husserl makes a distinction between rigorous and exact sciences. Mathematics and natural sciences are exact sciences, e.g., 2+2=4 holds true everywhere. These sciences are based on measurements and calculations. To contrast, the answers to questions such as bombings and shootings in Kashmir, are they a terrorist activity or freedom movement? Or say, in Sri Lanka, until recently, when the government was fighting against the Liberation Tigers of Tamil Elam (LTTE), was it a rebellion or an independence movement? The answers depend on one's subjective inclinations and on one's own personal propensity, usually upheld vigorously by the individual. Social sciences and philosophy in general, are rigorous sciences.

Phenomenological descriptions are presuppositionless[1], i.e., it does not allow a presupposition to remain stagnant, instead it is clarified in the best possible manner. In fact, the only major presupposition is that, there exists an entire world out there, totally unrelated to and independent of consciousness, with its own independent existence and meanings. Here, I prefer to use the term, 'nature' instead of 'world', as the latter is what it is only in context of its relationship to consciousness. Devoid of consciousness, 'nature' is a more befitting description to the former. But does anything exist in the absence of consciousness? Consciousness does not create anything *ex nihilo*, rather, it creates the world from nature. Nature can be considered to be the matrix, from which the world is created by consciousness. The question of origin is not an ontological, phenomenological problem, but a metaphysical one, for which there are no solutions, and therefore fruitless to continue this discussion. On further reflection, one can also state that nature is what it is only due to consciousness. According to Descartes, a thing becomes an object only in the presence of consciousness. Similarly from a phenomenological perspective, nature becomes world in the presence of consciousness. To speak

---

[1] Please refer to Chapter 11 for further understanding of presuppositionless in phenomenology.

of the world devoid of consciousness is meaningless. World is 'created' by consciousness from out of nature. For example, did Newton's laws exist before Newton? Definitely not, but that does not mean that the operational part of the laws did not exist before him; they were just not known as Newton's Laws, but as the operations of the phenomenon of gravity. Newton's laws can exist only when formulated by Newton, who created them from the experience of the phenomenon of gravity. Similarly, phenomenology creates the world by means of consciousness experiences. Nature is ontic or empirical, whereas the world is ontological, and it is consciousness that recognises whether something is ontological or ontic. The presence of consciousness is so overwhelming that we need consciousness to even understand its lack thereof. Insofar as a dead man is unaware that he is not conscious, one must conclude that there is no end to consciousness.

Phenomenology is a project of sober reflection, of how the world is experienced. The kind of reflection we examine here is not a reflection akin to empirical psychology that leads to psychologism, to eliminate which, Husserl proposes the methodology of epoché (suspension) and (phenomenological) reduction. Phenomenology analyses the sense or meaning of an experience (e.g., a tree), and not its essence (that is the business of the botanist), it examines my consciousness (of the tree). The tree belongs to the biological species; that species, with its defining features and characteristics, are analyzed in botany. By contrast, my experience (of the tree) belongs to an experiential species that is evaluated in phenomenology, independent of botany.

Figure 2.1 Relationship between the ego, consciousness and object

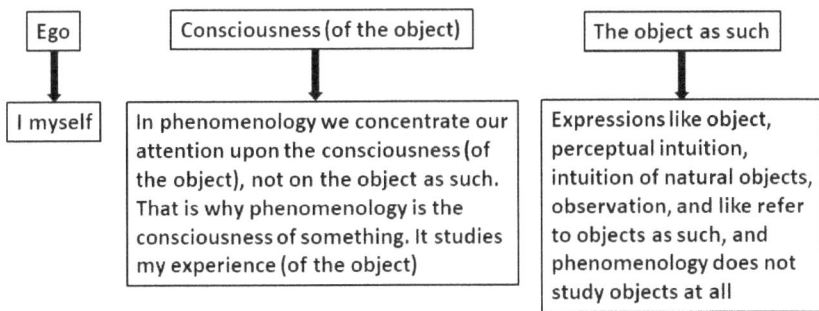

Ego	Consciousness (of the object)	The object as such
I myself	In phenomenology we concentrate our attention upon the consciousness (of the object), not on the object as such. That is why phenomenology is the consciousness of something. It studies my experience (of the object)	Expressions like object, perceptual intuition, intuition of natural objects, observation, and like refer to objects as such, and phenomenology does not study objects at all

When a botanist studies an individual tree (say e.g., a mango tree), his concern is not limited to that particular, solitary tree; instead, he aims to examine and establish the salient features of the mango tree, and those that link that particular species of the tree with the botanical characteristics of mango trees as a whole. Similarly, Newton arrived at his universally applicable gravitational theory by his personal experience of gravity. Likewise, phenomenology studies *my* individual conscious experiences in order to develop laws about consciousness in general. Universal general laws are the horizon of particular experiences according to the conceptualist theory of the universals. A phenomenologist's interest lies, not merely in an individual's conscious experience (of an object), but extends to the very structure of consciousness. It is in this sense that Husserl defined phenomenology as the science of the essence of consciousness, and the need for eidetic analysis. Husserl believes that phenomenology combines the best traditions of several disciplines such as transcendental idealism, realistic empiricism and descriptive psychology.

There are four characteristics to be considered while defining Husserl's phenomenology, namely, 1) it is rigorously descriptive, 2) it utilizes the techniques of epoché and reduction, 3) it explores the intentional relation between the so-called subject (*noesis*) or the transcendental ego and the so-called object (*noema*), and 4) it discloses the essence/meaning immanent in human experience by way of imaginative variation. Phenomenology has been sought to answer at least three of these questions namely, 1) how does consciousness relate itself to the world? 2) How is mental phenomenon differentiate from the physical phenomenon? And, 3) how can mental phenomena be distinguished from each other?

The term phenomenology is the combination of two Greek expressions, *phainómenon* (thing appearing to view) and *logos* (science), i.e., science of appearance. According to Husserl's article on phenomenology in *Encyclopaedia Britannica* (1927) (Husserl, 1971), it was introduced to designate the philosophical movement that arose at the turn of the 20th century. Some scholars claim to have found phenomenology as far back as the writings of Aristotle, and in the Socratic approach to philosophy, though this seems a bit far-fetched. But it is known for sure that Euclid used the term '*phainómena*' in his astronomical treatise to describe the movement of heavenly bodies. After several centuries, in 1637, Friedrich Christoph Oetinger, a theosophist and alchemist, used 'phenomenon' in three different ways in his book entitled, *The Philosophy of the Ancients* to explain 1) phenomenology, 2) the phenomenological way of thinking and 3) the phenomenological method of inference. He used the expression, 'phenomenology' in the sense of relation between things in the visible world. It is unsure if Husserl was aware of the expression, 'phenomenon,' used by Euclid and Oetinger. But he knew of the use of phenomenology by Johann Heinrich Lambert in his book entitled, *Neues Organon* (Lambert, 1762), according to whom, phenomenology meant the study of appearance, as opposed to the study of truth. Lambert also added that phenomenology signified a science of appearance that allows us to proceed from appearance towards truth. The point is this, neither Oetinger nor Lambert gave the impression that they were inventing a new terminology or assigning a new meaning to the term phenomenon. They used it as if it was already prevalent in the vocabulary of academicians. Ernst Mach, a German physicist, used the term phenomenon in reference to natural sciences, and Husserl acknowledged his indebtedness to the same in the Amsterdam Lectures (1929) (Husserl, 1997), where he identified the latter as a forerunner to phenomenology. Later on, Leibniz and his disciple Christian Wolff used the term in a philosophical sense. However, it was Kant who did enormous service for the development of the term phenomenology by using it as an integral part of his book entitled *Critique of Pure Reason* (Kant, 2007). Kant also wrote a number of letters to Lambert to clarify the expression, phenomenon. Another leap for the development of phenomenology came from Hegel and the Hegelians, especially so, due to his classical book, *Phenomenology of Spirit* (Hegel, 1976). It must be said that it was Hegel who bestowed legitimacy to the term phenomenology in the philosophical consciousness of scholars.

Despite all these, Husserl was inspired to use the term, 'phenomenology' by his mentor, Franz Brentano, who distinguished between physical and psychic phenomena in his book, *Psychology from an Empirical Standpoint* (Brentano, 1995). The physical phenomenon is a dead and an unchanging one, whereas the psychical phenomenon is characterized by what scholastics described as the intentional (mental) inexistence of the object or intentionality. It also indicates the directedness of consciousness to an object; this being the case, is phenomenology a form of psychology? Husserl, following his teacher Brentano, did state at one point during the early stages of his thinking that phenomenology is a form of descriptive psychology. But in the later stages, when the question of meaning became the central theme of Husserl's concern, he deviated from Brentano, and insisted that meaning is the significant content of experience and the fulcrum of phenomenology. It is meaning, not lexicographical meaning, but meaning rooted in lived experiences, that distinguishes our experiences and transforms consciousness into the consciousness of something.

Husserl never defined phenomenology along the Aristotelian lines, but rather described it in divergent ways, and discussed it on different occasions. But for a student of phenomenology, a definition is a must, for which, given below, is a descriptive, elucidatory definition to the same.

Phenomenology is a cognitive approach to a field of study aimed at scientifically rigorous and interpersonal knowledge by way of,

1.   Description of the intentional act and the intended object.

2.   Study of the modes of experiencing the phenomenon, and

3.   Examination of the way in which the phenomenon is constituted in (my) consciousness or by (my) consciousness.

To explain the various terms used here, intentional act is that which conveys the problem, say an intriguing phenomenon in physics, or what phenomenology is all about, etc. Intended objects are words, phrases or utterances used to elucidate the problem. It also includes all the devices used to discuss the problem that convey the intentional act. Modes of experiencing the phenomena discuss the issue of problem comprehension in the manner in which the problem's solution constitutes itself in my consciousness, which is the final state of mind when the solution is comprehended.

Let us say there is a student who is very much interested in the theory of quantum mechanics. On his own initiative, he reads a few chapters on the topic; during the process of his comprehension, he raises several questions, to clarify which, he approaches his teacher, who resolves these problems, thus expanding his horizon on the subject. The teacher suggests certain books and articles that would shed further light on his queries, and also suggests that the former attend certain lectures and seminars to aid in further understanding. At the end of this laborious process, the student is in a position to state that he has grasped quantum mechanics to a certain extent. What this actually means is that quantum mechanics has constituted itself in his consciousness, or in other words, his consciousness constitutes quantum mechanics in his mind. In this scenario,

1.   **Intentional act** stands for the student's desire to learn quantum mechanics.

2.   **Intended object** covers the books, articles, seminars and lectures, etc., i.e., the student's efforts to solve the problem

3.   **Modes of experiencing the phenomena** are the ways in which the student gradually grasps quantum mechanics after each effort. Quantum mechanics constitutes itself in him slowly, i.e., he understands the subject bit by bit, enabling him to understand the same.

In conclusion to this section, I wish to state that there are a number of themes discussed in phenomenology, some of them being,

1.   Phenomenology seeks to establish and develop a presuppositionless science.

2. Phenomenology demands, what can be described as a return to things.

3. Phenomenology accepts the Cartesian and Leibnizian ideal of universal sciences (*mathesis univerlais*).

4. Phenomenology accepts the ideal style of the Kantian transcendental philosophical method of *Critique of Pure Reason* (Kant, 2007), though Husserl proposes to go beyond Kant in this regard.

5. Phenomenology seeks to reconstruct the total range of the life of consciousness from the standpoint of transcendental subjectivity.

6. Phenomenology presents a new theory of meaning intimately bound to the doctrine of essence.

7. Phenomenology seeks to reconstruct Life world (*Lebenswelt*) that each one of us is born with, exists and dies.

8. Phenomenology presents a unique method of pursuing its ends by developing a theory of epoché (bracketing or suspension) and (phenomenological) reduction.

9. Phenomenology proposes a radical theory of consciousness and intentionality.

10. Phenomenology presents a new conception of evidence in terms of self-givenness.

11. Phenomenology articulates a theory of transcendental consciousness in terms of which a constitutive activity of transcendental ego emerges.

2.2 The Phenomenology of Self

Has the word 'self' been used so far? The answer is both yes and no. No, because it has not been used as such, and yes, since the expression, 'transcendental ego', the term equivalent to self in Husserl's transcendental phenomenology, has been used several times. It may be noted that, in Husserlian phenomenology, we find at least three phases, (excluding the pre-phenomenological phase), namely,

1. The realist phase represented by the book, *Logical Investigations*.

2. The transcendental phase represented by the book, *Ideas*.

3.   The genetic phase represented mainly by two books: The *Cartesian Meditations* and *Crisis of European Sciences*.

Husserl discusses 'transcendental ego' in the second phase, but rarely uses it in the third phase, preferring to use the expression, 'self' to refer to the same reality. In the post-*Crisis* (*of European Sciences*) period, Husserl continued his phenomenological investigations into various themes that captured his attention in the so-called realist and transcendental phases all the more vigorously, bringing them all into utmost unity and matchless coherence.

The term, transcendental ego or transcendental self is not used in *Logical Investigations*, instead, we find a non-egological concept of consciousness elucidated in an anti-metaphysical, anti-transcendental language, following Humes' empiricist philosophical style, where Husserl located consciousness as completely contained and fulfilled through intentional acts. At this point, he did not feel the need to have a foundation for consciousness, which changed when he published the II edition of *Logical Investigations*. In one of the significant footnote additions to the latter, Husserl wrote that he had discovered an ego, akin to Kant's transcendental ego. *Ideas I* includes an elaborate discussion of what he means by the transcendental ego, following which, he insists transcendental ego to be the origin of conscious or intentional acts, and the very condition for the possibility of empirical egos. It can be considered the single, unique and distinct ground for all individual conscious acts. Phenomenology as an eidetic science, is possible only by virtue of the discovery and disclosure of the transcendental sphere.

2.3 Beyond the Self

The conception of transcendental ego in *Ideas I* was just the beginning for Husserl, who, as an archaeologist of the mind, continued to explore consciousness further. He delved deeper into transcendental ego, looking for its basis for justification. On closer scrutiny of the same, Husserl realized that there were two diverse philosophical strands constituting it. One of the characteristics of transcendental ego is that it is a solitary, reclusive and totally isolated monad, and can be grounded only in a transcendental inter-subjective relationship. This led Husserl to *Cartesian Meditations* (especially the V meditation) (Husserl, 1977f). Another dimension of transcendental ego that Husserl noticed was that it was abstract, abstruse and irreal. He also realized that such a transcendental ego can be grounded only in something that is concrete, definitive and explicit. And such are the fundamental characteristics of Husserl's *Crisis of European Sciences*, especially the notion of Life world and post-*Crisis* writings. Life world, according to Husserl, is totally concrete and absolutely definitive. It is the medium through which transcendental ego can relate itself to 'facticity' and 'everydayness' (expressions from Heidegger). It may be noted that Heidegger in his 1925 lectures to his students, remarked that he hoped Husserl would take up his suggestion for radically transforming phenomenology. And it appears to me that the latter did take up Heidegger's suggestion, the result being Husserl's transition from transcendental to genetic phenomenology of *Cartesian Meditations, Crisis of European Sciences and Transcendental Phenomenology* and post-*Crisis* phenomenology, where notions such as Life world, lived time, history, etc., play a prominent role (Buren, 1989). And in fact, a transcendental inter-subjective relationship is itself grounded in Life world. So then, what is the difference between transcendental inter-subjectivity of *Cartesian Meditations* and Life world of *Crisis* insofar as grounding is concerned? Life world is the justification for transcendental inter-subjectivity, and the steppingstone to the former. So, is Life world founded on anything at all? Yes, it is founded upon life itself, upon human life and authentic living (note Heidegger). Husserl, in the early part of *Ideas I*, spoke about the difference between naturalistic and phenomenological (or philosophical) attitude, and urged us to follow a life of the latter. He demands a life of authentic attitude (i.e. authenticity) from us, but what, or of which kind? Spiritual and religious life for some, academic life for some others, social life and service of others for yet others, depending upon one's choice and attitude. The question is not 'what' kind of life we choose, but rather 'how' that life is chosen and lived.

Do phenomenological developments stop with Husserl's notion of Life world? The true culmination of Husserl's transcendental phenomenology is existential phenomenology. Heidegger, Marcel and several others had reservations about the term, existentialism, and in fact, Sartre did not know the meaning of the same at the time of the publication of his book, *Being and Nothingness*. However, I use the term in a different sense. According to Husserl's *Crisis of European Sciences* and *Cartesian Meditations*, existential phenomenology consists in drawing out in detail, the conclusions of transcendental phenomenology of *Ideas I*, following which, *Crisis of European Sciences and Transcendental Phenomenology* and *Cartesian Meditations* can be considered his everlasting contributions to existential phenomenology. Several authors also contributed to existential phenomenology, namely, Heidegger (*Being and Time*), Sartre (*Being and Nothingness*), Merleau-Ponty (*Phenomenology of Perception*), Paul Ricœur (*Husserl: An Analysis of his Phenomenology*). Heidegger's *Being and Time* was published in 1927, almost a decade before the publication of Husserl's *Crisis of European Sciences* and *Cartesian Meditations*. Heidegger studied *Ideas I* in depth, and even read Husserl's manuscripts of *Ideas II* and *III* long before they were published, all of which enabled him to propose a version of hermeneutical phenomenology dealing with *Dasein* (human existence) and being-in-the-world. I also believe that Heidegger obtained his initial base of *Being and Time* from all three *Ideas* and the *Logical Investigations* especially Investigation VI (Husserl, 1977r)

Further scrutiny of transcendental phenomenology allowed Husserl to produce various dimensions of phenomenology, including his own genetic phenomenology. Husserl and Heidegger have different approaches and varying perspectives in phenomenology. This in itself is the greatness of phenomenology, that it can accommodate differing viewpoints, and account for their ingenuity as well. While Heidegger discussed the hermeneutical phenomenology of *Dasein* and being-in-the-world world, Husserl laid foundations for human existence in general, including Life world, in his genetic phenomenology and post-*Crisis* writings. To conclude, Life world is the matrix in which lived experiences of an individual are rooted. Only upon Husserlian foundations can we ever have Heidegger's hermeneutic phenomenology and existentialism in general; such is the give-and-take between Husserl and Heidegger. This in no way minimizes the latter's importance, nor his contributions to hermeneutic phenomenology in particular, or to existential philosophy in general.

2.4 References

Brentano, F. (1995). *Psychology from an Empirical Standpoint* (A. C. Rancurello, D. B. Terrell, & L. L. McAlister, Trans.). Routledge.

Buren, J. V. (1989). The Young Heidegger and Phenomenology. *Man and World*, *23*(3), 239–272.

Hegel, G. W. F. (1976). *Phenomenology of Spirit* (A. V. Miller, Trans.). Oxford University Press.

Husserl, E. (1971). "Phenomenology" Edmund Husserl's Article for the Encyclopaedia Britannica (1927): New Complete Translation by Richard E. Palmer (R. E. Palmer, Trans.). *Journal of the British Society for Phenomenology*, *2*(2), 77–90.

Husserl, E. (1977a). Fifth meditation. Uncovering of the sphere of Transcendental being as Monadological Intersubjectivity. In D. Cairns (Trans.), *Cartesian meditations: An Introduction to Phenomenology* (pp. 89–150). Martinus Nijhoff Publishers, The Hague.

Husserl, E. (1977b). Investigation VI: Elements of a Phenomenological Elucidation of Knowledge. In J. N. Findlay (Trans.), *Logical Investigations Volume 2* (pp. 181–348). Routledge & Kegan Paul.

Husserl, E. (1977c). *Logical Investigations, Volume 1* (J. N. Findlay, Trans.). Routledge & Kegan Paul.

Husserl, E. (1981). *Husserl: Shorter Works*. University of Notre Dame Press.

Husserl, E. (1997). The Amsterdam Lectures on Phenomenological Psychology. In T. Sheehan (Ed.), & R. E. Palmer (Trans.), *Psychological And Transcendental Phenomenology And The Confrontation With Heidegger (1927-1931): Husserliana: Edmund Husserl-Collected Works Volume 6* (p. 220). Springer-Science+Business Media, B.V.

Kant, I. (2007). *Critique of Pure Reason.* Penguin Classics.
Lambert, J. H. (1762). *Neues Organon.* Wentworth Press.

2.5 Further reading

Atkinson, M. (1972). A Precise Phenomenology for the General Scholar. *The Journal of General Education, 23*(4), 261–297.

Berrios, G. E. (1989). What is Phenomenology? A Review. *Journal of the Royal Society of Medicine, 82*(7), 425–428.

Chapman, H. M. (1966). Realism and Phenomenology. In M. Natanson (Ed.), *Essays in Phenomenology* (pp. 79–115). Springer, Dordrecht.

Ehrich, L. C. (2003). Phenomenology: The Quest for Meaning. In *Qualitative Educational Research in Action: Doing and Reflecting* (pp. 52–79).

Gallagher, S. (2012). *Phenomenology.* Palgrave Macmillan UK.

Husserl, E. (1981). Pure Phenomenology, its Method, and its Field of Investigation. In P. McCormick & F. A. Elliston (Eds.), *Husserl: Shorter Works.* University of Notre Dame Press.

Mall, R. A. (1993). Phenomenology-Essentialistic or Descriptive? In *Husserl Studies* (Vol. 1, pp. 13–30).

McNamara, M. S. (2005). Knowing and Doing Phenomenology: The Implications of the Critique of 'Nursing Phenomenology' for a Phenomenological Inquiry: A Discussion Paper. *International Journal of Nursing Studies, 42*(6), 695–704.

Merleau-Ponty, M. (2005). Preface. In C. Smith (Trans.), *Phenomenology of Perception* (pp. vii–xxiv). Routledge.

Ricœur, P. (1973). Existential Phenomenology. In R. Zaner & D. Ihde (Eds.), *Phenomenology and Existentialism* (pp. 87–98). Capricorn Books.

Wojnar, D. M., & Swanson, K. M. (2007). Phenomenology: An Exploration. *Journal of Holistic Nursing, 25*(3), 172–180.

Chapter 3

Consciousness and Intentionality: The Perspective of Husserl

3.1 Man, World and Intentionality

Man is aware of himself; he is also aware of the world[1] around him and his surroundings. That is his way of living. Thus, while *being-in-the-world*, his awareness is enhanced and amplified by his cultural ties, religious quests and intellectual search, expressed through his philosophical questions, scientific concerns and transpersonal relationships. Contents within and without the world form the domain of his consciousness, allowing him to have an intimate and personal relationship with it. This world, this environment, is nothing in particular. The environment, '*Umwelt*', a terminology popularized by Heidegger in the recent past, is constituted by him, as well as revealed to him by his consciousness. Consciousness is the binding force, establishing an organic unity, an intrinsic relationship between man and his world. Man's world is not fleeting like a cloud or ephemeral like vapour or transient like the wind; instead, it is the foundation upon which the edifice of man's everyday existence is constructed. It may also be noted that man cannot be conscious of the world unless it already exists prior to his existence, and precedes his awareness of the world. However, there is a significant difference here. The world that exists prior to his awareness is only a 'what' world, i.e., the material, physical, impersonal, and the so-called objective dimension of the world. However, his awareness transforms it into a 'how' world, i.e., a world with a unique, personal, subjective, intuitive relationship with him. The how

---

[1] The expression, 'world' has been bestowed different meanings throughout history. The Greeks understood the world as cosmos. The Bible speaks of the world as that which was created by God at the beginning of creation. Science apprehends the world as that which results from the big bang. Descartes comprehends the world as a collection of things standing over against a consciousness, raising them to the level of objects. Kant assumes the world as a phenomenon. However, Husserl grasps the world as a horizon of meanings, whereas Heidegger interprets it in terms of one's praxis and interests. Finally, we have common sense, which recognizes the world as that which contains all things, the place of our residence. Intellectual history, thus, tells us that the expression, 'world' does not have any one single meaning at any given time; it has different senses and varied meanings.

designates that the world is constructed upon foundations of consciousness, transforming it. In other words, consciousness makes the world my own (i.e., mineness, according to Heidegger). Since consciousness transforms the world, it is not just immanent, but also transcendent to it. This is human consciousness, something that is fundamentally intentional. This intentionality that demonstrates the tending character of consciousness, is its very essence.

The intentionality of consciousness is the very substratum upon which the entire edifice of Husserlian phenomenology rests. To clarify the intimate relationship between consciousness and intentionality, let us look at an example. I go to the sports goods shop to purchase a football. What I get from the shop is a flat, toneless, lifeless, empty leather case. I bring it home, pump an optimal amount of air, and take it to the football pitch. Until the match begins, the ball lies in the corner of the pitch. During the match, the ball is kicked around, far and wide, up and down, moving from place to place, depending on the force of the kick and the direction of the pass. The ball now gets direction, a thrust, an orientation. The ball is alive only in the context of a match, when it is kicked around to achieve a goal, to obtain a result, and during the course of the match, the ball is never at rest. So, what is the relationship between the ball and the air in it? The air is what makes the ball a ball. The air sustains it, infusing life into it, bringing it alive. Air gives meaning to the ball, without which it is dead and obsolete, an entity to be discarded. In other words, the ball that I purchased from the shop is only a potential ball, to use an Aristotelian expression, that begins to act only when filled with air. The relationship between consciousness and intentionality is something similar. Intentionality is the very essence of consciousness, never existing without the former. Intentionality infuses life into consciousness. While it is intentionality that sustains consciousness, consciousness makes intentionality what it is. Although this seems to be the case, the example of the football and air cannot be applied directly into the domain of consciousness and intentionality, primarily because the former cannot exist without the latter. The two are so intimately and intrinsically interconnected, that they can only be distinguished but never separated. The relation between the ball and air on the one hand, and consciousness and intentionality on the other, is something like this. Inasmuch as there can be more or less air in the ball, one can speak of degrees of consciousness (Heidegger). Consciousness is *a priori*, in the sense that man is born with consciousness. Consciousness is the condition for the existence of man, the constitutive component of man's being-in-the-world. The same principles apply to intentionality as well. When consciousness ceases to be, his intentionality also disappears, and that is the end of man as well.

Intentionality is the principal theme of Husserl's phenomenology. Husserl's thought can be adequately grasped only if we understand what he means by consciousness. Consciousness is characterized in its pregnant sense only through intentionality. Fundamentally, Husserl is a philosopher of consciousness and intentionality. Phenomenology offers an examination of consciousness, leading to the analysis and description, not of just consciousness, but also of the phenomenon, viz., the object of intentionality. Phenomenology involves the structural description of objects of the intentional act, and as a result, it is a renewed elucidation of the direction of consciousness known as intentionality. All conscious acts have direction. They point towards an object, irrespective of its physical or material objectivity. By stating that consciousness is the consciousness of something, it is implied that it is intentional, and that intentionality is built upon consciousness itself. This does not mean that intentionality is an accidental property, or a superstructure built on the foundations of consciousness; rather, it is the necessary outgrowth of consciousness in different directions due to various experiences. Consciousness is not a one-dimensional realm composed merely of psychic acts; instead, it is a correlation between the domain of acts and the field of objects, constituting the province of meaning, i.e., *noema*. This *noetic-noematic* correlation is what intentionality signifies when we say that consciousness is the consciousness of something.

The Husserlian notion of consciousness does not refer to the Freudian understanding of consciousness or unconscious. In everyday language, an action performed intentionally implies that it is performed on purpose. But in Husserl, the term, intentionality, is a technical one, not limited to perception, volition, etc., but includes intentionality in the ordinary sense. An act indents an object, i.e., the intentional object. Nevertheless, not all experiences are intentional, e.g., dizziness or nausea. Most of our experiences transform into the consciousness of something, and take their place in a structured temporal stream of experiences. While the distinction between intentional and non-intentional experience is crucial in phenomenology, the former is emphasized.

Only the conscious self is aware of the intended object. Consciousness thus, as an intentional relation, is internal to the subject. This relation is one-sided, springing from the subject and directed to the intended object, but not vice versa. The domain of intentionality is central to the study of phenomenology, and it may be stated here that phenomenology is the study of the essence of consciousness as lived. Hence, it looks into the intentionality of conscious experiences such as imagination, volition, judgement, experiences of other people, etc. Therefore, phenomenology is mostly concerned with experiences expressed in acts directed towards the world. Husserl's theory of intentionality forms the centre of new science, viz., rigorous science. Phenomenology offers analysis that leads to the description of the essential structures of the phenomenon and constituents of consciousness. It is the structural description of the consciousness of things, which implies that intentionality occupies a central role in this study.

Intentionality is the primary feature of Husserl's phenomenology. It is independent of casual relationships with external things. It does not explain how mental states relate themselves to the world; this is a question of causality, but how do we discover meanings at all? A mental state is intentional by virtue of its relation to the extra-mental state, i.e., meaning, *noema*. Consciousness has a fundamental directional character, i.e., they point toward certain objects, be it real, physical, or material, implying that all thinking refers to thinking about something, and all remembering is remembering something. Every act of consciousness is the consciousness about something, implying that the subjective aspect, the *noesis* of experiences, is aware of it. Therefore, a thinking act of consciousness is related to a thought object, a desiring act of consciousness is related to the desired object, and similarly for other acts. By saying so, we turn our reflections to the structure of consciousness as we experience it. This property of consciousness, called intentionality, demonstrates that consciousness/intentionality is directed at the object, i.e., it has a projective, directional activity. Intentionality, therefore, is the purposeful directedness of consciousness. All such directed acts are intentional experiences, intentionally related to objects. The inquiry into consciousness has two sides: the subject pole, i.e., the *noesis*, and the object pole, the *noema*, that cannot be separated, though distinguishable. *Noesis* is a particular act of consciousness by which the object is apprehended. No intentional experience can ever occur without a correlation between *noesis* and *noema*.

Intentionality in Husserl's sense refers primarily to the phenomenological structure of the act. The structure of intentionality from Husserl's point of view is purely *a priori*, and refers fundamentally to the experience of meanings. Consciousness is a continuous and interrelated act, bound together in the unity of inner time, and as William James puts it, flows like a stream. These acts do not require an actor, inasmuch as a consciousness does not require a consciousness-er. Acts have their grounding and origin in the transcendental ego. Consciousness arises from conscious experiences or rather, they co-exist. Consciousness is *swayambhu*, it is self-existing and the necessary condition for the existence of a self, i.e., a transcendental ego. It is *a priori*. Consciousness is intentionality, intentionality is transcendental ego, and transcendental ego is consciousness. Is there a difference between transcendental ego, consciousness and intentionality? Consider the previous example of the football. What is the difference between the football purchased from the shop, and the one into which air was pumped? It is the one and the same, except that now air is inside, making it ready for action. The ball purchased from the shop, the ball filled with air, the ball resting in the corner of the pitch, and the ball bouncing around, are all one and the same. All we see are different dimensions of the same ball; similarly so is it with transcendental ego, consciousness, and intentionality. They are all one and the same, and yet functionally different, named differently, each mode, a facet of the other.

Within the structure of consciousness or intentionality, Husserl points out that there is an interrelated polar aspect, namely *noesis* and *noema*, or subjective and objective dimensions respectively. The transcendental ego or *noesis* assigns meaning to *noema*, which is the perspective adapted to an object. Consider the example of a chair. The meaning given to the chair currently is a place where I can sit. Then I notice that the ceiling fan above is stationary, so I bring the chair below the fan, climb on it, and jerk the fan, whence it begins to rotate. Now, the chair is transformed into an elevated platform. A lecture hall, filled with students, has no empty chairs. When the principal enters, a student immediately offers his/her chair to sit. Here, the chair symbolises a place of honour. A terrorist enters a classroom with intention to attack. The teacher quickly throws the chair at the terrorist, intending to disarm him and protect the students. Here, the chair is transformed into a protective weapon. These scenarios reveal varying uses for the chair, implying that it does not have a fixed meaning, but varies depending on our perspective, that I, the transcendental ego, assigns to it. Depending upon my intention, the chair is assigned/acquires new meanings, signifying its essence, namely, the *noema*. *Noema*, therefore, is the perspective adapted to an object (here chair) at the moment, and as intended.

Intentionality is the relation between the mental states of the experiencer and the extramental state of affairs, i.e., the event, all of which are called objects. This is the general relational theory of intentionality, wherein, it is not essential for the object to have physical, material existence; we are talking about existence independent of intentional objects. The most obvious problem with this relational view of intentional relational is that, the object of the intentional state need not always be an actually existing object. Consider the following, pegasus, mermaids, centaurs, dreams, hallucinations, etc., can be objects of intentionality/consciousness, although none of them have material, real existence like that of a table, chair or fan. The question now is: how does Husserl justify the contention that consciousness is in fact the consciousness of something, a dictum he obtained from his teacher, Franz Brentano, when he himself considers non-existing realities also as objects of intentionality?

3.2 Brentano's Notion of Intentionality

Psychology diverged from philosophy and took an empirical turn in terms of the notion of introspection and various other kinds of experiments, since Wilhelm Wundt and his followers. Arguing against crude empirical direction, yet firmly rooted in the empirical dimension of psychology, Brentano held that psychology studies psychic life, for which, he contended that empirical methods cannot be used without reservation. The entire world of appearance, he remarked, was divided into two categories: the psychic and the physical. The psychic phenomenon refers to psychic activities such as belief, doubt, judgement, desire, love, fear, etc. There is no possibility of error whilst dealing with these. Psychic phenomena are processes or activities that are complex, stratified and inwardly cohesive. They are intentionally directed to the object. To summarize, inner perceptions, through which all the above mentioned are perceived and apprehended, can be termed psychic phenomena, according to Brentano. Physical phenomena, on the other hand, are colours, sounds, odours, etc., i.e., sensations that are not physical things. The physical remains constant, while the psychic transcends itself. And there is a possibility of erroneous determination while dealing with sensations, in the sense that inner perception is always true, whereas, there is always a possibility of error with outer perception. Theodore de Bore made a detailed study of Brentano in his book, *The Development of Husserl.* Brentano formulated his celebrated notion of intentionality during the process of distinguishing physical and psychical phenomena. Husserl quotes Brentano in *Logical Investigations Vol. 2,* who uses terms such as mental inexistence, inner objectivity, internal inexistences, direction towards the object or content, to explain intentional inexistence, all of which demonstrate the distinguishing characteristics of psychic phenomenon (Husserl, 1977c). It may be noted that scholastics used 'intentionality' both in the conative as well as in the cognitive sense. Although Brentano was committed to scholastic philosophy, being a catholic priest himself, he rejected the conative, accepting only the cognitive[2]. The most important property of consciousness, according to him, is striving towards an object, which implies, having a direction towards the same. This is the most decisive and indispensable feature of consciousness. Brentano affirmed two

---

[2] I have come across several students writing in their dissertations that Brentano is the originator of the notion of intentionality. This is totally wrong and completely false. In fact, Brentano himself acknowledges that he borrowed it from scholastic philosophers, who in turn obtained it from Avicenna (980-1037), a great Islamic scholar and a philosopher. It may further be noted, remarks Prof. Richard Sorabjee of University of London, that Avicenna formulated the notion of intentionality based on his study of Aristotle. However, there is no mention of Avicenna, either in Brentano or in Husserl.

aspects of intentional relation; on the one hand, he spoke of relation as directedness, from which arises the object theory of intentionality. There is also the notion of the object, which is the basis for Brentano's object theory of intentionality. Husserl was not enamoured by the latter, and rejected it, since it did not serve his purpose. But he accepted the relational theory of intentionality with modifications. The problem with Brentano's object theory of intentionality was something like this. I am conscious of the chair, which implies that I am conscious of a material, physical, object existing in space and time. In the next moment, I am aware of a mermaid or a centaur or a dream. None of them have a material, physical existence, yet, I am conscious of both sets, and my intentionality is directed towards both. In the first case, the object exists materially and physically in space and time, while, in the second, they have no existence, yet my consciousness and intentionality are directed to them. How is this possible? Brentano could not solve the problem. But Husserl solved it by stating that intentionality is not directed to the object as such, but to the meaning of the object, or the *noema* that exists, irrespective of whether the object exists physically or not. Thus, Brentano and Husserl differ with respect to the position of states of intentional relation. For Brentano, intentional relation was the same as any other relation, and the difference between the relational and the object theory of intentionality was based on the nature of the object, which Husserl disagreed with. According to the latter, intentionality is a very distinctive kind of relation, found nowhere else, arising from the very possibility of meaning, *noema*. In this regard, Husserl rejects Brentano's object theory of intentionality completely, for whom, intentionality consists in distinguishing the physical from the psychical (Mohanty, 2002a). But, according to Husserl, intentionality has a constitutive role to play, and an epistemological function. Brentano was deeply rooted in empirical psychology, mainly of Wundt, despite his serious reservations about the same. He also believed that his acceptance of intentionality did not necessitate him from giving up his empiricist commitments, as is clear from his book, *Psychology from an Empirical Standpoint*. All these were anathema to Husserl; his transcendental viewpoint never allowed him to accept them. He rejected all such views, for intentionality leads to bracketing, constitution, horizon and Life world, none of which exist in Brentano. Husserl's radical interpretation of Brentano's psychology and notion of intentionality led him to formulate his own notion of relational theory of intentionality.

According to Husserl, intentionality of consciousness involves a threefold distinction among act, content and object. Consider the following example. Dr Amartya Sen is the object of my consciousness, the intentional object. The various characteristics of Dr Sen such as, he was a Bengali by birth, he was a professor of economics who taught in highly esteemed universities in India,

Europe and the USA, he is the acclaimed author of highly reputed books, he was awarded the Nobel Prize in economics, etc., form the content of the intentional object called Dr Sen. The object as such is hollow and empty. Its contents make it vibrant, lending it solidity, defining its horizons. The content distinguishes not just objects in general, but also similar objects. There could be different people by name Dr Sen, but the contents of Nobel Laureate, Dr Sen, are unique. The content infuses life into the object, and speaks for it. The object as such is dead, but is given life by the content. When we say Dr Sen, we mean all those mentioned in the content, we do not just refer to the object Dr Sen. And when someone refers to the object, Dr Sen, he in fact, refers to its contents; this is the reason as to why Husserl states that content articulates the meanings (*noema*) of the object, giving the act (*noesis*) its direction; this is called intentionality, i.e., intentionality of an act is its directional content. The intentional object is the transcendent object. But the *noema* is the immanent object, the transcendental object, or the meaning of the transcendent object, i.e., the meaning assigned to the same by *noesis*. The *noema* is the abstract and ideal entity. It is by virtue of *noema* that *noesis* intends an object. The act, *noesis*, is directed to the object via an intermediate entity called *noema*. The object of consciousness is a transcendent object. But intentionality is possible only through the immanent object, *noema*, meaning. This means that the mode of givenness of the transcendent object is different from the mode of givenness of the immanent object, implying that every process of consciousness is given immanently to consciousness. Husserl's theory of intentionality is not an object theory, since it emphasizes not the object, but its content. Intentionality is explained by the intrinsic features of the consciousness of the act and the directedness of the conscious act (to the object). For Husserl, intentionality stands for the relational property of having an orientation.

3.3 The Basic Features of Husserl's Intentionality Theory

1. Intentionality involves a referent, which does not require physical, material existence. It refers primarily to meanings, *noema*, and not to the object as such, which was how Husserl sorted out Brentano's cumbersome problem. The referent is independent of my consciousness, my mind. The intentional object is the sense, due to which the directional aspect of the intentional phenomenon appears.

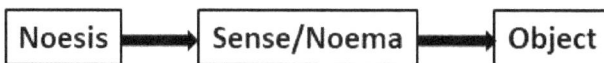

$$\boxed{\text{Noesis}} \longrightarrow \boxed{\text{Sense/Noema}} \longrightarrow \boxed{\text{Object}}$$

2. The act and content are distinguished from the object, which undergoes suspension (epoché) and phenomenological reduction. The object is intended, but not the content. The object is approached perspectively, but not the content. The content is the *noema*, revealed by phenomenological reflection.

3. It is the content that establishes the relationship of intentionality between the act and the object. On the other hand, the relationship between the act and the object can also be represented in the following manner.

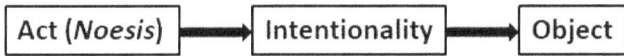

Act (*Noesis*) ⟶ Intentionality ⟶ Object

4. Even if the object does not exist materially and physically, there can be a content related to the *noesis* (example mermaid, pegasus, centaur, etc.), which means that the intentional character of the act is independent of the (non) existence of the intended object. The object of the act is transcendent in the sense that the object is outside my cognitive framework.

5. The content of the act is closely connected to the ways conceiving the object.

Intentionality, as a property of our experiences, has a subjective dimension, and is independent of other ties to the external world. Husserl constantly maintained that intentionality was a feature of phenomenological philosophy. He considered the same to be a feature of mental states, independent of our casual relationships to extramental things and states of affairs. The problem of intentionality, for Husserl, is not to explain how mental states relate themselves to the world, but to explain how they possess a phenomenological or an intentional character of relating to anything at all. A mental state is intentional in character, by virtue of its relation to *noematic Sinn*. Since *noematic Sinne* are meanings, they simply have an intrinsic and irreducible property of meanings. In this context, Husserl holds a version of Frege's theory of meaning. Intentionality, the central issue of Husserl's phenomenology, examines the nature of relationships amongst mental acts, their content and the external world. Mental acts here refer to mental experiences, and not activity; the opposite of the word, act, does not mean passivity, but potentiality.

Intentionality is the ability of the human mind, i.e., consciousness, to refer to an object. It is something we understand fundamentally from self-knowledge and personal experiences, making it nearly impossible to explain it purely from a third person point of view. This is because such a point of view cannot accommodate the internal subjective character of our experiences. This is known as the phenomenological character of intentionality. The important phenomenological problem around which the notion of intentionality revolves is related to how our acts of consciousness and their internal character relate to the external world that Husserl deals with in his notion of naturalistic attitude. The objects to which our acts refer, exist independent of ourselves. Moreover, our mental states and experiences are related to our belief.

Phenomenological problems involve questions about the acts' internal character and structure. Intentionality requires three ingredients: the intending subject, the intentional consciousness and the intended object. Consciousness is wholly internal and immanent to the subject. Intentional relation, therefore, is internal to the subject, but external to the object. Thus, the relation is one-sided, directed from the subject to the object. It is a subjective exploration of the how of the problem. Intentionality refers to the objectification, or the object-related/directed-function of consciousness, and consists in assigning the object with a sense or meaning, which is the most fundamental and universal structure of consciousness. Husserl also states that intentionality is a characteristic feature of our mental states and experiences, especially evident in what is commonly referred to as the consciousness of, or being aware of. Each mental state or experience in a way, relates itself to something other than itself. The proper understanding of intentionality requires phenomenological reduction. Transcendental reduction explicitly reveals that the structure of consciousness is of major importance in phenomenology. Phenomenological consciousness is not the natural consciousness that has a relation to the pre-given transcendent object; instead it is the transcendental consciousness that constitutes sense, arising only as result of transcendental reduction. The mundane being is the being which is, and undergoes phenomenological reduction. However, transcendental consciousness posits being as *noema*, i.e., it is dependent on the former, i.e., *noesis* or transcendental ego, not just for meaning, but also for being. Positing a being is by way of instituting sense, i.e., to arrive at the *noema*.

In Husserl, we find notions of static and dynamic intentionality, both in *Logical Investigations* and *Ideas I*, according to which, they do not exclude, but support each other. Static analysis of intentionality refers to an intentional or mental state, whereas, the dynamic notion of intentionality highlights three consequences of the intentional act, namely, 1) fulfilment and realization inbuilt in intuitional act, 2) temporal dimension of the intentional act, and 3) elucidation of absolute givenness, i.e., examination of total intuitive grasp. To indent in Husserl is aimed at, or directed towards something, i.e., subject intends an object in an experience. The content of experience is the meaning of experience. Consciousness is always consciousness of something, i.e., intentionality. Consciousness does not occur in isolation, rather, in a stream, according to William James; this stream belongs to the 'I', the transcendental ego. In every occurrence of the act of consciousness, i.e., *cogito*, a radiating glance is directed from the transcendental ego to the object through the content.

3.4 Characteristics of Intentionality

Intentionality has several characteristics, a few of which are listed below:

1. Acts of consciousness are experiences and not events. The event is momentary, whereas the experience is long-lasting. For example, let's assume that I am involved in a motorcycle accident. The event itself, i.e., the accident lasts just a few seconds, but is experienced in the following way, broken limbs, hospitalization and surgery, repeated visits to the hospital, money spent on treatment, recuperation and rest for an extended duration, inconvenience caused to the family and friends in addition to mental disturbance to everyone concerned in my intimate circles.

2. The object of the experience is out there, it is transcendent. The subject of experience, the I, the ego, is the individual who experiences the object; it is the transcendental.

3. An act has its content and is different from the object of intentionality (This was illustrated using the example of Dr A. Sen.).

4. The content presupposes that I am aware of the object's background, giving me information of its how (this means that I already knew something about Dr Sen).

5. The background illuminates the horizon of possibilities.

6. The totality of the content describes the 'what' of the object. So, is it possible to have a totality of contents leading to the objects? It is not possible; the totality of previously known contents produces the objects. It is although possible to enrich them further with the discovery of new content. Sartre's expression, trans-phenomenality of phenomenon, becomes all the more meaningful here.

Noesis is both psychological and transcendental; it is psychological, being the real component of the act, i.e., a real subject, I myself, and it is transcendental, since it is capable of assigning meanings. There is no *noetic* phase without a *noematic* phase. The *noema* is the intentional correlate of *noesis*. The discovery of the *noetic-noematic* phases is of significant importance in Husserl's philosophy. Each *noetic* act has its *noema*, and a manifold of appearances can refer to the same transcendent object. The *noema* is irreal, beyond space and time, and stands over against real acts of the *noesis*. The relation between *noesis* and *noema* is unlike that between the subject and the object, for the latter is real, transcendent, existing in space and time, whereas *noema* is irreal, immanent, not existing in space and time.

In *Logical Investigations*, intentionality is explained as a self-transcending phenomenon, but in *Ideas I*, it is expounded through the correlation between *noesis* and *noema*. Post-*Ideas I*, especially in *Ideas II*, intentionality is described mostly through the notion of constitution. Ignoring all other meanings of constitution such as *Sinngebung*, it becomes all the more important in the context of intentionality. Husserl emphasizes constitution as productive and constitutive. Yet, he was very suspicious about production as creation, since, according to him, phenomenology is not a philosophy of production, creation and freedom, especially, there is no creation *ex nihilo*; rather, it is a philosophy of meaning and sense. However, it may be noted that, while discussing the notion of constitution, Husserl brings forward notions such as passive synthesis, genetic constitution, operative intentionality, horizon, intentionality etc., notions of passive synthesis and horizon intentionality that can be seen in *Ideas I* as well.

Noesis-noema is another intentional relation. Every *noesis* has its own intentional correlation to *noema*. *Noesis* bestows meaning or sense to *noema*. The *noetico-noematic* structure permeates all forms of mental activity. The concept of constitution also refers to the correlation between *noesis* and *noema*, inasmuch as meaning is constituted. *Noetic* acts are necessary for *noematic* results. Constitution is a production, since *noesis* acquires a kind of productivity by way of the former. The constituted, i.e., the *noema*, is a product of constitution. The production, i.e., constitution, is a transcendental creation, or a creation by transcendental consciousness. It is not creation *ex nihilo*, but a creation in the sense of bestowing meaning, assigning a sense. I constitute the *noema*, the sense, not materially or physically, but intentionally and transcendently. To explain the intentionality of the acts, we need to explicate the intentionality of experiences, the *noematic Sinn* and the horizon. Objects are experienced only on account of meaning, which in turn, render meaning and coherence to our experiences. Without *noematic Sinn*, we have no consciousness of objects; they are meaningless. *Noematic Sinn* conceived by Husserl, are intentional, since they are entities whose very nature is to represent meanings.

Consciousness and intentionality lead to the notion of constitution, vaguely mentioned in *Logical Investigations*, but acquire precise meaning in transcendental phenomenology and later works. Constitution implies that the appearing object is not a simple occurrence, but modes of appearance that require an identifying synthesis, so that in the course of unification, the object presents itself as one and the same. Constitution is a matter of sense bestowal. *Ideas I* imposes limits on the constitutive function of pure consciousness, but these are thrown to the wind in *Ideas II* and *Phenomenological Psychology*. A conscious act is an act, i.e., consciousness is defined by its reference to a sphere of sense; to experience an act is akin to actualize a sense. Hence, every act of consciousness must be treated in terms of the relation to the *cogito-cogitatum* as *cogitatum*. This *noematic* structure enters into every form of mental activity.

3.5 Temporality of Intentionality

To be aware of an object is to be aware of it as being the same as that of which I was aware of in the past experiences, and as that which I may be/will be aware of, in an indefinite number of presentative acts in time to come, or acts that will make it present in the future. The first part of the above statement means that my awareness of the object is from an indefinite past until now; the second part means that my awareness also has a temporal dimension of the past, present and future. It also means that the identity of the object has a temporal dimension without which, my awareness cannot stand the test of identity. Further details on the temporality of intentionality can be found in Chapter 10.

3.6 Human Body in the Context of Intentionality

The human body is brought into the midst of the discussion on consciousness and intentionality, in the context of the elucidation of constitution. The human body that Husserl considers here is not bound to a naturalistic attitude (*Körper*) but is liberated to the transcendental level (*Leib*), and this enables Husserl to speak about the intentionality of the human body. In *Phenomenological Psychology*, Husserl states that the treatment of the intentionality of consciousness in *Ideas I* does not do justice to the notion as a whole. This acknowledgement is an indication of Husserl's mind on these issues, who later describes the relation of intentionality of the human body to degrees of intentionality, horizon intentionality, constitutive intentionality, intentionality of knowledge, intentionality of emotion and affectivity, etc.

Hyle is a Greek word used by Aristotle to refer to the material principle formed by the formal principle to produce the material thing. In *Ideas I*, *hyle* is regarded as a component of human consciousness, and in Section 85

(Husserl, 1976k), Husserl uses the expression *hyle* or *hyletic data* to refer to the sensuous constituent of our intentional experience such as acts of perceiving, acts of cognizing, all of which have a sensible content apart from inbuilt content. Prof. Mohanty in his book *Explorations in Philosophy* (Mohanty, 2002a), used the term, 'uninformed matter' to characterize *hyle* or *hyletic data.*

Husserl progresses in his understanding of body, and its role in the context of consciousness and intentionality as he moves from *Ideas I* to *II*. In the former, he considers the human body as a link between pure consciousness and the world, whereas, in *Ideas II* (Husserl, 1989g), he is engaged in a systematic analysis of the human body, pointing out that there are different levels of understanding the same. Human body is not merely material, but has psychic layers too. In fact, that which we describe as the physical body is the field of localization, the seat on which everything is situated.

In conclusion, I wish to quote *in toto*, *Intentions of Intentionality: 20 Theses* (Mohanty, 2002b). I wish to discuss Theses 1, 3, 15 and 20, with which I have a few difficulties.

1. Something is intentional if it is directed towards some object or other.

2. To an intentional act, belongs inextricably an intentional object.

3. There is a many-one correlation between acts and their contents.

4. Every intentional act has a sense or meaning through which its object is intended.

5. Every intentional act is meaning-giving or interpretive.

6. Intentionality is either cognitive or practical or affective, as also are their meanings.

7. An intentional act, if it is not an original beginning, functions within a culture.

8. A culture is but a system of sedimented meanings.

9. Every meaning must be, in the long run, originally, a gift of intentionality.

10. Intentional acts originate from the subject, who refers to himself as I, (and in this sense, from an ego).

11. An ego is not just the source of one's intentional acts, but as one performs these acts founded upon earlier acts, they modify the life of the ego.

12. To be distinguished from I-intentionalities are We-intentionalities or collective intentionalities.

13. To be distinguished from acts performed by an ego or a collectivity are those which operate anonymously.

14. Intentionality constitutes the world.

15. The world constitutes intentionality.

16. The truly transcendental principle is the consciousness of the world.

17. Objects as presented to consciousness are results of interpreting the given data.

18. Perceptual objects are passively constituted.

19. Theoretical, mathematical and logical objects are actively constituted.

20. The empirical is the transcendental.

3.7 Discussion on Mohanty's Theses 3, 15, 20 and 1

3.7.1 Thesis 3: There is a many-one correlation between acts and their contents

I find it difficult to see this correlation as Prof. Mohanty suggests between acts and their contents. Let's reconsider the examples of the chair and Dr Sen mentioned earlier to clarify my point. There are different kinds of acts of consciousness mentioned with respect to the chair and Dr Sen, each of which gives rise to distinct contents. One act of consciousness with respect to the chair is that, it is an elevated platform, which gives rise to a corresponding content of my consciousness. But when my act of consciousness is that of the chair as a weapon, then the content of my consciousness is now that of a weapon, and no longer an elevated platform. Similarly, when my act of consciousness changes into a place to sit, the content also changes, and so on with each act of consciousness. Thus, each act of consciousness has a corresponding content, i.e., one-one relationship, i.e., it cannot be a many-one relation as Prof. Mohanty holds. Similarly, in the case of Dr Sen, when my act of consciousness of him is that of him being a Bengali, surely, the content of my consciousness agrees with the acts of my consciousness. But when my act of consciousness of him is a Nobel Laureate, my content of consciousness corresponds to him as a Nobel Laureate, different from all other contents of my consciousness. This implies that each act of consciousness has its corresponding content, the correlation being one-one, and not many-one, as stated in Thesis 3. In fact, Thesis 5 of Føllesdal (*vide* Chapter 6) also speaks against this contention of Prof. Mohanty.

3.7.2 Thesis 15: The world constitutes intentionality

Thesis 15 says that the world constitutes consciousness. In my opinion, the correct formulation should instead be, consciousness constitutes the world (as stated in Thesis 14). When we understand the world in the Husserlian sense, as the horizon of meanings, or in any other sense, we cannot state that that the world constitutes consciousness. It is the 'I', the transcendental ego that constitutes the world. Otherwise transcendental phenomenology does not have much of a meaning.

3.7.3 Thesis 20: The empirical is the transcendental

My response to the above statement is an emphatic no. It should instead be, the empirical is transcendent; it is ontic, spatio-temporal and undergoes epoché and phenomenological reduction. On the other hand, pure consciousness is the transcendental ego. It is the *noesis*. It is the final term of all reductions, in the sense that no reduction can go beyond it.

3.7.4 Thesis 1: Something is intentional if it is directed towards some object or other

I do have some reservations with Thesis 1, though not very serious. It is indeed true that Husserl uses neutral gender with respect to the transcendental ego. But can we use the same when we speak of consciousness and intentionality? I believe that a log of wood, or a piece of rock is not conscious. Only a follower of Sri Aurobindo will state that consciousness is in a dormant state in them, but I do not accept the same. I believe that consciousness and intentionality are possible only for a human being, implying that consciousness and intentionality are available only to a male/female, i.e., a he/she, and therefore cannot be *something*, as noted by Prof. Mohanty, but rather, *someone*. True, this is only a minor oversight, but others need clarification.

3.8 References

Husserl, E. (1976). Sensile ὕλη, intentional μορφή, Section 85. In W. R. B. Gibson (Trans.), *Ideas: General Introduction to Pure Phenomenology* (pp. 246–250). Humanities Press.

Husserl, E. (1977). Consciousness as intentional experience. In J. N. Findlay (Trans.), *Logical Investigations Volume 2* (pp. 94–127). Routledge & Kegan Paul.

Husserl, E. (1989). The Constitution of Psychic Reality Through the Body, Sections 36-42. In R. Rojcewicz & A. Schuwer (Trans.), *Ideas Pertaining to a Pure Phenomenology and to a Phenomenological Philosophy: Second Book, Studies in the Phenomenology of Constitution* (pp. 152–169). Kluwer Academic Publishers.

Mohanty, J. N. (2002a). Can Intentionality be Explained Away? In B. Gupta (Ed.), *Explorations in Philosophy: Essays by J N Mohanty* (p. 30). Ohio University Press.

Mohanty, J. N. (2002b). Intentionality of Intentions: 20 Theses. In B. Gupta (Ed.), *Explorations in Philosophy: Western Philosophy* (pp. 123–124). Oxford University Press.

Chapter 4

Husserl's Investigation of Meaning

4.1 The Question of Meaning: Preliminaries

How does meaning originate? It is often recognized that phenomenology in general, and existentialism in particular are concerned, not with things, but with their meanings; they are not concerned with lexicographical or linguistic meanings, but with personal and subjective kind of meanings. This may not be very much in line with Husserl's early writings on meaning, especially in *Logical Investigations* and *Ideas*. But the veracity of the statement is beyond doubt when we examine his later writings like *Cartesian Meditations* or *Crisis of European Sciences* or post-*Crisis* writings. It is equally true of Heidegger's hermeneutic phenomenology or Sartre's descriptive phenomenology or the existential phenomenology of Merleau-Ponty. Phenomenology is not concerned with physical objects like natural sciences, but instead with their sense or meaning as physical objects, which it seeks to clarify, by returning to intentional experiences that constitute these meanings. In other words, the constitution of meanings is an essential component of the phenomenological enterprise. Meanings are constituted, both in the acts of understanding, as well as in the correlation between the understanding-use of expressions by speakers and the understanding-grasp by listeners. In other words, meaning-assigning acts arise, not just from acts of understanding, but also from interpretative acts. To put it in proper perspective, if the sense of the physical objects is constituted in the perceptual experience, the sense of meaning is constituted in the acts of understanding, i.e., in the correlation between the understanding-use of expression by speakers and the understanding-grasp by listeners.

4.1.1 Generalities and Universals

Meaning is signified by an expression. There are essential distinctions between meaning and the object meant. Sometimes different expressions with different meanings may refer to one and the same object. For example, we have expressions like the morning star and evening star, both referring to the same planet, Venus. Similarly, we speak of Napoleon Bonaparte as victorious at Jena and vanquished at Waterloo. There are also instances where multiple acts of meaning refer to a single object. This is known as identical or ideal meaning, referred to by Husserl as the 'ideal entity'. It was this problem of ideal or identical meanings that led Husserl to the problem of generalities and universalities. Let us look into some expressions and analogies that we use in our daily life to understand the problem. Consider the analogical expression, faithful. A man is faithful to his wife, God is faithful in His promises, a dog is faithful to its master, a soldier is faithful to his country. In each case, the word faithful has a different sense. In contrast, let's look at a univocal expression like heaven or hell. Heaven, in ordinary parlance, refers to a place of happiness and joy, a paradise, seventh heaven, a world of fulfilment of one's heart's desires and longings. For some, heaven consists in having several good books to read, for someone else, heaven may mean a lot of money, and yet for some others, physical wellbeing. Hell on the other hand, refers to suffering, perdition, torment, agony or ordeal. Heaven, hell and other such univocal expressions have a primary, identical meaning that does not change depending on context; Husserl refers these as generalities or universalities. General essences are given only in the intuitive apprehensions of such generalities. Grasping of general essence or ideas is called ideation, which are the original kind of immediate, intuitive experience. It should be noted here that universal propositions can be grasped only by the admission of general essences. These essences or entities are *sui generis*, but have a mode of being that makes it possible to formulate true propositions about them.

4.1.2 What Meaning is, what Meaning is not?

The meaning that Husserl refers to, is neither the object, nor the representation of objects, nor a mental picture, nor even an intuition of the object. Husserl's basic thesis with respect to meaning is that, it is an ideal entity. No other thesis of Husserl has been subjected to so much unfavourable criticism. By making this assertion, Husserl has the following three points in mind.

1. Meanings retain identity in the midst of varying contexts (**identity**).

2. Meaning can be communicated from one person to another (**communicability**).

3. The same or different speakers can retain the same meaning in different speech acts and contexts (**repeatability**).

These three, referred to as identity, communicability and repeatability of meanings, constitute the objectivity of meanings. These are internally related (i.e., thought, feeling and intuition) to the mental life of the person participating in them. Though meanings do not belong to the real order of temporality, spatiality and individuality of events, they are incarnate in physical expressions, words and sentences that are extrinsic to meanings. Yet, they are united with meanings. Consider the following example. Recall the colour white, present in various things in the room, and the meaning of white in our understanding. The meaning of white that is the colour of the roof, the white that is the colour of the switch board, the white of this sheet of paper are all instantiations of white in understanding.

4.1.3 What is Meaning?

For Husserl, meaning is always the meaning of an act, an act of intentional experience. Meaning consists in understanding words and sentences. If I do not understand them, they are not meaningful to me; they are meaningful only to the person who understands them. The sense in which a physical inscription (a written text) or an oral discourse is meaningful, is derived from the primary sense, inasmuch as we posit one thing or the other as being the source of that meaningfulness. To say that an act is intentional means that an object is intended in a certain manner of being; it ascribes a certain meaning and reference to it. For Husserl, meanings are contents of acts. I perceive something, on the basis of which, I state that it is white, implying that the meaning of the sentence is the content of my act of perceptual judgement. Hence the content grasped is the meaning. The sentence is not limited to the few words that I utter, neither is it limited to the gestures that I make while uttering the sentence; it consists in understanding the sense or contents of what I said. Meaning is the ideal content of words and gestures. This implies that the real component of an experience is such that each component is a real bit of that experience, or an intentional correlate that necessarily accompanies an act. What is *not* meaning? Meaning is not a private particular, neither is it the object towards which an act may be directed, i.e., the intended object.

4.1.4 Meaning and Linguistic Expression

Expressions are meaningful signs that Husserl defines through their meanings. According to Husserl, "the essence of an expression lies exclusively in its meanings" (Husserl, 1977o). Expressions are not just names. Speech shall count as an expression when it has communicative motive. In other words, Husserl's primary concern is speech, neither the written word, nor the documented language. He examines the act of speaking, not from the hearer's viewpoint, but from the speaker's. If meanings are rooted solely in intuition, then the symbolic way of thinking should be held questionable; and if meanings were identified solely by objects, then imaginary ones such as mermaids would be meaningless. Hence Husserl invented a third method of discovering meaning in speech acts, which was later accepted by Heidegger[1] as well, since both attached meaning to the spoken language. Speech, as an expressive act, is the primary phenomenon. It is a rule-governed behaviour, an intentional act containing both meaning and reference. Speech, as a demonstrative mode of consciousness, is a living act; it is both animating and an animated context of expressive act.

4.1.5 Extension of the Theory of Meaning to all Intentional Expressive Acts

Husserl extended his theory of meaning, rooted in the act of speaking, to include various kinds of expressive acts, such as acts of perceiving, imagining, thinking, remembering, hoping, desiring or loving, all of which have a certain kind of expressive character. Husserl justifies these contentions and claims by stating originally that these words relate only to the sphere of speech (Husserl, 1976o). Originally, these words relate only to the sphere of speech. This extended concept of meaning is described as *Sinn*, retaining the word *Bedeutung* to explain the meaning of expressions at the linguistic and conceptual level.

4.1.6 Conditions for Assigning Meaning

Husserl holds that linguistic utterances acquire meaning on account of the conscious acts of the speaker. Assigning a linguistic expression with meaning cannot be capricious or whimsical; it is determined by individual, personal, communitarian and cultural considerations of language. The expressions and acts that animate them with meaning are not detached or divorced from each other; instead, they are bound up with one another, forming two sides of the same coin.

4.1.7 Meanings are Intentional

Being intentional, meanings are directed to an object, and hence a referent is required for it to be complete, implying that the intentionality thesis suggests meaningfulness. Meaning demarcates experiences in which an object is meant or intended. Husserl speaks of the transformation of the 'object tree' to the '*noema* tree' as a result of intentionality (Husserl, 1976h). But the difference between tree as an object and as a *noema* is extrememly radical. The object tree can be destroyed, but not the *noema* tree. Meanings are

---

[1] Heidegger, in his book, *An Introduction to Metaphysics*, wrote that interpretation occurs through language. The true foundation of language from the point of view of hermeneutic phenomenology is not proposition, judgement or statement, but the phenomenon of speech. The hermeneutic function of language shines forth in speech, which is the living context of language.

intentional in the sense that they are directed, and this being the case, a referent is required to complete the directions. Meanings are acts of consciousness. How objects appear to us depend on how they are given to us, and when our consciousness encounters it. Someone appears to us as a stranger or friend only because of the manner in which we are conscious of him. It depends on the type of experience within which he appears to us.

4.1.8 Meaning is the Meaning of an Act

For Husserl, meaning is primarily the meaning of an act, i.e., an intentional act or experience. To say that an act is intentional implies that it is intended in a certain manner. It ascribes both meaning (sense) and reference to it. When Husserl states that meanings are (ideal) contents of a conscious act, it means that they are intentional correlates that necessarily accompany an intentional act. It is important to stress that meanings thus conceived by Husserl are not objects of normal acts, but of linguistic acts. Further, the identity of meanings from act to act is the identity of species.

4.1.9 Meaning and Species

Husserl speaks of meanings as ideal entities or species. If meanings are described as species, then it must be understood as species of acts and not as species of objects. In the ontology of *Logical Investigations*, meanings are considered as species. We can speak of the same meanings from speaker to speaker, from one occasion to another, by virtue of the fact that there are numerically different individual moments of meanings in the relevant acts, e.g., acts of presentation or of judgement serve to instantiate identical species. Meaning is one, acts are many, meaning is identical with itself, and acts are concrete instances of this self-identical meanings. Meanings are ranged above acts that instantiate them. Meanings are a kind of meta-knowledge. They are ideal, universal. It may be remarked that it is meaning-acts rather than meanings that are responsible for object directedness.

4.2 Meanings and Monologue (Non-Linguistic Expressions)

4.2.1 Meaning in Non-expressive and Non-Linguistic Contexts

Does the assertion that expressive linguistic expressions exclude non-linguistic expressions such as gestures, smiling or groaning (in pain) from the purview of meanings? Sometimes these non-linguistic expressions may not convey anything at all unless interpreted. So, the question of interpretation becomes essential here. These non-linguistic expressive behaviours, viz., a person groaning, is interpreted as a sign of pain, while smiling as a sign of happiness. But they need not mean exactly as what they appear outwardly, for a person can very well pretend to be in pain. They may not express genuine thought. Non-linguistic expressions would mean that one has turned away from communicative to confirmative speech, i.e., to inner monologues, soliloquy or some sort of silent speech to oneself. In *Logical Investigations*, Husserl remarks that although meaning can be expressed only outwardly, articulated words can be dispensed with, as in the case of monologue or soliloquy or silent inner self-speech. Husserl writes (Husserl, 1977n) that it is not communicative speech in the sense of speaking to others, but confirmative speech through which one interacts with oneself before finally confirming or deciding for oneself, the core or essence of speech to the other. Heidegger uses the expression *Rede* in this sense. The essential core of speech consists in 1) expressing meaning or thought, and 2) it refers to some object. This kind of eidetic variation by way of rudimentary eidetic reduction of expressive speech is a must to arrive at confirmative speech. The speaker's inner monologue or expressions is a lived experience of the same.

The switch from communicative to inner confirmative speech may be regarded as a decisive step for Husserl's subsequent philosophizing. Inner speech can be made a constant presence to oneself, which is not possible with communicative speech, the latter being evanescent, flowing and passing, and therefore always new and unrepeatable. The reduction of communicative speech to inner speech conforms to the general trend of transcendental phenomenological reduction. It is true that *Logical Investigations* does not bring in the notion of phenomenological reduction. However, in transforming communicative speech to confirmative speech, in converting expressive speech to monologues and soliloquy, Husserl gives an indication of the eidetic reduction about which he speaks in detail, both in *The Idea of Phenomenology* (Husserl, 1999) and in *Ideas I* (Husserl, 1976d). It is a sort of initial practice of eidetic reduction. In communicative speech, words uttered disappear, since each uttered word is evanescent. But in confirmative speech, words do not disappear, instead, they sink into one's consciousness and is ever available to the speaker, on account of self-presence. In other words, the now or the present gnaws at the already said in the past, and that which is going to be said in the future. And moreover, the pre-requisite for the ideality thesis (meanings are ideal entities) is not the repeatability of inner speech, but their meanings; since the latter are shareable (others can understand and participate in it), the so-called allegation of privacy of the transcendental ego (the person) is thus overcome.

4.2.2 Transformation of communicative speech to confirmative speech and establishing meaning in the living context of human reality

Husserl reduces communicative speech to monologue, though this transformation appears to run the risk of psychologism and relativism. It must be kept in mind that Husserl's motive in turning to monologue is precisely to avoid and even eliminate the dangers of psychologism by eidetic reduction. The reduction of communicative speech acts to confirmative speech acts makes the acts of meanings almost indistinguishable. The soliloquising thinker understands his words, which is simply an act of grasping the content, which is the meaning. Meaning, meanwhile, consists in understanding words and sentences. If I do not understand them, they are not meaningful to me. They are meaningful only to the person who understands them. Husserl's move towards monologue is a move that needs to be supplemented by the thesis of objectivity of meanings, the identity of language, and finally the intersubjectivity constitution of language. On account of the shift in emphasis from written to spoken language, from the act of speech to monologue, meaning is re-established in the living context of human condition. Husserl's thesis does not require non-empirical consciousness for an ideal meaning, but implies that real temporal acts of consciousness are correlated to ideal meanings. The inner monologue is as much a real, temporal event as an instance of overt speech.

4.3 Ideality of Meanings

4.3.1 The difference between Meaning and Essence

There are at least four strands of thought in Husserl's phenomenology of meaning, namely,

1. Phenomenology began as a programme of describing essence on the basis of intuition, and essential structures of the various regions of phenomena.

2. It was initially concerned with the meaning of words and expressions in language, i.e., a semantic concern; but later, this concern for meanings overshadowed other concerns (viz., the concern for essence).

3. Thereafter, meaning and essence were identified with species; the genuine identity that we assert can be the identity of species (Husserl, 1977m).[2]

---

[2] The essence of an expression is identified solely by its meaning.

4. Finally, they were both sharply distinguished from each other, and the importance of meaning stressed over that of essence. Meaning does not coincide with the object. The object never coincides with the meaning (Husserl, 1977m).

Since the time of Plato and Aristotle, essence always remained a metaphysical concept, held superior to meaning. Though meanings had a semantic character in the early part of *Logical Investigations*, it has been considered phenomenological, ever since meanings were linked to intentionality, epoché, phenomenological reductions and other phenomenological concepts. Husserl also holds that meanings are irreal, adding that only irreal meanings can defy individuation by spatio-temporal ingredients, and irreality alone can maintain identity in multiplicity. For Husserl, meanings are not a part of ontology, but essences are. Meanings spring from a phenomenological attitude via epoché and reductions, and therefore turn away from the object-oriented ontological point of view. It must be added that any entity that we admit into ontology must be such that it can be referred to, and only individuals and essence can be referred to in this manner.

4.3.2 Ideality and Objectivity of Meanings

Husserl emphasized the ideality of meanings, which implies three things, 1) meanings retain an identity in varying contexts, called the identity or context independence of meanings, 2) meanings can be communicated from one person to another, called shareability or communicability of meanings, and 3) the same speaker(s) can return to the same meanings in different contexts, called the repeatability of meanings. These three, viz., identity, shareability and repeatability, are collectively called objectivity or ideality of meanings. Plato's theory of meaning has all the above characteristics, but errs in separating meanings from concrete meaning-experiencing acts by substantiating the former into entities existing in the world of ideas. By doing so, he cut off meanings from the subjective life of persons, and also from experiences that bear them. To grasp the totality of Husserl's understanding of meanings, the following five points are helpful.

1. Meanings are characterized by identity and context independence.

2. Meanings are sharable/communicable from one person to another, and this enables us to say they are objective in the phenomenological sense, i.e., objectivity is subjective shareability.

3. Meanings are internally related to the mental life of a person, to thought, feelings, and intuition.

4. Though meanings are different from the real order of temporally individuated events, they nevertheless serve as a medium (*noema* is medium) of reference for things, events, processes or places.

5. They are incarnated in physical expressions, such as words or sentences, all of which are conventional signs (and therefore extrinsic to words), and yet united with the meanings that they signify.

4.3.3 The Presumptive Ideality of Language vs Ideality Proper of Meanings

The ideality of language or linguistic expressions is different from the ideality of meanings, called presumptive ideality. Language has an objective being handed down by tradition. As a persisting and abiding system, '*the*', the definite article, (a syncategorematic expression) occurs repeatedly in the English language, both in writing and speaking. Each inscription or uttering is a distinct occurrence and a separate event, and there seems to be no way of bringing them under the same linguistic umbrella, Although distinct, 'the' is always a definite article with the same meaning, and therefore, has an identity within itself, described by Husserl as a presumptive or corporeal ideality, its function being that it retains its meaning in the varying multiplicity of contexts. This presumptive ideality of language is not the same as the ideality of meanings that words and sentences express. Ideal meanings are contents of acts, called meaning-intending or meaning-conferring acts.

4.4 Meaning and Reference

Expressions, their meanings and references are crucial in Husserl's elucidation of meaning. It indicates not just Husserl's close familiarity with his contemporaries who contributed to the development of the notion of meaning but also his serious reservations with them, especially Frege. Husserl begins his examination of meaning, stating that, "each expression, not merely says something, but says it of something" (Husserl, 1977p). This implies the following things,

1. Every expression has meaning and reference. Meaning, from the Husserlian point of view, initially means that the meaning of a linguistic expression and the reference is the reference to an object.

2. There is a clear distinction between the object and meaning, and meaning transcends the object.

3. Meaning and reference spring from linguistic expressions, i.e., expression is the source of meaning; it is a meaningful sign (Husserl, 1977n).

4. Meaning is the content (refer to Dr Sen's example to explicate the sense of content).

5. The distinction between content and object is the same as the distinction between what is meant and what is spoken of.

4.4.1 The Ontological Divide

Husserl, in his early phenomenological period, was working against a dominant understanding of meaning, linking it with reference, of which Frege was a major proponent. The referential theory of meaning refers to a linguistic expression, an object, or in other words, to a referent. It states that a linguistic expression has meaning by virtue of its reference to certain objects, properties or relation to the world. Although reference is an important factor, Husserl is totally against the identification of meaning and the referent, stating that "the object never coincides with meaning," which implies that the object and its meaning belong to two different categories or regions namely, the regions of ideality and reality. This is an ontological divide between meaning and object. Meanings exist neither in properties, nor objects, nor entities.

4.4.2 What does a Sign Mean?

To be a sign is to be a sign for something, which in turn, is to point something out. But all signs do not exhibit meaning, i.e., not all expressions are signs. It also means that expressions are meaningful signs. The concept of a sign is wider than the concept of expressions. In this sense, speech is an expression or an expressive act. Distinguishing expressions from signs, Husserl proceeds to state that expressions function as signs in communicative speech acts, whereas in communicative speech, the speaker's expressions serve as signs of thought to the hearer, which he describes as the pronouncing-function. Communication is the original function of language; but there is also a meaning-function in communicative acts. It may be noted that communicative expression has three functions namely, 1) meaning function, 2) naming function and 3) pronouncing function, among which, the first two are prominent, for they make expressions truly expressions, i.e., expressions-qua-expressions. And, it is this meaning and naming function that lead us directly to the Frege-Husserl controversy.

4.4.3 Schröder, Lotze, Frege and Husserl

Husserl published his book *Philosophie der Arithmetik* (Philosophy of Arithmetic) (Husserl, 1970b) in early 1891, wherein he committed the error of psychologism. Frege reviewed the same in 1894, pointing out the error and criticising it. Fortunately for Husserl, he had caught the error and corrected it in late 1891 when he reviewed Schröder's book, *Algebra der Logik* (Schröder, 1890). Husserl understood his error when he asked himself two questions, 1) whether there belongs to a name, a meaning (*Sinn*), and 2) whether or not an object corresponding to it (a reference) exists; the second question was more crucial than the first. According to Husserl, Schröder got confused while dealing with these two questions, and Husserl corrected his own erroneous thinking to such an extent that he refused to publish the second part of his book. It was such a radical conversion for Husserl that he reconsidered his position and reviewed his entire philosophical commitment. Fortunately, this revaluation augured well for phenomenology, originating from this reassessment. In fact, when Frege's review was brought to Husserl's notice, the latter remarked: "External influences are without significance, my course was already marked out by *Philosophie der Arithmetik*. And I could do nothing other than to proceed further" (Farber, 1940). The first point to be noted here is that Husserl realized the error of psychologism himself, prior to, and independent of Frege's intervention. In all probability, the logician, Lotze, could have been instrumental behind this, for Husserl went on to study him immediately after publishing his habilitations. The second point is that a cursory glance at *Philosophy der Arithmetik* can tell us that psychologism was not the major issue for Husserl in that work. So, there was no need for Frege to make such a hue and cry on a non-issue. But several of Husserl's earlier students and disciples harbour the misconception that he changed his views on psychologism due to Frege's criticism. We are ever indebted to Prof. Mohanty for clarifying several difficult issues in the Husserl-Frege controversy.

4.4.4 Frege and Husserl on Sense and Reference

There is commonality and difference between Frege and Husserl with regard to the notion of sense and reference, which is as follows. Both asserted the objectivity of meaning, as opposed to the subjectivity of meaning and privacy of mental states. Both consider the objectivity of meaning incompatible with any thesis, making them real components of mental states. However, the differences are much more serious than their similarities. For Frege, mental states are imminent, private episodes. Meanings are to be apprehended in mental acts. But they are neither real constituents of the mind, nor in any way related to it. In contrast, Husserl held that mental states are intentional, founded on imminent private experiences, while an act, insofar as it is intentional, has a correlative meaning that is objective. This peculiar and decisive intentional correlative character gives him a concept of objectivity, completely different from Frege's. Most importantly, meaning, according to Frege, is *Bedeutung*, i.e., meaning of words, sentences, logical concepts and conceptual meanings. But for Husserl, meaning is the meaning of expressive speech acts, i.e. *Sinn*. In other words, Husserl's theory of meaning is concerned with both linguistic and conceptual meanings (*Bedeutung*), as well as with *noematic* sense, i.e., *Sinn*. For Husserl, meanings are ideal contents, intentional correlates of acts, whereas, according to Frege, meanings belong to ontology. For Husserl, meanings do not belong to any ontology, but to intentional consciousness. From these discussions, we can understand that Husserl's full-blown notion of intentionality had a great advantage in comprehending the notion of meaning, which Frege lacked. It also enabled Husserl to develop his views on meaning successfully, without which Frege could not sort out several traditional problems with respect to meaning.

4.4.5 Frege's Notion of Sinn and Husserl's notion of noema

Frege's notion of *Sinn* is close to Husserl's understanding of *noema*. But there are several differences too. One major point of intersection is that, both in Husserl and Frege, we find objectivity of meanings, distinguished from subjectivity, variability and privacy of mental states. And, the objectivity of meanings rules out meaning being a real component of mental act. However, Husserl insists on intentional correlationship. In fact, all objectivity, according to Husserl, consists in intentional correlation. Some differences between them are as follows. The Husserlian *noema* are first conceived to be ideal contents, and subsequently to be correlative of subjective acts. But Frege's notion of *Sinn* has no such relationship to acts apprehending them. In fact, all objectivity according to Husserl consists in intentional correlation. Further, the difference between Frege and Husserl on *Sinn* is that Frege's *Sinn* are meanings of linguistic expressions; they are conceptual meanings, which Frege refers to as *Bedeutung*. However, Husserl's *noemata* are meanings of acts, both conscious and speech acts. Husserl's notion of *Bedeutung*, which in *Logical Investigations*, is the counterpart of Frege's notion of *Sinn*, is the meaning of expressive acts, or of linguistic expressions. Right from the beginning of his phenomenological career, Husserl's concept of meaning was clearly related to his concept of intentionality. His interest in the first investigation of *Logical Investigations* was not in words or sentences, but in the acts constituting them, namely, intentional acts. The ideal, objective meaning of the first investigation of *Logical Investigations* is the intentional correlates of real meanings of intending acts of expressions. It is this notion that enters into *Ideas I* as well. In Frege's thesis, it is *Sinn* that becomes the object of reference. But Husserl does not regard *noema* as the object of reference; *noema* is the medium of reference. Thus, the Fregean *Sinn* refers to metaphysics. But Husserlian *Sinn* does not find place in any ontology. Husserl also claims that ideal meanings are *noemata* and contents of intentional acts. In Husserl, meanings are not objects, but a media of reference; they are *noema* through which objects are referred to or arrived at. In the final analysis, it needs to be pointed out that for Husserl, strictly speaking, there is nothing like linguistic meaning, which Frege has been harping about. From a phenomenological perspective, the meaning of the object is *noema*, the object as meant. Meaning is the demarcator of those experiences in which an object is meant or intended, and *noema* is the meaning of the object. When 'tree' is used as a *noema*, Husserl often encloses it in quotes to indicate the change of meanings from object to *noema* (Husserl, 1976h).

4.5 Platonic Theory of Meaning-Ontology and Ideality

4.5.1 Platonic and non-Platonic Theories of Meaning

Husserl's theory of meaning is an attempt to take into account, the various facets of our encounter with the experience of meaning. Broadly, theories of meaning can be classified into Platonic and non-Platonic; non-Platonic is further divided into psychological and non-psychological theories. The former emphasizes the ontological character of meaning conceived as entities which subsist, and they are substantial entities existing in the world of ideas. Words signify them contingently, but the mind inspects them while thinking about them and understanding them. Non-Platonic theories, while denying the subsistent character of meaning, reduce meaning to a kind of mental life of the speaker and the hearer. But they rescue meanings from the privacy of mental life, and account for the meaningfulness of words in terms of rules of their use in a given language. They are right in not cutting meanings off from the meaningful life of persons, but unfortunately, they do not have a notion of mental life, and hence there are serious drawbacks.

4.5.2 Does Husserl accept Plato's Ontology?

Husserl's acceptance of the Platonic theory of meaning concerns the fulfilling of meaning in/of intending acts. In fact, Husserl is far from indulging in any kind of ontology, for he is not concerned with the existence of entities; they undergo, due to phenomenological procedure, eidetic reduction. He is instead concerned with the intentional correlates of the meaning of intending experiences. After all, phenomenology does not claim to go beyond the given. The given object is the intended object. The object-intended is the *noema*, and the act of intending is the *noesis*, which is the *noetico-noematic* correlational context. Return to the object is not a commitment to any ontology. The *noema* or the intentional correlate is inseparably linked to subjective, *noetic*, experiences. From another point of view, *noetic* acts reveal themselves as merely leading to the intended object (*noema*). They stand together, and by doing so, they have meaning enriching each other. They offer, not a conflicting, but a complimentary description of phenomenon.

4.5.3 Can Husserl be called a Platonist?

Husserl's point is that meanings of universal propositions can be satisfied only by the admission of general essences. In this context, Husserl has been accused of Platonism. All that Husserl states is that universals are entities of their own. He never exclaimed them to be real, eternal, changeless or even superior to particulars. He also goes on to say that universals are constituted by one's own subjective consciousness, derived from the perceptual experience of particulars.

4.5.4 What kind of Platonism did Husserl accept even if he is called a Platonist?

In Husserl's phenomenology, there is a kind of Platonism, an expression Husserl used very unwillingly due to lack of a better expression. But what kind of Platonism was it? The Platonic hypostasizing (substantializing) of essence, which thereby becomes a reality, occurs in two different forms, according to Theodore de Boer; only one form can be found in Husserl, i.e., hypostasizing something outside thought, also referred to as metaphysical hypostasizing (de Boer, 1978a). Husserl finds fault with Plato for attributing substantiality or real existence to ideas. The second kind of hypostasizing is assigning substantiality to something within thought, which Husserl refers to as conceptual hypostasizing. In this case, essence is hypostasized to form a reality within consciousness, the real existence of the species within the bounds of thought. Against conceptual hypostasizing, Husserl points out that there is no universal triangle in consciousness other than the one within the real world, i.e., outside consciousness. What is absurd in reality is also absurd in the mind, since psychological being is also a reality. Similar to Brentano, Husserl rejects any Platonizing conception of universals as a separate reality beyond things (de Boer, 1978b). Husserl completely rejects the metaphysical hypostasizing of Platonism, despite which, he occasionally calls himself a realist due to the lack of a better term to characterize himself in this regard. Moreover, when he calls himself a realist, he places the term within quotes. In other words, Husserl's version is a revised Platonism, which conceives the so-called reality as ideality. Both Prof. Mohanty and de Boer point out that Husserl arrived at this interpretation of Plato on account of Lotze, whose interpretation of thinking exercised deep influence on him. We can use the term realist, with respect to Husserl, only insofar as he accepts a being, independent of consciousness. But can there be a being independent of consciousness from a phenomenological perspective? I am of the firm opinion that, from a phenomenological point of view, the so called being, independent of consciousness, cannot be accepted by any stretch of imagination. Husserl repeatedly said that existence itself, and not just meanings, is dependent on consciousness. Consciousness is the fulcrum of phenomenology, around which everything moves, giving them both meaning and being. The intentional object is an intentional mode of being, but the Platonic ideal object is independent of consciousness, and this cannot be accepted by Husserl.

4.6 Meaning and Essence

4.6.1 Medium and Reflective Reflection

Two major points discussed here are: 1) are Husserlian meanings essences? And 2) are Husserlian essences meanings? To answer the first question, we need to know the functions of meaning, *Sinn* and *noema* in Husserl. *Noema* originates from an act of consciousness, and is arrived at by perceptual reflection or perspectival glance; here the chair as an elevated platform or weapon is not the object of intentional consciousness, for the object is the chair itself. *Noema* is the medium/agency[3] through which the object is arrived at. The act of consciousness is directed towards the object, the chair, for intentional consciousness is always directed to the object. It is an act of reflection that is directed towards the *noema*. What does this reflection mean? We need to distinguish between an act of consciousness directed to the object and the reflective glance towards the *noema*. *Noematic* reflection is a reflective one directed to oneself. It is a higher order consciousness compared to the object's consciousness. Sartre's notion of pre-reflective and reflective consciousness is useful to understand these concepts. Consciousness of an object, according to Sartre, is pre-reflective consciousness, whereas one's reflection of oneself is reflective reflection, aimed at discovering the depths of meaning assigning self. It is an internally directed reflection that is contemplative, meditative and self-revelatory, which indicates the how of reflection. It is a reflection returning to oneself for the sake of discovering or elucidating oneself; it is my attempt to understand myself. It is such a reflection that can unravel the mystery of the self. It is a reflection to understand the manifold layers of the constitutive powers of the self; such a

---

[3] The expression, 'medium' requires a little clarification. We speak about medium through which a living person can speak to his departed near and dear ones. We speak of oil paint as the medium by which a painting is brought to life by an artist. The medium, i.e., the paint used by the artist, or the person through whom we speak to departed ones, is not the object or the end that we arrive at or aim to achieve; they are a means to an end, the object. Surely there is immense difference between the medium and end, and Husserl is interested only in the medium, i.e., *noema*, for *noema* is meaning.

reflection points towards the unfathomable depths of discovering meaning, even in the apparently meaningless phenomenon of death confronting human existence (death from the perspective of Sartre vs Heidegger). It is a creative and regenerative reflection aimed at innovation, and a realization of the profundity of the self. It is a meditation upon myself revealing my spiritual relationship to others, and to the world in general, or creation at large. It is a reflection that reveals that I am not just the foundation of my world that I have brought into existence, i.e., my world, (mineness from the perspective of Heidegger) but that, my world is dependent on me for its meaning as well. It is an authentic, internally directed reflection. But consciousness of an object is externally directed, revealing the what of reflection. It is directed outward; externality characterizes the reflection of the object. It is the kind of reflection studied in different kinds of philosophies, and also in (empirical) psychology. It is the ordinary, mundane, everyday kind of consciousness regarding entities and external realities. It is founded on the Platonic and Aristotelian logic.

4.6.2 Husserl on Meaning and Essence

To answer the first question above, as to whether Husserlian meanings are essences, meanings do exhibit identity, non-temporality and independence of real occasions; these they share with ideal entities or essences as well, but that does not imply that meanings are essences. The distinctions are as follows. Consider an example, the meaning and essence of red (or redness). What is the meaning of a red patch on my cheek? It might mean that I got drunk last evening, got into a brawl and got beat up. My red cheek indicates my drunkenness and misbehaviour; but the essence of redness is something else. Red is a part of the colour spectrum; when a ray of light passes through a prism, it splits into a range of constitutive component colours depicted by VIBGYOR. All these colours have frequency and wavelength, of which red has the lowest frequency, and is at the end of the visible spectrum, next to orange. It is one of the primary colours along with blue and green. These properties form part of the essence of the colour red. However, from the perspective of meaning, red is the symbol of danger, anger, it is a sign asking us not to proceed further. It indicates violence, bloodshed, and even a sort of sadism. It refers to a particular political ideology that promotes aggression at least implicitly. In each of these cases, red has been assigned a unique meaning, with essence flowing outward from the object. To put it in the Aristotelian language, essence is metaphysical, it is part and parcel of the object itself. However, meaning is phenomenological. To say that a thing exists implies that it can be referred to. Essences are entities, and are real, like things. But meaning is not an object of reference, but a medium of reference, through which we refer to something. Meaning-qua-meaning is not an entity.

As to the second question, as to whether are all Husserlian essences meanings, the answer is definitely in the negative. Essences are objects of possible reference, and are one and the same, referred to through different meanings. For example, a bench, a bed, a door or a table are all different things with the same essence (wood) manifested in all these entities. But meaning-qua-meaning, chair as an elevated platform or weapon or comfortable seat are not entities; meaning is a transcendental phenomenological category, but essences are objects of reference.

4.6.3 Meaning and Essence: Robert Solomon's Position

Robert Solomon, in his book, *From Hegel to Existentialism* (Solomon, 1987), contradicts what has been said so far about the distinction between meaning and essence, instead, strongly identifies meaning with essence. He points out that Husserl denies the distinction between meaning and essence, and affirms that the latter introduces the concept of meaning as *Sinn* in *Logical Investigations* in order to explain the relation of necessary concepts (essences) to meanings. He adds that essence is independent of matters of fact, and that the intuition of essence is different from the experience of matters of fact. Husserl speaks of necessary being whenever he refers to essences. Solomon also affirms that in *Ideas I*, Husserl uses the hyphenated, compound word, meaning-essence, to demonstrate the unity of meaning and essence. Thus, Solomon concludes that both in *Logical Investigations* and *Ideas I*, meanings and essences are not separate from each other, but instead, intimately linked to the other. He justifies his position, quoting Husserl, "The essence of an expression lies exclusively in its meaning" (Husserl, 1977o). In view of this and such other assertions, the strong denunciation of the identification of meaning and essence, as stated by Prof. Mohanty, must be taken with a pinch of salt.

I agree with Solomon in stating that meanings are related to objects since object-as-meant is the *noema* or meaning. Surely the object-as-meant, the *noema*, is not real or spatio-temporal; but one cannot deny the strong relation between the object and the object-as-meant, for there cannot be an object-as-meant, without the existance of the former. The object-as-meant can only arise conditional to an object, for it is from the latter that one constitutes the object-as-meant, the *noema*. But it is to be noted that the object undergoes phenomenological reduction, whereas the object-as-meant or *noema* is constituted. Moreover, as Husserl defines an expression by its meaning, a linguistic unit can be described as an expression only because it is meaningful. Prof. Mohanty's position appears to be correct despite the fact there are texts that can be adduced to support Solomon's position as well.

Essence arises from the object. But from Husserl's phenomenological perspective, the object undergoes eidetic reduction. What we have then, is not the object as such, but the object-as-meant (*noema*/meaning). Insofar as this is the case, an object cannot be same as the object-as-meant; both are very different. Solomon's position with regard to the distinction between object and object-as-meant needs revision, since Husserl writes: "the object never coincides with meaning"(Husserl, 1977n). Solomon cannot ignore passages from Husserl himself contrary to his position. It may also be noted that Prof. Mohanty authored an article (Mohanty, 1970), in which he does not refer to meaning at all. True, the point of that article was not to discuss meaning; but Prof. Mohanty, being a phenomenologist par excellence, had he believed that there was some relation between meaning and essence, would have discussed it, or at least, hinted at it. His silence speaks volumes about his conviction and position regarding the difference between meaning and essence. Had there been any relation between meaning and essence, there could have been some remarks on it in the above-mentioned article. And, that clearly shows that essences cannot be identified with meanings.

One cannot deny the fact that there are passages in Husserl that describe identity, as well as the difference between meaning and essence. Prof. Mohanty acknowledges the fact that Husserl identified meaning and essence, and he later refers to this when he speaks of the four stages in Husserl's development in the understanding of meaning; though he leans more towards asserting the fact that that Husserl maintains a very strong separation between the two. Unfortunately, Solomon does not even acknowledge the difference. Prof. Mohanty selected such passages from Husserl that suited him, similar to Solomon. To summarise, phenomenology is a perspectival study of a subject matter, which when undertaken could result in a position contrary to one's own. One cannot reject or ignore such a position, but only strive to discover the means to account for it. The ingenuity of an author consists in exploring common grounds despite differences; ignoring the opposite position is not the solution. The positions of both Prof. Mohanty and Solomon can be justified on the basis of texts from Husserl.

4.6.4 Meaning-Intention and Meaning-Fulfilment

In his elucidation of meaning, Husserl does not give us any criterion for the same, instead he aims at describing what it means for an expression to be meaningful. In this regard, Husserl's theory centres around meaning-intention and meaning-fulfilment. An expression has meaning-intention, provided it has meaning. A meaningless expression, say for example, abdefu (a collection of a few Latin alphabets) lacks meaning, and therefore carries no meaning-intention. It is this feature of meaning-intention that constitutes the core of an expression-qua-expression. Expression-qua-expression, a genuine expression, is constituted by meaning-intending acts. All meaningful expressions are meaningful by virtue of the meaning-intention that they embody. According to Husserl, thinking consists in meaning-intending acts, and insofar as meaning-intention is not fulfilled, we have no knowledge. But his position regarding meaning-fulfilment is this, knowing consists in the fulfilment of meaning-intentions; insofar as meaning-intention is not fulfilled, we do not have knowledge, which is an intuitive apprehension that is symbolically thought of. Meaning-intention and meaning-fulfilment are correlative concepts. The former accounts for our understanding of an expression, while the latter to the difference between mere thought (symbolic understanding) on the one hand, and knowledge on the other. Meaning-fulfilment is meant to absorb all that is valuable in our knowledge. Thinking, meaning-intention and meaning-fulfilment are also intuitions in a narrow sense. Knowledge, as distinguished from thought, consists in an intuitive fulfilment of an intention. Corresponding to meaning-intention and meaning-fulfilment, we may speak of contents of those acts which intend meaning and which fulfil meaning. Both meaning-intention and meaning-fulfilment are acts of awareness.

4.6.5 Meaning in Later Husserl

In his later works, especially in *Crisis of European Sciences*, and to a certain extent in *Cartesian Meditations*, Husserl brings forward the notion of the genetic phenomenological theory of meaning instead of the static theory of meaning, discussed in *Logical Investigations* and *Ideas I* without major alterations, which can be noted in his Origin of Geometry (Husserl, 1970g). The notions that play crucial roles in the genetic phenomenology of meanings are, horizon, temporality, history and tradition, wherein Husserl no more considers history an empirical science or a set of previously occurred events, but as the present interpretation of the past, in view of the future. He goes on to add that actual history is the history of meanings; it is the unity of co-existence of the formations of meanings arising from time to time for human purposes. The historicity of meanings reveals that there can be no absolute meanings and totally new beginnings of meanings. In this context, language and tradition have a major role to play, for meanings evolve as language develops. Tradition depends on the creative reproduction of the past, for otherwise, tradition is a dead and irrelevant collection of events that occurred to someone in the past. Insofar as meanings refer to language, and the latter has a social dimension, social world determines specific meanings that cater to the individual life. Meanings originate from already existing meanings, and develop further by addition of more and more scales of meanings to it, similar to a ball of ice rolling down a slope collects more snow, gaining in weight and momentum. Meanings gain greater significance in the context of meanings. In *Cartesian Meditations*, Husserl asserts that consciousness is possible only in the context of a meaningful world, while our experiences can be understood only in the horizon of a meaningful world. Meanings create and recreate horizons, allowing us to delve deeper into meanings, though these meanings essentially possess an individual and personal character, i.e., what is meaningful is meaning for me alone. To conclude, meanings are communitarian, since they account for a community of people communicating with one another.

4.7 References

de Boer, T. (1978a). Husserl's 'Platonism' or 'Realism'. In T. Platinga (Trans.), *The Development of Husserl's Thought* (p. 264). Martinus Nijhoff Publishers, The Hague.

de Boer, T. (1978b). Recapitulation of the Problem. In T. Platinga (Trans.), *The Development of Husserl's Thought* (p. 235). Martinus Nijhoff Publishers, The Hague.

Farber, M. (1940). Edmund Husserl and the Background of his Philosophy. *Philosophy and Phenomenological Research, 13*(1), 1–20.

Husserl, E. (1970a). *Philosophie der Arithmetik: Mit Ergänzenden Texten (1890–1901) (Husserliana: Edmund Husserl – Gesammelte Werke-XII)* (L. Eley, Ed.). Martinus Nijhoff. The Hague. Netherlands.

Husserl, E. (1970b). The Origin of Geometry. In D. Carr (Trans.), *The Crisis of European Sciences and Transcendental Phenomenology* (pp. 353–378). Northwestern University Press.

Husserl, E. (1976a). *Ideas: General Introduction to Pure Phenomenology and to a Phenomenological Philosophy* (W. R. B. Gibson, Trans.). Humanities Press.

Husserl, E. (1976b). Real (*reelle*) and intentional factors of experience. The noema, Section 88. In W. R. B. Gibson (Trans.), *Ideas: General Introduction to Pure Phenomenology* (pp. 257–259). Humanities Press.

Husserl, E. (1976c). The Noetic-noematic Stratum of the 'Logos'. Meaning and Meaning Something, Section 124. In W. R. B. Gibson (Trans.), *Ideas: General Introduction to Pure Phenomenology* (p. 346). Humanities Press.

Husserl, E. (1977a). Investigation I: Connection between Meaning and Objective Reference, Section 13. In J. N. Findlay (Trans.), *Logical Investigations Volume 1* (p. 289). Routledge & Kegan Paul.

Husserl, E. (1977b). Investigation I: Continuation: The Objective Correlate of an Expression, Section 12. In J. N. Findlay (Trans.), *Logical Investigations Volume 1* (p. 287). Routledge & Kegan Paul.

Husserl, E. (1977c). Investigation I: Expression and Meaning. Expressions in Solitary Life, Section 8. In J. N. Findlay (Trans.), *Logical Investigations Volume 1* (p. 279). Routledge & Kegan Paul.

Husserl, E. (1977d). Investigation I: The Act-character of Meaning and the Ideally Unified Meaning, Section 31. In J. N. Findlay (Trans.), *Logical Investigations Volume 1* (p. 330). Routledge & Kegan Paul.

Husserl, E. (1999). *The Idea of Phenomenology: Husserliana: Edmund Husserl-Collected Works, Volume 8* (L. Hardy & R. Bernet, Trans.). Kluwer Academic Publishers.

Mohanty, J. N. (1970). Individual Fact and Essence in Edmund Husserl's Philosophy. In *Phenomenology and Ontology* (pp. 152–162). Martinus Nijhoff Publishers, The Hague.

Schröder, E. (1890). *Algebra der Logik.* Teubner.

Solomon, R. C. (1987). Sence and Essence: Frege and Husserl. In *From Hegel to Existentialism* (p. 207). Oxford University Press, New York/Oxford.

Chapter 5

Natural Attitude, Epoché and Reductions

This chapter examines Husserl's transcendental phenomenological methods. They involve three steps: 1) Elimination of Natural Attitude, 2) Epoché and 3) Phenomenological Reductions.

5.1 Natural Attitude

By raising the question of self via *cogito, ergo sum*, Descartes commenced a radical way of philosophizing. But, instead of leading cogito to its profound and logical conclusions, he went astray with his God-talk and other things primarily outside the domain of philosophy. Phenomenology starts with an explicit methodological decision to attend exclusively to that which presents itself in the full range of one's perception exactly as it (i.e., object or that which presents itself) presents itself. The phenomenologist cannot assume that which is presented to his senses is real. Our basic assumption is the belief that there exists an external world independent of my consciousness. This is the most primary, or in fact, the only assumption/presupposition that we possess according to phenomenologists. Husserl wants to eliminate this presupposition from our consciousness in order to arrive at the 'presuppositionless' starting point of philosophy. He does not deny or exclude the external world; there is no nihilism in phenomenology. All that he does is suspend the contention regarding the existence of the external world thought to exist independently of my consciousness. The reality of the external world in which events are rooted is taken for granted. In other words, Husserl places in abeyance, the general thesis of the natural standpoint or common belief in the independent existence of the external world. This belief is neither stated in a proposition, nor is it a formulated article of faith. It is an unstated, implicit theme in our common sense related to nature. Husserl proposes to suspend this proposition, describing it as epoché, a Greek terminology originating from the sceptic tradition. This suspension enables my awareness of the very meaning of the natural standpoint, shifting my attention from the object of my consciousness to consciousness itself. This shift does not erase the world and my everyday dealings with it but instead, shifts my focus from their existence to their meanings and essences. Epoché is a necessary condition for all phenomenological procedures.

5.2 Suspension of Natural Attitude

It is in natural attitude that we live a life of presuppositions, either metaphysical or epistemological. Husserl wishes to suspend all such presuppositions; from his perspective, there is only one major epistemological presupposition, viz., there exists a world independent of my consciousness. The Aristotelian contention that subject, object and predicate leads to substance is an excellent example of epistemological presupposition. There can be cultural presuppositions as well, assumptions regarding the validity of the central concept of predeccessors as is the case of Marx-Hegel and the dialectical method, suppositions regarding the purpose of philosophy, etc. There are also metaphysical or existential presuppositions regarding body and bodily life; one such presupposition is that smoking leads to cancer, but it is not true all the time. Religious beliefs have a metaphysical or existential strand of presupposition as well. Such presuppositions are technically described by Husserl as those with natural attitude or natural standpoint. He demands that all such presuppositions, no matter their origin, must be suspended. A presuppositionless philosophy, according to Husserl, does not mean a lack of presuppositions, but instead, they are rendered explicit, and elucidated through phenomenological inspection and evaluation to the best of one's ability. With this in mind, this chapter examines the following, 1) Husserl's treatment of natural attitude, 2) how to suspend natural attitude (epoché), and 3) how to establish the primacy and primordiality of consciousness, i.e., the transcendental ego, which Husserl collectively describes as phenomenological reduction. There are four points built into the notion of natural attitude namely, 1) a world exists around me independent of consciousness; 2) I then shift my consciousness, away from the world and its transcendence, toward my consciousness of it; 3) I attend exclusively to my consciousness, one that is reflexive and turning upon itself, and finally, 4) I describe my consciousness.

The epistemological issue that led Husserl into framing the phenomenological notion of reduction is the concept of natural attitude, which one needs to relinquish in order to enter the domain of philosophy and assume a phenomenological point of view. Are there any compelling reasons to do so? What does natural attitude designate? Husserl renders a thoughtful and modern interpretation to the traditional distinction between opinion (*doxa*) and knowledge (*episteme*). Natural attitude is a naïve, pre-philosophical attitude lacking in subject relatedness. It affirms the independence of nature from consciousness. A philosophy that believes in it is bound to it; it can operate on a realistic level, and therefore cannot critique transcendental philosophy. This was Husserl's weapon against those heretics who wished to continue with the principles of transcendental philosophy without accepting the consequences of natural attitude or reduction. Natural attitude is our normal, engaged, absorbed attitude that conceals the extraordinary in the ordinary, the strange in the common, the hidden in the obvious, the precious in the cheap. It is a complex constellation of attitudes that underlie our ordinary sense of the world.

Natural attitude is a standard belief in the real or actual existence of a world out there. It is the fundamental, unstated thesis that holds that there is a real, external world in space and time familiar to all men. All our doubts, fears, anxieties, questions, hypotheses and assumptions presuppose natural attitude, which arises due to a deeply rooted prejudice in the natural sciences. Natural attitude is a general philosophical orientation that treats the total range of all mental activities as essentially related to, and a part of events occurring in nature, as a consequence of which, natural sciences and their methodology begin with a set of philosophical presuppositions and implicit metaphysical commitments. In natural attitude, we are interested in things in terms of qualities and properties, with what objects are; we are absorbed in our mundane projects and earthly plans; in it, we ignore their modes of manifestation.

First and foremost, there is the natural attitude that we live in, which forms a part of our daily experiences, namely, the attitude of mundane experiences. In it, 'I', experiences itself and experiences other I's; this attitude of experience is natural. The natural concept of the world is the concept of the world in natural attitude, where 'I' is experienced as a member of nature, as an object of spatio-temporal existence. Descartes also brings into question the legitimacy of natural world, and points out that a grounding of natural attitude is necessary.

Critical analysis of natural attitude and its pitfalls led Husserl to do away with it completely, and replace it with a philosophical, phenomenological or transcendental attitude. This technical process is called epoché, i.e., bracketing or suspending natural attitude, in which, we propose to shift our attitude from the ordinary natural standpoint to a philosophical one, focusing on the content of consciousness, rather than the object of thought. Instead of remaining in natural attitude, we propose to alter it radically; we set it out of action, we disconnect it, bracket it, and do not use it. In so doing, we do not deny the world like the sophist, nor do we doubt it like a sceptic. All that we do is to bar ourselves completely from judgements concerning the actual, spatio-temporal world, as opposed to the conscious.

5.3 Epoché

Epoché is the suspension of metaphysical and epistemological presuppositions and judgements about the world and its entities. It is to withhold our judgements about the truth or falsity of our belief. It is to abstain from making judgements concerning the existence of the world; it means to suspend our judgements, not refuse, not reject, not deny the external world and its objects. It is to not pay attention to the existents therein, they being irrelevant and not of my concern. I pay attention only to my consciousness (of objects), i.e., consciousness itself becomes the object of consciousness. This is not a second consciousness, but a reflexive or reflective consciousness. Bracketing involves staying away from or setting aside preconceived notions and biases about phenomena, since things cannot be understood via external frameworks or structures, but only through (internal) reflection. Epoché provides the original vantage point to clear the mind of what experience leads to.

Husserl compares epoché to bracketing done in mathematics (remember, he was a mathematician himself). Contents within brackets are outside my immediate consideration. However, the bracketed material does not cease to be within the equation. It only means that it ceases to be of action; it is removed from consideration for the time being so that attention can be focused on another part of the equation. It means that I refuse to affirm it, neither consent nor decline. It is a negative expression, indicating that several things are unclear, allowing me to focus on aspects clearer to me. Husserl borrows the notion of epoché from the Greek sceptical tradition, but modifies it to his requirements, and aims to arrive at an unbiased view of theories to achieve metaphysical neutrality. For Husserl, epoché is an epistemological issue, and that which leads him to epoché is nothing but natural attitude. In *Ideas I*, Husserl considered epoché as a turn away from the external world and its experiences to the realms of consciousness, a move away from transcendence to imminence, a turn away from the object to the subject. Husserl's epoché is not a Cartesian doubt. In epoché, I do not deny the world, nor do I doubt it. All I do is bracket it to intensify my consciousness of it. For example, there are a large number of chairs made of steel, wood or plastic, manufactured by workmen in a factory, and eventually sold at a shop in town. These indicate various factors regarding the existence of the chairs; but how do I consider the chair now? While attending a lecture, it appears to be a comfortable seat. I notice that the overhead fan is not rotating; I climb on a chair to give it a quick jerk to get it to rotate, here, it appears as an elevated platform. The Principal of the college enters the crowded hall that has no vacant chairs. However, someone gets up and offers him a seat, whence the chair appears as a place of respect. Today it is my friend's birthday, and I gift him a beautiful chair; now it appears as a gift. Someone attacks me, whence I use the chair as a weapon for my defence. From the point of view of existence, it is the same chair, made of steel, wood or plastic, produced by workmen in the factory, and purchased from the shop. But it appears differently to different people, either as comfortable seat, an elevated platform, a place of respect, a gift or a weapon. I am unconcerned about the make of chair or its construction materials, be it steel, wood, plastic, etc. I am concerned solely by its mode of appearance. My interest in the chair is limited to its meaning and relation to me. My focus is now on the chair's appearance to me, while factors connected with its existence are ignored and modalities of its existence set aside; so, there is a shift in my mode of attention. When I focus on the chair's appearance to me, I am not rejecting, refusing or denying its existence, I just impart no importance to it, considering them to be irrelevant. According to Husserl, paying attention to existence is an expression of natural attitude, whereas paying attention to meaning is phenomenological, philosophical or transcendental attitude. My natural, ordinary everyday approach to existence is suspended. The materiality of the chair indicates the existence of a real, objective world, independent of my consciousness. Therefore, epoché is the suspension of at least three things, 1) everything originating from unquestioned philosophical conception, 2) scientific theories, and 3) popular beliefs.

Epoché enables us to shift our attention away from the objects of the natural world, towards our inquiry on the fundamental evidence, on which rests our natural belief in objects. This shift towards evidence leads to consciousness, and this search for evidence centres not on the object, but on the subject. The purpose of epoché is to explain the phenomenological features of the acts of consciousness. It is an invitation to ignore the relationship between the mind, the world and its objects, and focus our attention on the *noema* and the relationship amongst *noemata*.

When I focus on the appearance of the chair given to me personally and directly, I concentrate on the meaning or essence of the chair, while the transcendent object, i.e., the existing chair that is outside my consciousness is presupposed. All that occurs in epoché is a shift in the mode of consciousness of objects external to my consciousness, a transition from transcendence to imminence. The reality that was taken for granted in the naïve natural attitude is now diverted towards a phenomenological transcendental attitude. The actual world of every day experiences does not vanish under epoché, but instead it creates a new perspective, a new relationship with the same. In natural attitude, my consciousness is concentrated on objects, for consciousness is the consciousness of the very same objects. On account of epoché, I now possess a reflexive consciousness, one that comes back upon itself. Epoché is the necessary condition for phenomenological procedure, for it guarantees freedom from natural attitude. Epoché points out that no opinion is to be accepted as philosophical knowledge, unless adequately established by consciousness, and any belief incompatible with the evidence of consciousness is to be rejected. Epoché is reflexive/reflective in nature, i.e., attention is turned away from the consciousness of objects toward consciousness itself. Bracketing is a first-person reflective process involving diversion from the naïve understanding of the mundane world towards an intuitive understanding of it.

Epoché ensures that we do not utilize natural and perceptual knowledge as a premise in our transcendental investigations. It purifies my reflection, acquainting me with the transcendental import of things before me. It establishes a transcendental territory in which I should be interested in, while doing phenomenology. Epoché is a change in attitude, a shift in interest, a revision in standpoint, a modification in outlook, in which the world is not lost, but only its transcendence. Certain salient features of epoché are, 1) my consciousness is the consciousness of something, initially being the consciousness of the object. I bracket the world and its objects to shift my attention away from them, after which, 2) I direct my attention towards my consciousness, 3) resulting in a change of attitude from objects. It is not a second consciousness, but a reflective one. Since presuppositions about the world and its objects no longer exist, it is by nature a presuppositionless description. In short, by being cognizant of natural attitude, we become aware of our own weaknesses to the material, physical world; but epoché allows us to recover ourselves and return to our consciousness of it. Therefore epoché and phenomenological reduction enable us to gain a phenomenological attitude, allowing us to focus on transcendental ego, the source of consciousness.

5.4 Phenomenological Reductions

After epoché, the next step in phenomenological procedure is phenomenological reduction, one of the most crucial notions in Husserl's transcendental phenomenology. In *Ideas I*, Husserl strongly asserts that phenomenology cannot be done without phenomenological reduction, proceeding to adding a preface regarding the same to the English translation of *Ideas I*. But unfortunately, none of Husserl's prominent disciples, such as Heidegger, Sartre, Merleau-Ponty accepted it. They accepted his phenomenology as presented mainly in *Logical Investigations*, but rejected the transcendental phenomenology of *Ideas I*, which led Husserl to agonize over the fact that he was like a leader without any followers.

1. The history of philosophy reveals that different philosophers proposed various kinds of reductions. Reduction is a way to define or eliminate one category in terms of some others. Some of them are, 1) epistemological reduction (Descartes), 2) ontological reduction (Berkeley), 3) empiricists' reduction of physical objects to sense data, where values are reduced to facts, and finally 4)

phenomenological reduction (Husserl). It can be seen that Husserl was not the first to speak of reduction in philosophy.

2. Husserl is not consistent in his writings as to the numbers or names of reductions. In his book, *The Idea of Phenomenology* (Husserl, 1999), he speaks of just one reduction namely, the eidetic reduction. In *Logical Investigations*, when Husserl speaks of the transformation from communicative to confirmative speech, one notices eidetic reduction in its rudimentary stages. During his 1910-11 winter semester lectures, published as *The Basic Problems of Phenomenology* (Husserl, 2006g), he speaks explicitly of eidetic reduction. But one can notice psychological reduction in its embryonic stage in at least two sections (Husserl, 2006i, 2006j, 2006e, 2006a, 2006b). In these lectures, he speaks in depth about intersubjectivity and empathy (Husserl, 2006e), which later appears as reduction by way of Life world in *Crisis of European* Sciences. In *Ideas I*, he speaks of three reductions namely, eidetic, psychological and transcendental. In *Cartesian Meditations*, he speaks of transcendental-psychological reduction(s). Is it a single reduction or two interrelated reductions? Commentators differ in their views. However, it has been pointed out that in *Crisis of European* Sciences, he speaks of eight reductions namely, 1) phenomenological, 2) transcendental, 3) phenomenological-psychological, 4) transcendental-phenomenological, 5) psychological, 6) positivistic, 7) behaviouristic and 8) universalistic. Several commentators like Dermot Moran have pointed out that the last three cannot form part of transcendental phenomenology (as they are a part of natural sciences) and therefore should be rejected from transcendental phenomenological procedures (Moran, 2000b).

3. Joseph J. Kockelmans, a close disciple of Husserl, holds there are seven reductions in his book (Kockelmans, 1967), 1) phenomenological, 2) philosophical, 3) psychological, 4) eidetic, 5) transcendental, 6) ethical, 7) intersubjective. Other eminent scholars like Marvin Farber and Maurice Natanson speak only of two, eidetic and transcendental reduction, but go on to add that these are not the only ones (Husserl, 1977n).

4. Husserl's first-generation commentators have several differences of opinion. Iso Kern (Kern, 1977), who edited three of Husserl's lecture series (1910-11 and 1923-24) into three books, speaks of four reductions in his paper's introduction (Husserl, 1977n)

namely, 1) reduction by the Cartesian Way, 2) reduction by intentional psychology, 3) reduction by the ontological way and, 4) reduction by critique of positive sciences. Immediately thereafter, he modifies his statement sans explanations, stating that reduction by the ontological method and by critique of positive sciences are one and the same, resorting to a final of three reductions

5.   Second generation commentators, or present-day scholars have very different opinions on reductions. Sebastian Luft, along with Søren Overgaard (Luft, 2004, 2012), speak of three reductions namely, Cartesian, psychological and reduction via Life world. This begs the question, what about Husserl's transcendental reduction in *Ideas I*? It is far more interesting to note that in footnote 31 in his article, he speaks of apodictic reduction, "in order to gain absolute foundation within the sphere of transcendental life" (Luft, 2004). Is this a fourth reduction? Despite quoting from Husserl's 1922-23 lectures, he does not elaborate on it any further, neither does Iso Kern. This also begs the question as to the reason Luft omitted it from the body of reductions mentioned in his own article? However, in his second article (Luft, 2012), he speaks exclusively about the three above-mentioned reductions, with no mention of apodictic reduction, sans explanation. Several other authors fail to mention apodictic reduction as well. Søren Overgaard, meanwhile, describes seven reductions in his article (Overgaard, 2002) namely, 1) primordial, 2) solipsistic, 3) eidetic, 4) transcendental, 5) Cartesian, 6) psychological, 7) reduction by way of Life world. However, scholars like David Smith, Robert Walsh, Langsdrof, Michael Atkins, Lisa Catherine Ehrlich and several others speak only of three reductions, though there is a lack of unanimity as to which three.

Though Kockelmans and Overgaard both speak of seven reductions in Husserl, there are hardly any similarities between them. Bossert claims eight reductions, which have nothing in common with the reductions mentioned by the former (Moran, 2000b). In light of these difficulties and my reflections over them, I wish to put forth my conclusions as follows.

It is to be noted here that 'reduction' refers to different things in different instances. For example, in eidetic and psychological reductions, it eliminates something; my assertion of existence is removed in eidetic reduction, while my belief systems are deleted in psychological reduction. However, 'reduction' in the case of transcendental reduction, adds something; here, meaning is assigned to *noema* by transcendental ego. In the case of reduction by way of Life world, 'reduction' assigns meaning to a community, or it can refer to a search for a communitarian meaning. To conclude, one should be very careful while using the word, reduction in the context of phenomenological reduction.

Phenomenological reduction is absolutely crucial to Husserl's transcendental phenomenology. It was instrumental in driving away several of his disciples, which led Husserl to mournfully state that he was a leader without followers. It makes us wonder how there was no unanimity amongst those Husserlian scholars with regard to the number of reductions. Several justify their discord to Husserl's inconsistencies with the number of reductions and their names; he spoke of one reduction in *The Idea of Phenomenology* (Husserl, 1999) three in *Ideas I*, further appending the list in *Crisis of European Sciences*. These scholars also point out that the exact numbers of reductions are unimportant. The only requirement is to acquire the spirit of phenomenological reductions and practise them rigorously to arrive at the essence of the phenomena, which was what led Husserl forward in his inquiries into phenomenological reductions, they add.

So, where do I stand with regard to this problem of reduction? In the light of my studies and reflections on the topic, I accept that there are four reductions in Husserl, namely 1) eidetic reduction, 2) psychological reduction, 3) transcendental reduction, based on *Ideas I* and, (4) reduction via the ontology of Life world, based on *Crisis of European Sciences*. The first question regarding reduction is: why should there be any reduction at all? The reason is that phenomenology is an eidetic science, a science of essence; it only aims to arrive at essences, and in doing so, it is unconcerned with existence.

5.4.1 Eidetic Reduction

Reduction brackets existence; this does not mean that we deny, reject or refuse existence during the course of phenomenological procedure, but choose to ignore it, and focus our attention on essence. Once the unnecessary is removed, i.e., existence, essence will shine in its pristine purity. The entire transcendental procedure is to arrive at essence, which when arrived at, is assigned meaning by the transcendental ego. Eidetic reduction consists in suspending, and not asserting our judgements regarding the existence or non-existence of the objects of consciousness, so as to enable us to concentrate our attention on essence. Consequently, we consider existence to be irrelevant.

5.4.2 Psychological Reduction

Psychological reduction is fundamental to Husserl's phenomenology, for he erroneously upheld the position of psychologism during his pre-phenomenological days. After having liberated himself from its deadly clutches, Husserl fought against it vehemently, thereby making it a part of phenomenological reduction. Psychological reduction stands against the Cartesian attempt to neutralize consciousness. Husserl holds that consciousness or transcendental ego assigns meanings to objects. However, Descartes held that consciousness merely reflects objects, and in doing so, does not add to or subtract anything from the same, and therefore, remains neutral like a mirror. Psychological reduction refrains from looking at the origin of objects from the perspective of theories, hypotheses, cause-effect relations and other such frameworks.

Eidetic and psychological reduction allow us to arrive at the essence pre-consciously, spontaneously and instantaneously. For example, during a terrorist attack in a classroom, how does the teacher throw a chair at the terrorist to disarm the former, protecting the students and himself? The teacher does not waver, nor does he make any elaborate calculations, nor does he care for premises and conclusions; he does not waste a moment. The need to protect himself and the students is his primary motive, driving his swift action of throwing the chair at the terrorist. Decision-making and execution occur almost simultaneously, i.e., awareness of the chair's use as a weapon, and the act of throwing it at the terrorist. The teacher discovers the essence of the chair as a protective weapon preconsciously, instantaneously and spontaneously, and he acts on it immediately. According to Husserl, the teacher instantaneously discovered the essence of the chair as a weapon, and quickly assigned meaning as a defensive weapon.

5.4.3 Transcendental Reduction

Transcendental reduction assigns meaning to the above event through transcendental ego. It is in fact, the constitution of a phenomenon by consciousness or transcendental ego, such that the phenomenon is dependent on the latter, not just for meaning, but also for being. From the above example, it is demonstrated that the teacher constituted the chair's being as a weapon, assigned it meaning as a defensive weapon to protect the students and himself.

5.4.4 Reduction by Way of the Ontology of Life world

What does Husserl mean by Life world? (*vide* Chapter 7). The world of science is a world of abstraction, not in consonance with our pre-scientific attitude. It is the world encountered in natural attitude. However, we do not accept the general thesis of natural attitude. Husserl discusses reduction by way of the ontology of Life world only in *Crisis of European Sciences*. However, he states in *Ideas I* that everything in the natural world is acceptable, except the general thesis of natural attitude. This sentence was prophetic in terms of the direction of his future works. This implies that there is no contradiction between his statements in *Crisis of European Sciences* and *Ideas I*. Life world is a subjective, pre-scientific world that is the foundation for all human action, natural as well as scientific. It is the task of phenomenological reduction to rediscover Life world by uncovering the abstract character surrounding it. The modern, scientifically-oriented man has forgotten life, since he bears the massive burden of the primarily theoretical and abstract scientific world.

Husserl's position in *Crisis of European Sciences* does not contradict his insight from *Ideas I* as he already envisaged such a possibility. He holds that everything in the natural world is acceptable to phenomenology except the general thesis of natural attitude. Moreover, from a higher transcendental point of view, Husserl incorporates the initial form into a later form. One form is neither lower nor higher, since both exist in the transcendental sphere. In conclusion, this is a reduction that allows us a glimpse into Life world, revealing the spheres of life fundamental to philosophy. How does Life world relate to the other three reductions? I arrive at my subjective meanings through the first three reductions, they being strictly individual and personal. The fourth reduction teaches us that subjective and personal meaning has relevance to the community, allowing us to arrive at a communitarian or universal meaning. This is because Life world is concerned, not just with the individual, but the community as a whole.

In *The Idea of* Phenomenology, Husserl discusses only eidetic reduction. In his lecture series of 1910-11, he was sure about one reduction, but drops clues to the psychological reduction, in addition to discussions on intersubjectivity and empathy, not considered a reduction then, but which later became one. Finally, in *Ideas I* (1913), he confidently elaborates three reductions, eidetic, psychological and transcendental. In the French edition of *Cartesian Meditations*, he discusses transcendental-phenomenological reduction. Are they two reductions or just one? There is no definitive answer. In *Crisis of European Sciences*, does Husserl have eight reductions as claimed by Philip Bossert (Moran, 2000a) or just a few reductions as claimed by Iso Kern, Luft and others? Moreover, though Kockelmans and Overgaard describe seven reductions in Husserl, there are hardly any similarities among them. Bossert's claims of eight reductions have nothing common either with Kockelmans and Overgaard. In light of these difficulties and my reflections, I wish to add the following concluding remarks.

5.5 Concluding Remarks

1.   Though Husserl spent his entire life writing continuously and ceaselessly, he never felt completely satisfied with any of them and, therefore refused to publish them. He refused to publish *Logical Investigations*, as he was of the opinion that *Investigation VI* was unsatisfactory. But his friends collected them from his table and sent it to the press, as a result of which we now have a wonderful book. He went for a holiday with his assistant Ms. Edith Stein, with the intention to revise the time consciousness lectures. But instead of revising them, Husserl proceeded to work on something new on time and individuation (*vide* Chapter 10). Similarly, he withheld publication of the second and third *Ideas*, though finished manuscripts were given to Heidegger and Edith Stein to be read and commented upon. His constant and continuous work meant that he was left with no time to revise his manuscripts, although he had a desire for it; in the end, they were left to his succours and students. He was a pathfinder, constantly discovering new roads, seldom stopping to look back. 33,000 pages of his *Gabelsberger* shorthand writings were smuggled out of Germany and airlifted overnight to Brussels, Catholic University of Louvain by Frau Husserl and his student H. L. Van Breda after his death, due to Nazi antagonism to Husserl due to his Jewish origin.

2.   The notion of phenomenological reduction explicitly pervaded Husserl's mind for about thirty years from the time of *The Idea of Phenomenology* (1907) to *Crisis of European Sciences* (1936). It is but natural that one forgets certain things with the passage of time, for which Husserl can also be excused, owing to the large time gap. But it is yet to be seen as to whether a favourable acceptance of this excuse can be found amongst his critics.

3.   There are also serious mistakes with the commentators who insist on the exact numbers of reductions. They forget the purpose and essence of phenomenological reductions, and the reasons for which Husserl instituted them. The primary reason for reductions was to establish the primacy and primordiality of the transcendental ego, and demonstrate that *noema* is dependent on *noesis*, not just for its meaning, but also for its very being. It was to explicate the constitutive powers of the transcendental ego that Husserl formulated reductions. Once the primordial and constitutive powers of the transcendental ego are established, the number of reductions is immaterial.

4. Husserl occasionally thought that a single reduction was sufficient to establish the pre-eminence of the transcendental ego, and at other times felt the requirement for multiple reductions, all of which depended on his state of mind and topics being worked on at the time. Context has a lot of importance. He was not bound by rules or yard sticks; he was his own master. Remember his response to Frege's comments: "External influences have no bearings on me." His only criterion was his faithfulness to his vocation as a master phenomenologist.

5. Despite such justifications, I humbly submit the following. Phenomenological reduction is a crucial theme and a major issue in Husserlian philosophy. It was due to this problem that Heidegger remarked on the occasion of Husserl's 70th birthday celebrations (on 8 April 1929) that, "you (Herr Geheimrat, the reverential title used to address Husserl) are our master, but we are not your followers," which I interpret as: 'we accept you as the sole founder of phenomenology, but we have formulated our own phenomenological positions in the light of your insights and teachings, because we have differences with your elaborations', to which Husserl agonizingly wrote in his letter (on 6 January 1931) to Pfänder, "I am a leader without followers." This being the case, Husserl should have been more careful in speaking about reductions. The number of reductions, be it 1/2/3/4 may be irrelevant. He should not have spoken about positivistic, behaviouristic and universalistic reductions in the context of phenomenology. Their inclusion amongst other reductions cannot be justified by any stretch of imagination.

6. I refrain from commenting on the number of reductions referred to by Husserl's direct students, Kockelmans or Marvin Faber or his good friend Alfred Schütz, or his faithful disciples, Iso Kern, Adolf Boehm, Sebastian Luft. If asked to give a number and names to the reductions, I am of the opinion that there are only four reductions: three from *Ideas I*, eidetic, psychological and transcendental reductions, and one from *Crisis of European Sciences*, by way of the ontology of the Life world. Every other reduction described in *Crisis of European Sciences* (eight reductions), or the reductions his disciples and followers speak about, seem to be corollary to these four. These four reductions are exemplars for all others.

5.6 References

Husserl, E. (1977). Investigation I: Continuation: The Objective Correlate of an Expression, Section 12. In J. N. Findlay (Trans.), *Logical Investigations Volume 1* (p. 287). Routledge & Kegan Paul.

Husserl, E. (1999). *The Idea of Phenomenology: Husserliana: Edmund Husserl-Collected Works, Volume 8* (L. Hardy & R. Bernet, Trans.). Kluwer Academic Publishers.

Husserl, E. (2006a). Appendix VIII. In G. H. James & F. Ingo (Trans.), *The Basic Problems of Phenomenology*, (pp. 149–152). Springer Netherlands.

Husserl, E. (2006b). Appendix XII. In R. Bernet (Ed.), & G. H. James & F. Ingo (Trans.), *The Basic Problems of Phenomenology*, (pp. 165–176). Springer Netherlands.

Husserl, E. (2006c). Phenomenology's Move Beyond the Realm of the Absolute Given. In G. H. James & I. Farin (Trans.), *The Basic Problems of Phenomenology* (pp. 56–57). Springer Netherlands.

Husserl, E. (2006d). *The Basic Problems of Phenomenology* (F. Ingo & G. H. James, Trans.). Springer Netherlands.

Husserl, E. (2006e). The Natural Attitude and the 'Natural Concept of the World'. In R. Bernet (Ed.), & H. James G & F. Ingo (Trans.), *The Basic Problems of Phenomenology*, (p. 5). Springer Netherlands.

Husserl, E. (2006f). The Uncovering of the Phenomenological Multiplicity of Monads. In R. Bernet (Ed.), & H. James G & F. Ingo (Trans.), *The Basic Problems of Phenomenology*, (pp. 82–86). Springer Netherlands.

Kern, I. (1977). The Three Ways to the Transcendental Phenomenological Reduction of the Philosophy of Edmund Husserl. In F. A. Elliston & P. McCormick (Eds.), *Husserl: Expositions and Appraisals* (pp. 126–149). University of Notre Dame Press.

Kockelmans, J. J. (1967). *A First Introduction to Husserl's Phenomenology*. Duquesne University Press.

Luft, S. (2004). Husserl's Theory of the Phenomenological Reduction: Between Life world and Cartesianism. *Research in Phenomenology, 34*(1), 198–234.

Luft, S. (2012). Husserl's method of reduction. In S. Overgaard & S. Luft (Eds.), *The Routledge Companion to Phenomenology* (pp. 243–253). Routledge (Taylor & Francis), London and New York.

Moran, D. (2000a). *Introduction to Phenomenology*. Routledge (Taylor & Francis), London and New York.

Moran, D. (2000b). Notes no. 20, Husserl's Discovery of the Reduction and Transcendental Phenomenology. In *Introduction to Phenomenology* (p. 493). Routledge (Taylor & Francis), London and New York.

Overgaard, S. (2002). Epoché and Solipsistic Reduction. *Husserl Studies, 18*(3), 209–222.

Chapter 6

Husserl's Treatment of Noesis and Noema: Conflict and Convergence

6.1 Introduction

The notion of *noema* is central to Husserl's phenomenology, and is intimately linked to the problems of consciousness, intentionality, meaning, essence, and a whole bunch of such issues. The crucial question that Husserl raises here is, 'how can consciousness be involved with an object?' The problem has its origin in Husserl's understanding and interpretation of his teacher, Brentano's notion of intentionality. Husserl writes in *Logical Investigations*, "Every mental phenomenon is characterized by what mediaeval schoolman called intentional (or mental inexistence) of an object, and by what we, not without ambiguity, call the relation to a content, the direction to an object (by which a reality is not to be understood) or an immanent objectivity" (Husserl, 1977q). This text contains the crux of Brentano's position, which Husserl strongly differs from. Two important points in Brentano are, he assumed that the relation between the real (i.e., a material, physical object existing by itself) and immanent object is a casual one, which led him to yet another assumption regarding the intentional inexistence of the immanent object. It may be noted in this context that Husserl was concerned with the direction to an object.

David Hume, to whom Husserl imparted a lot of importance in his philosophy, taught him that causality cannot provide sure and certain knowledge. He also rejected the validity of the first part of Brentano's thesis based on his notions of natural attitude, epoché and phenomenological reductions. His position on the second part of the thesis was as follows. It is in the very nature of consciousness to be involved with an object, i.e., consciousness is the consciousness of an object. Husserl interprets this as intentionality. It is akin to the following, water flows downstream, heat expands bodies, sugar sweetens, i.e., one is inseparable from the other, and so too with consciousness, which is inseparable from its object. In other words, the directedness of consciousness is inextricably linked to its consciousness, inasmuch as spreading light is inherent to a lit candle. This directedness also implies that intentionality does not require a material, physical object to which it is directed, rather, it just needs an intended object (e.g., my happiness, or the schizophrenic condition of a person). This directedness of consciousness to an object has a peculiar mode of orientation, a remarkable manner of preference, a unique style of interest that enables the object to reveal itself in perspectives, to manifest itself from a position, and to disclose itself from a standpoint.

This perspectival manifestation of the object arises due to my personal interest and specific orientation to the object, implying that no object can ever remain neutral before my consciousness; no object can exist in a detached manner or disdained fashion before consciousness. Every object is linked to my consciousness in a very personal and distinctive manner. Moreover, no object can reveal the totality of its perspectives to my consciousness at any one time. It also implies that an object is what it is, only in terms of its appearance to me; I make the object appear in a precise manner. From Husserl's point of view, it is my perspective to an object that gives rise to *noema*, it is my attitude towards the object that generates *noema*, it is my peculiar kind of preference that provokes the manifestation of *noema*, it is my choice of a particular mode of object that gives rise to *noema*. What this means is that, to be directed to an object in a particular manner is to have a *noema*. *Noema*, in other words, arises in my (*noesis*) peculiar kind of relation to an object. It also means that there can be no *noema* without an intentional relation originating from the *noesis* to the transcendent object. This would imply that in the genesis of *noema*, *noesis* has both ontological and epistemic priority, ontological, because *noema* is dependent on *noesis* for its (intentional) coming to be, and epistemic, since *noema* gets its meaning from *noesis*. It may also be noted that the directedness of consciousness to the object generates *noema*. Different kinds of relations between the subject (*noesis*) and the (transcendent) object can engender different kinds of *noema*.

Consider the following example of a chair, a material object in front of me. I am now very tired, my legs cannot carry my weight, I need to rest, I am about to collapse. I see a chair lying nearby, which now appears as a place where I can sit comfortably and relax. I feel warm and sweaty. I need a little extra breeze. Unfortunately, the overhead fan is stationary. I drag the chair under the fan, climb on to it, and jerk the latter into motion so that it can generate breeze to soothe me. Presently, the chair reveals itself to me as an elevated platform. Consider the next example of a lecture hall packed with students attending a lecture. The Principal walks into the hall, and finds himself without a seat. So one student offers his seat to him, at which instant, the chair manifests itself as a place of respect proffered to the Principal. In another examples, a terrorist enters a classroom with the intent to attack the teacher and students. The brave teacher throws a chair at the former to disarm him, wherein the chair discloses itself as a weapon of defence. To the carpenter who built the very same chair, it acts as a means of his livelihood. From the point of existence and existential characteristics, it is one and the same chair, constructed out of steel, wood or plastic, assembled by workmen in a factory, purchased from a shop on payment, and finally delivered by the porter to the college. In each instance, the chair appears differently to different people, appearing as a comfortable seat on one occasion, as an elevated platform at another, as a place of respect at another instance, and on yet another, materializing itself as a weapon. In none of these cases am I bothered with the existential characteristics of the chair, i.e., whether it is made of steel, plastic or wood, if its colour is red, blue or white, its weight, and the like. All that concerns me is its mode of appearance, i.e., what it means to me now, or how it is related to me. It appears to me as a seat to sit and relax, or as an elevated platform, or as a place of respect to a senior person. In other words, my concern is with the meaning of the chair.

Noema studies how the chair appears to me on different occasions, i.e., as a comfortable seat, as an elevated platform, as a place of respect, as a weapon of self-defence, etc. In all these cases, *noema* is the meaning that I assign to the chair. In other words, the chair as a seat, or as an elevated platform, or as a place of respect, or as a weapon, emerge only on account of my intentional relation to the material object called the chair, without which it remains as an unidentified, anonymous, nameless, material object. Therefore, it is my intentional relation to the object that makes it a chair, or in other words, in the presence of consciousness, there is no neutral object, in the presence of which, the object is no more a 'what', but a 'how'. Despite a transition from 'what' to 'how' in the context of consciousness, I do not ignore the 'what', i.e., the existence or the existential characteristics that constitute the 'what' of the chair, rather, in the phenomenological context, I am just unconcerned with it, which is described by Husserl as natural attitude. I do not reject, deny, decline, or refuse to accept the material existence, or the transcendent characteristics of the chair; they definitely exist, but is irrelevant to me, and that which concerns me is the 'how' of the chair. I am concerned with the meaning of the chair, which translates itself into having a phenomenological attitude and transcendental concern, which in turn generates *noema*. *Noema* is the meaning or sense of the transcendent object. *Noema* is the ideal entity belonging to the sphere of meanings; the *noema* is called the 'meant-object' according to Husserl. This implies that in the absence of a transcendent object, a *noema* cannot be produced by *noesis*. The transcendent object need not always be material. It is the object outside my cognitive structure, outside the framework of my consciousness, exterior to my mental makeup. It is the matrix that constitutes the *noema*. Our attitude to every transcendent object we confront in our everyday life constantly produce *noemata*. All that is required for the production of a *noema* is our imagination, which is the basis of the epistemic generation of *noema*. The source of one's imagination is one's wants, desires, needs, wishes, etc. I, myself, am the source of my imagination, and therefore, of the *noema*. This implies that *noema* can be found not just in my perception and imagination, but also in my memory, expectation, thinking, judging, volition and presentation, i.e., my consciousness in general.

Noema is not a property, determination, or predicate of the (transcendent) object undergoing the phenomenological procedure, rather, it is one of the components of experiencing an object, one that refers to the mode of the intended object. *Noema* teaches us that there are no neutral objects. Can I be indifferent to an object? I can be, in which case, the meaning that I assign to the object is that of my indifference. This is my attitude right now, which might change later on, resulting in a positive or negative attitude toward it. This fluctuation of attitudes is common in our everyday life. Husserl's reference to putting something into brackets alludes to this attitude, which does not concern me right now. My interest in an object is always perspectival, which comes to the forefront depending on my interest in the same. In other words, *noema* is the perspective that I adapt to an object based on my interest. No object can reveal itself in the totality of all its perspectives at one time; the fullness of the object can be arrived at only as the sum total of all perspectives.

The expressions, *noesis* and *noema* originate from the Greek term *Nous*, meaning mind or intellect. Roughly, *noesis* is the meaning-assigning aspect of the act of consciousness, whereas *noema* is the meaning-receiving dimension of the act. Husserl gives a detailed description of the notion of *noema* in various sections of *Ideas I*, although certain preliminary notions appear as early as in *Logical Investigations*, in which he distinguished among three concepts: the (intended) object, the (intentional) content and the real content (*noesis*). In the example of the chair mentioned above, the material, physical object called chair is the (intended) object of my thought, but the (intentional) content of my thought assumes various forms according to when the chair is a seat, or an elevated platform, or a place of respect, or a weapon, or a means to one's livelihood. These form the (intentional) content of my thought of the object, the chair, while I myself, am the real content (*noesis*). The intentional content (*noema*) exists only for a *noesis*. Surely, one can immediately notice the similarity between *noema* on the one hand and (intentional) content on the other hand.

In terms of intentional content, i.e., *noema*, 'I' (*noesis*) assign meanings to the intended object called chair. These meanings are ideal, in the sense that they are beyond space and time, yet they are assigned to an intentional content. It may be noted that it is within the framework of real and intentional content, that Husserl formulates his notion of *noema* and *noesis* in *Ideas I*.

Every intentional act includes a *noesis*, the meaning assigning component, and *noema* that acquires meaning from the *noesis*. The example of the chair illustrates that various kinds of *noemata* can be attached to the same *noesis*. It may be noted that while *noema* can be grasped only in transcendental phenomenological reflection, the intended object is transcendent, it is a part of the natural attitude, and undergoes phenomenological reduction. Hence, they both belong to two different categories.

Is essence the same as *noema*? The answer from a phenomenological point of view must be in the negative. They are essentially different concepts, unrelated to each other, coming from two entirely different philosophical traditions. Essences are instantiated in the objects; they, essence and objects, are inseparable, and can only be distinguished. As a thing exists in nature, the object has physical characteristics such as colour, height, weight, etc. It involves what Husserl calls naturalistic attitude. It can be created or destroyed. Even now, our philosophical reflection on things are very much rooted to the Greek manner of Aristotelian thinking. Essences are grasped in eidetic intuition by way of abstraction and studied in regional ontologies (Aristotle). Essences belonging to the transcendent object can be analysed and compared. The material object, the chair, from the Aristotelian point of view, will have an essence that exists in space and time. It is a thing in nature. It has chemical composition and can be destroyed (Husserl, 1976c, 1976f, 1976p). Consciousness can be directed to it; it is the object intended. However, *noema* has a very different nature and function. Primarily, it needs to be stated that *noema* is to be found, grasped and studied in Husserl's transcendental phenomenological reflection. *Noema* is an integral part of consciousness. *Noema* is the object as perceived in a particular manner. It is the meaning of the object perceived, a meaning that I assign to the object. This meaning is ideal in the sense that it is non-temporal and beyond space. *Noema* arises from our ways of experiencing the object and presents it in a particular way (Husserl, 1976n, 1976q, 1976l). The same object can give rise to different kinds of *noemata*, i.e., each appearance or perspective of the object is a *noema*. The example of the chair instantiates and validates this claim. One can discuss *noema* only in relation to *noesis*. Therefore, are *noesis* and *noema* the same or different kind of entities? *Noesis* is the transcendental ego; it is the real, temporal component of experience, the meaning-giving, sense-assigning component of experience. It has both ontological and epistemic priority over *noema*, since *noema* is dependent on the *noesis*, both for its being and meaning.

However, it may be noted that *noesis* does not create *noema ex nihilo*, it merely fashions or devises *noema* on account of its constant urge and continuous striving to discover meaning in experiences, a yearning cotemporaneous with the existence of *noesis* itself. Moreover, *noema* is non-real, it is not in space and time, not in temporal flow. *Noema* is the ideal entity, or ideal meaning; it is the ideal content. The question then arises, how can the non-temporal, ideal meaning of *noema* be linked to *noesis*, which has very different qualities? In other words, how can a *noema*, an ideal entity, a non-temporal, non-spatial entity be linked to *noesis*, a real, temporal entity? How can there be a link between temporal and non-temporal entities? Husserl answers this query by stating that it is part of the essence of experience to include in it (experience), a sense, a *noema*. By asserting such a position, Husserl clearly follows Plato and Platonic logicians like Frege (although I refer to Plato, there is nothing akin to the Platonic world in Husserl). Let's consider the example of the following classroom. Its ceiling is white. The walls are white. The colour of the ceiling fans rotating above is white. The tube light is white. The switch board is white. Some students are wearing white clothes. The chalk piece that I use to write on the board is white. The students scribble their notes on white sheets of paper. All these are white, yet not all of them are equally so. But we consider all of them to be white. All these are just instances of a perfect or ideal white; these are all more or less white. Then where is the perfect white? It is not seen or experienced or exemplified anywhere, it lies in my understanding of white. The perfect white is the source from which these instances of white proceed. Ideal white is non-temporal; it does not exist anywhere concretely, it is irreal, and exists only in my thought. All instances of white are said to be white, only in comparison to that ideal white. All instantiates of white are described to be more or less white. The link between the various instances of white and the ideal white indicates the relation between *noesis* and *noema*. This implies that *noematic* meanings are ideal entities realized in temporal experiences, or in other words, *noema* is a unique ideal entity that enters into temporal experience. Thus, meanings are realized in temporal experiences. This is the novelty of Husserl's theory of meanings. The mode of being of the *noema* is ideal, but dependent on experience. *Noema* belongs to an act of consciousness. It is an ideal entity that enters into temporal relations.

Noema is the meaning of the object as intended. It is the object as the subject, *noesis*, is aware of it. *Noema* and the object are completely distinct entities that belong to two radically different dimensions, and linguistically, to two different kinds of givenness. True, *noema* is related to the transcendent object. The possibility of turning away from the object-oriented attitude (intentionality) to the *noema*-directed standpoint is inherent in the very structure of consciousness. This is because consciousness considers everything perspectively; it is a correlation between *noema*, the plane of meanings, and *noesis*, the plane of the transcendental ego, such that corresponding to each act, there exists a *noema*. *Noema* is different from acts of consciousness and does not constitute itself as a part/element of the act; the act exists within consciousness. *Noema* is distinct from the acts of consciousness. It is the meant-correlate of the intentional act, the intending meaning presented by the intentional act, i.e., *noesis*.

6.2 The Conflict: Gurwitsch and Føllesdal on the Notion of *Noema*

6.2.1 Gurwitsch on Perceptual *Noema*

Perceptual *noema*, according to Gurwitsch, refers to a thing perceived exactly, and only as it appears to the perceiving subject through an act of perception (Gurwitsch, 2010). Husserl characterizes perceptual *noema* as perceptual meaning or significance. Perceptual *noema* is the perceived thing, as it presents itself through a given series of acts of perception in a particular manner of presentation. It denotes the material thing perceived from a given standpoint in a determinate orientation, with regard to the perceiving subject. Since perceived *noema* is the result of a certain perspective with regard to an object, one and the same material object can produce a multiplicity of *noemata* depending on the perspectives under which it is approached. And therefore, the perceived thing cannot be identified with any one single *noema*.

When we talk of perceptual *noema*, i.e., *noema* originating from a perceptual act, it cannot be totally divorced from the object of perception. Such a *noema* arises because the object has been perceived from different perspectives, and depending on the plurality of perspectives, we can have a multiplicity of perceptual *noemata*. And, therefore, *noema* must be distinguished from sensorial acts. Whatever be the relation between the acts of sense perception and its corresponding perceptual *noema*, the *noema* must not be mistaken for a part, element, moment or constituent of the act.

Perceptual *noema* is the perceived meaning that is perceived as such. It belongs neither to the real domain, nor to the material and physical object, nor to the event, nor to the act of consciousness as such. On account of *noema*, a given thing is not a perception of a certain specified thing, i.e., perception of a determinate thing. Perceptual *noema* is a sense, a significance or meaning of perception. This becomes abundantly clear from the passage in the context of the example of the chair mentioned above. Perception is an act characterized essentially by intentionality. Sense or significance does not denote real features or constituents of the act of perception; rather, on the contrary, it denotes an ideal unit. The notion of *noema* is not found explicitly in *Logical Investigations*, yet exists in its embryonic stages as notions of 'quality' and 'matter'. Quality is the factor of act rendering a presentational character to the same. Matter on the other hand, denotes the component of intentional act that determines not just the objective reference to a particular thing, but also the manner in which the object is apprehended. The definition of matter of the intentional act prepares us for the later notion of *noema*. we have an incipient version of notion of *noema-noesis* in *Logical Investigations* that attained maturity in *Ideas I.*

From the distinction between the perceived thing and perceptual *noema*, it follows that *noema* is not affected by any changes in/of the thing. Husserl's discussion of the tree consumed by fire (Husserl, 1976c, 1976f, 1976p) is an affirmation of it. However, it may also be noted that Husserl's concept of *noema* is dominated by his notion of epoché and phenomenological reductions, under which perceptual *noema* corresponds to an act of perception, i.e., the perceived object appearing in a certain manner of presentation. What does perception mean in the context of perceptual *noema*? *Noema* simply designates the portion of the organized structure of our experiencing pertaining to the experienced object; in contrast, *noesis* pertains to the experiencing subject in that structure. I perceive the material, transcendent object, i.e., the chair; I also perceive the chair from different perspectives, as a place of honour, an elevated platform or weapon, all of which perceive the chair as a *noema*. When I perceive the chair as a material, physical, transcendent object, it has reference to my sense organs, for I can perceive it as an object only through them. However, when the chair is perceived as a *noema*, sense organs are not involved, implying that there is a difference in meaning in both perceptions. When the chair is perceived as a *noema*, it is not a perception by sense organs, but occurs via an intellectual perception; it is my intuition of grasping the meaning of the chair. Hence, perception in the context of the intellectual perception of *noema* needs to be distinguished from sensorial perception. But unfortunately, word perception, like word grasping, has been misused to the point of absurdity by several authors, scholars and philosophers claiming to be an authority in the proper use of language and determination of meaning. Several of them annihilate the original etymological sense of the word, ruining its pristine purity and sublime context. The following contention of analytic philosophy is worth noting, that language is no one's private property or personal wealth, and that it is to be utilized with utmost care and a high degree of precaution. The contention of phenomenology that argues that there exists a transcendent reference for everything, also means that language cannot be used according to one's imagination and fantasies. Gurwitsch's treatment of perception refers to sense perception, i.e., perception by way of sense organs, though not confined exclusively to the same. His understanding of perception goes beyond the limits of sense organs to the very meaning of perception. His understanding is like a spiritual vision (spiritual level as opposed to the mundane, worldly level), belonging to the ideal realm. If a chair, a material transcendent object, is conceived to be the same as *noema*, then the chair as a seat of respect or elevated platform or weapon, would hold no difference amongst them. When perceptual *noema* originates and is articulated as the perceived, we cannot speak of sensual origin. *Noema* originates in my thought process and conscious acts. The perceptual *noema* is fully articulated and well-formed only in my knowledge and judgement and in my spiritual processes far removed from sensual perception.

6.3 Føllesdal's Treatment of *Noema*

This section on Føllesdal attempts to neither question the validity of his twelve theses, nor does it raise objections against them. It rather strives to understand these theses myself, and explain them with examples to my students and to phenomenology scholars in general, who wish to grasp them, as Hume said: "Understand the whole, do not criticise the parts." My programme is to instantiate and elaborate them in the most simplistic terms, so that students who are even beginners in phenomenology can understand and appreciate them. I wish to neither comment negatively, nor condemn these, for they are rooted in the rational grounds of Husserlian philosophy in exact and precise terminologies. After all, Føllesdal's quotes from Husserl's *Ideas I, Ideas III* and *Noema Und Sinn* illustrate that his position is deeply rooted in Husserl's writings, thereby demonstrating the validity of his position. In my view, phenomenology should not be a business of a few gifted scholars, but of common ordinary folk. Føllesdal elucidates his understanding of Husserl's notion of *noema* in twelve theses (Føllesdal, 1969). They are extremely precise and exact, devoid of ambiguity and confusion. Thesis 1 defines *noema*. Thesis 2 speaks of the composition of *noema*. Thesis 3 delineates that *noema* relates itself to objects. Thesis 4 denotes what *noema* is and what it is not. Theses 5 and 6 describe *noema's* relation to an object. Thesis 7 relates *noema* to acts of consciousness. Theses 8 and 9 explain the abstract nature of *noema*. Theses 10 and 11 disclose the way we realize *noema*, while Thesis 12 signifies its temporal determinations.

6.3.1 Thesis 1: The *noema* is an intentional entity, a generalization of the notion of meaning (*Sinn, Bedeutung*)

Føllesdal, in his analysis of *noema*, bases himself on Section 16, *Ideas III* (Husserl, 1980a). However, he is very much aware of the fact that one single reference to *Ideas III* is insufficient, and hence borrows from numerous sections of *Ideas I* (Husserl, 1976h, 1976f, 1976m, 1976e), in addition to Husserl's manuscript, *Noema und Sinn*. He builds up a structure based on *Ideas III*, not foundational by itself, therefore depends on extraneous sources for support. This also implies that he recognizes the succinct and well-articulated treatment of *noema* in *Ideas I*, relying on the same to support his views. At the very beginning of Thesis 1, Føllesdal states that this thesis and its consequences might go against the usual interpretation of Husserl on *noema*, which raises the query as to what the usual interpretation is; but he does not answer it anywhere. I am sure he must be referring to Gurwitsch,[1] for his was the only major interpretation of *noema* that arose before that time, implying that Føllesdal was aware of the historical development of the interpretation of *noema* by Gurwitsch, yet conveniently ignores to mention it. It is good to remember that every scholar sits on the shoulders of his predecessors, and no human creativity is absolutely new and so totally modern so as to begin *ex nihilo*. Føllesdal forgets this simple truth regarding human creativity on *noema* while working on his paper. Can we not say that Heidegger's treatment of understanding and pre-understanding has reference to it? My present understanding definitely has a reference to earlier (pre-) understanding. By concentrating exclusively on *Ideas III* to begin his elucidation of *noema*, Føllesdal commits the error of universalizing the partial; he fails to do his homework.

Føllesdal in Thesis 1 uses two German expressions: *Sinn* and *Bedeutung*, both of which broadly refer to meaning, albeit with a subtle difference. *Sinn* has the connotation of meaning in a very general sense, i.e., meaning as a whole, while *Bedeutung* refers only to linguistic meanings or conceptual significations, i.e., meaning of expressions in language or partial meanings. Føllesdal conveniently ignores such a distinction and identifies the meaning of *Sinn* (meanings in general) with the meaning of the expression *Bedeutung* which is quite incorrect. Consider the example, the part-whole distinction to clarify my viewpoint. The whole is abstract with no reference to any context. On the other hand, the part is contextual, concrete, an instantiation of the whole. Part is a component or a moment of the whole. I express this figuratively in the following manner.

The list of parts of course, is not exhaustive, for there can be a variety of other meanings too. To identify these partial meanings with the totality of meanings would be wrong, though they do have their characteristics and individualities. Nowhere does Føllesdal elucidate his reasons for identifying

---

[1] Husserl's *Ideas I* was published in 1913, and immediately thereafter, within a period of 10-12 weeks, he wrote both *Ideas II* and *III*, subsequently giving both manuscripts to Martin Heidegger and Edith Stein to edit. They were published in German in 1952 by Husserl Archives, Catholic University, Louvain. Gurwitsch wrote his book, *Field of Consciousness, Theme, Thematic Field and Margin* in 1962. However, Føllesdal published his paper on *Noema* only in 1969, which meant that both Gurwitsch and Føllesdal were fully aware of Husserl's writings, yet, the former appears to be ignoring *Ideas III*, whereas Føllesdal, though aware of Gurwitsch's work, pays little attention to it (Føllesdal, 1969).

Sinn with *Bedeutung*. The extreme complexity of the phenomenon of meaning might have forced him to abandon it without further elucidation, paving way for his successors to enter into polemics over it.

Table 6.1 Part and whole, explaining the relation between *Sinn* and *Bedeutung*

	Types of Meaning	Illustration
1.	Linguistic meaning	
2.	Existential meaning	
3.	Religious meaning	
4.	Meaning of secret codes	
5.	Social meaning	
6.	Artistic meaning	
7.	Hermeneutic meaning	
8.	Meaning of symbols	
9.	Meaning of gestures	
10.	Every other possible meaning	

Sinn stands for meaning as a whole

1, 2 and so on, stand for *Bedeutung*, meaning in particular cases, such as linguistic meaning, existential meaning, and so on

6.3.2 Thesis 2: Components of *Noema* and its Thetic Character

A *noema* has two components, the first of which is common to all acts with the same object possessing identical properties, oriented in the same way, etc., regardless of the thetic character of the act, be it perception, remembering or imagining. The second component of *noema* is different in acts with different thetic character. In Thesis 2, Føllesdal quotes *Logical Investigations* (Husserl, 1977c), stating that matter and quality come together to form *Sinn*, which I believe is incorrect. As stated in an earlier context, only matter from *Logical Investigations* refers to *noema* from *Ideas I*. These two different notions of *Logical Investigations* cannot be combined to form the basis of the very same *noema* due to their incompatible characteristics.

6.3.3 Thesis 3: The Noematic Sinn is that in virtue of which consciousness relates to the object

Thesis 3 signifies Husserl's radical deviation from Brentano, as he found it difficult to cope with Brentano's interpretation of the precept that consciousness is the consciousness of something (an object). Husserl raised questions regarding the status of an object, for example, now I am conscious of a chair, the object is in front of me, before my eyes, before my sense organs.

But when I am conscious of my happiness, joy, anxiety or nothingness (Heidegger), the object does not exist like in the earlier case. Then how do I justify the meaning of the claim that consciousness is the consciousness of an object? Husserl brought in the notion of *noema* to solve this dilemma, which refers to the meaning of my conscious act. In and through *noema*, Husserl justifies the contention that consciousness is the consciousness of an object (meaning is also considered as an object). Therefore, on account of *noema*, consciousness is directed, or in other words, to be directed is to possess a *noema*, while reference to an object springs from meaning (*noema*). One question that can be raised here is this: can anything be meaningless from a Husserlian or phenomenological point of view? The answer is a firm no. The endeavour of consciousness is to discover meaning, and consciousness does not fail in its attempt. To go one step further, Heidegger's hermeneutical phenomenology rules out the very possibility of meaningless experience of *Dasein*, whose strength lies in finding meaning, even in death, considered the most meaningless phenomenon according to Sartre. I do not agree with the position of Sartre for various reasons (Thomas, 1990). One can speak of meaningfulness in the domain of consciousness. However, all meaningfulness disappears when one is dead, since consciousness is absent in that dead individual.

6.3.4 Thesis 4: The noema of an act is not the object of the act (i.e., the object toward which the act is directed)

Thesis 4 has reference to 3 in addition to references to the object and the act. Let me reiterate the example of the chair. It functions as an object; it is material, physical, corporeal and transcendent, and is the object of my consciousness. But when conceived as a place to sit, an elevated platform, a place of respect, or a weapon, it becomes an immanent object, a *noema*. It is no more the material, corporeal, transcendent chair. I, as *noesis*, assign meanings to the immanent chair. The various conceptions of the chair as a *noema*, i.e., a seat, as an elevated platform, as a weapon, etc., spring from various acts of my consciousness.

6.3.5 Thesis 5: To one and the same *noema*, there corresponds only one object

When I consider the chair as a weapon (a *noema*), the spatio-temporal, material, physical object in its totality, is the weapon, the *noema*; similarly so in the case of the chair (the transcendent object) as an elevated platform (*noema*). There is a one-to-one relationship between the direction of *noema* to the transcendent object. Here, the argument originates from the *noema* and moves towards the transcendent object. But Føllesdal's statement that the converse is not true originates from the fact that from the same material, transcendent object (chair), one can arrive at a plurality of *noemata*. In the example of the chair, a single material, physical object (chair) can produce a plurality of *noemata*. A one-to-one relationship does not hold good when the argument is from the *noema* to the transcendent object, but it is valid when considering the inverse relation, i.e., from the transcendent object to the *noema*. This must be abundantly clear by now in the example of the chair, which is a single object and the source of a plurality of *noemata*, but not vice-versa. This demonstrates the invalidity of Thesis 3 of Prof. Mohanty (*vide* 3.7.1. in Chapter 3).

6.3.6 Thesis 6: To one and the same object, there may correspond several different *noemata*

Thesis 6 justifies our example of the chair and its various *noemata*. The chair transforms itself into a comfortable seat to sit, or it is a weapon, an elevated platform, each of which is a *noema*. This thesis is a tribute to the fertility of Husserl's philosophy regarding *noemata*, and allows us to appreciate the richness of the ordinary, mundane objects that we deal with in our everyday life.

6.3.7 Thesis 6*: To one and the same object, there may correspond several different *noematic Sinne*

Thesis 6* differs from 5 only in the substitution of *noema* by *noematic Sinne*, which serves to further strengthen the former. But why does Føllesdal think that Thesis 6* needs strengthening, and what is the difference between *noema* and *noematic Sinn*, since *noema* itself refers to meaning? Føllesdal does not give any answer to it.

6.3.8 Thesis 7: Each act has one and only one *noema*

Conceiving the chair to be a comfortable seat to sit down is a single act of consciousness, which is the meaning I assign to the chair, and hence the chair's *noema*. Similarly, grasping the chair to be a weapon is yet another act of consciousness. This demonstrates that each act of consciousness with respect to a material transcendent object leads to a single *noema*, implying a one-to-one relation or correspondence between the act of consciousness and the *noema* arising from the act.

6.3.9 Thesis 8: *Noemata* are abstract entities

The term, 'abstract' has several meanings; it could mean non-existent in space and time or devoid of spatio-temporal determinations. It could also mean conceptual, non-substantial, non-factual, non-real or non-tangible. Abstract could also refer to meaning, for meaning is not a perceptual, substantial entity. It can only be grasped intellectually or by way of intuition or in and through (non-sensorial) vision, i.e., meanings are inaccessible through sense organs. Abstract could also mean conceptual, which can be grasped only by understanding or intuition. It may be noted that spatio-temporal objects can be grasped only perspectively. Since *noemata* are not perceived through perspectives, they cannot be considered to be objects in space and time. For example, my act of conceiving the chair as a weapon is a thought within me, and as such, beyond space and time, or in other words, abstract.

6.3.10 Thesis 9: *Noemata* are not perceived through our sense

To avoid possible confusion with regard to the word 'sense', since sense can mean both sense organs as well as meaning, I wish to add organ to 'sense' as given in the thesis, thus describing the thesis as, *noemata* are not perceived through our sense organ(s). Thesis 9 is an immediate consequence of thesis 8. *Noema*, being meaning, cannot be perceived through sense organs, since meaning is an abstract entity, irreal and conceptual according to Husserl.

6.3.11 Thesis 10: Noemata are known through a special reflection, the phenomenological reflection and Thesis 11: The phenomenological reflection can be iterated

In Thesis 10, *noemata* are known through a special reflection, i.e., the phenomenological reflection, and Husserl says that such a reflection can be repeated. Theses 10 and 11 are combined together for elucidation since both focus on phenomenological reflection. How can we understand *noema*? Thesis 10 states that *noema* can be known through phenomenological reflection, in and through which we grasp meanings. Phenomenological reflection is not done using sense organs, rather it enables us to grasp meanings via epoché and phenomenological reduction. Thesis 11 states that this reflection can be repeated. Consider the example of the chair; my conception of the chair as a comfortable place to sit or as a weapon is the result of phenomenological reflection, which is performed by my consciousness pre-logically, pre-consciously, pre-verbally and spontaneously. This reflection is strictly subjective and ego-centric, but cannot be object-centric. It is a reflection that reiterates the primordiality and primacy of one's subjectivity and can be performed recursively.

6.3.12 Thesis 12: This pattern of determinations, together with the *Gegebenheitsweise* is the *noema*

Thesis 12 raises the question, is there an incompatibility between Theses 1 and 12? My answer is a definite no. Both provide different perspectives on *noema*; Thesis 1 states that *noema* is meaning, whereas Thesis 12 enables us to find them. We do find meanings in the already given, that is the past, gnawing into the present as well. The past and the present are not cut off from each other or from the future, like the Aristotelian chronometric understanding of time; rather, the present extends itself or gnaws into the past and future, i.e., it is such a present that extends itself into the future as well. So in the present, we find meanings of the past (the already given) and future, and in the manner of their givenness. In other words, Føllesdal accounts for temporality of meanings in Thesis 12, a central concern in Husserl's philosophy (Chapter 10 deals with temporality). Consider the example of a crow. The crow is black, it hops around, pecks prey and crows. These are the already given, i.e., the past and up to the present. In a moment from now (the future), it will fly away, make its nest, lay eggs and raise its young ones. Two crows would do these mentioned activities in a similar fashion, and their manner of doing so would reveal their individuality. The example of the chair can also be adduced to interpret Thesis 12, according to which, the *noemata* contains in itself, the past and the future in addition to the manner in which it is given. Since some *noemata* are always outstanding, the meaning of an object is always incomplete; thus Thesis 12 accounts for future possibilities of *noemata* as well.

This is how I understand Føllesdal's interpretation of Husserl's notion of *noema*. This is not the end of the story. Husserl's ideas on *noema* inspired several scholars, namely, Alfred Schütz, Marvin Faber, Joseph Kochelmans to explore the same. They followed in the footsteps of Gurwitsch, upholding the notion of perceptual *noema*, while Føllesdal's reflections attracted experts such as David Smith and Ronald McIntyre (McIntyre & Smith, 1975; Smith & McIntyre, 1982). Meanwhile, another group of phenomenologists, including, William McKenna (Mckenna, 1982), Lenore Langsdrof (Langsdorf, 1984) and Mary Jeanne Larabee (Larrabee, 1986), and a few others began to explore *noema* in yet another direction.

Føllesdal's treatment of *noema* is logical and analytical, which was later adopted by his disciples as well. His theses 8 & 9 do not explicate the term, 'abstract entities' in detail, probably owing to the complications that might arise from a clear explication of the same. But his disciples, Smith and McIntyre point out that Husserl identified *noema* with meanings expressed in language (Husserl, 1976n, 1976q, 1976l; Smith & McIntyre, 1982), though they are not the sole medium of expressing meaning.

Though meanings can be expressed through language, language is not the only medium of expressing meanings. There are other ways too. Consider the notion of the look expounded by Sartre in his celebrated book, *Being and Nothingness*. No word is uttered, no oral expression is exchanged, the situation is totally non-linguistic and completely non-verbal, yet the context conveys the enormous weight of meaning. It is a look that can freeze a person.

Consider Heidegger's understanding of nothingness. When nothingness is understood as an absence permeated by presence (note, this assertion does not involve any contradictions), it is terribly full of meaning, totally non-linguistic and completely existential. These examples show that meanings are not limited to language and can be communicated by other means too. Føllesdal's disciples, due to their commitment to logic and over enthusiasm to the analytical approach to meanings, ignore these subtle contexts and fine expressions of meanings via non-linguistic devices. Smith and McIntyre also ignore several insights of meanings by Husserl in *Ideas I* (Husserl, 1976j). Inasmuch as Føllesdal commits errors by universalizing the partial, his disciples follow in his footsteps doing the same.

Another fundamental question that I would like to address is, where does *noema* get its meanings from? Meanings are assigned to *noema* by *noesis*, i.e., *noema* receives meanings only from *noesis*, and not from any linguistic source. Smith and McIntyre ignore *noesis*, the transcendental ego as the source of meanings, and the fact that *noema* is dependent on *noesis*, not just for meanings, but also for its being, the dependence being both epistemological and ontological. Language is created by man (*noesis*), who assigns meanings to it. Conventions have a role to play in assigning meanings, but conventions are also created by man. Words and expressions (language in general) do not assign meanings unto themselves. Meanings of languages are not self-generative but man-made, which implies that the meaning of words and expressions is beyond language.

There is another group of Husserl commentators namely, William McKenna, Langsdrof and Larabee, who hold that *noema* is the same as the transcendent object or a functional replacement for the latter, which I consider erroneous for the following reasons.

1. *Noema* arises from the rigorous process of phenomenological epoché and reduction, which in turn results from an epistemological procedure and phenomenological reflection. But the transcendent object exists as what it is, devoid of human intervention. The material object is spatio-temporal and ontic. Phenomenological analysis begins from this material, physical transcendent object, reaching its conclusion in *noema*. The object exists here and now. It is ontic, and the ontic is what it is; it is the empirical, transcendent object. While *noema* is notional and theoretical, *noema* is irreal, immanent, and symbolizes the culmination of a quest for meanings. While a person can have various perspectives towards a material object, such a perspectival approach is not possible with *noema*, which is complete in every

possible way. But a material object is never complete, as ever new perspectives can be had or added to the object from time to time. Hence to replace one with the other is not possible.

2. *Noema* and transcendent objects belong to different categories and identifying one with the other would lead to a category mistake (Ryle, 2000).

3. If *noema* and object could be interchanged, there would have been no need for Husserl to work so hard and write ever so many enlightening pages specifically on *noema* in *Ideas I*. A large part of *Ideas I* (Husserl, 1976g) and *Noema Und Sinn* would have been meaningless if this were possible. There are also commentators like Hubert Dreyfus (Dreyfus, 1972), Theodore de Bore (de Boer, 1978c) and several others who differ from Gurwitsch, Føllesdal and other scholars who discussed *noema*. References could have been be made to their writings as well had this been an exclusive study of *noesis* and *noema*.

6.4 Possible Convergence of the views of Gurwitsch and Føllesdal

So far, we have seen that there are a large number of differing interpretations and alternative views on meaning and the purpose of *noema*, of which the main opponents seem to be Gurwitsch and Føllesdal, both of whom are outstanding commentators and leading analysts of *noema*, deeply rooted in Husserl. While Gurwitsch bases himself on *Ideas I* (Husserl, 1976c, 1976f, 1976p), Føllesdal roots himself predominantly on *Ideas III* (Husserl, 1980a). Later on, he realizes his inadequacies of being glued chiefly to *Ideas III*, and quotes extensively from *Ideas I* and *Noema Und Sinn*, that serves to demonstrate that the evidence and justification for Føllesdal's views on *noema* is beyond *Ideas III*. In fact, it may be noted that Føllesdal is the only commentator of *noema* to use *Ideas III*. Føllesdal's paper is extremely logical, both in appearance and content, wherein he demonstrates the origin of *noema* from Husserl's understanding of Frege's notion of meaning. Although Thesis 1 speaks of *Sinn* and *Bedeutung*, in the course of his analysis, he identifies them both, yet again emphasizing *Sinn*, stating from the very beginning, the close similarity between *Sinn* and *Bedeutung*; and, in fact, one follows the other (*vide* Thesis 1). On account of this, Richard Solomon points out that *Sinn* and *Bedeutung* are treated in tandem, and the remainder of Føllesdal's essay treats these two different senses of meaning cooperatively, one reinforcing the other (Solomon, 1977). Føllesdal's *noema* is a close relative of Frege's *Sinn*. Many scholars who follow Føllesdal ignore Gurwitsch totally, turning a blind eye to the notion of perceptual *noema*. At least Føllesdal refers to Gurwitsch indirectly by speaking of usual interpretation (*vide* Thesis 1) before elucidating his own understanding of *noema* as an intentional entity.

Despite these differing views and conflicting interpretations, my query is this: is there some way of bringing Gurwitsch and Follesdal, together? My endeavour in the remaining part of the chapter lies in this direction. Can we not demonstrate that Føllesdal's treatment of *noema* as a conceptual entity has some continuity with Gurwitsch elucidation of perceptual *noema*? After all, both positions are rooted in Husserl's phenomenology, nay, in Husserl's *Ideas I* and *Ideas III* and *Noema Und Sinn;* while my answer is in the positive, my views are interlaced with my comments as well.

1. Gurwitsch holds that perception establishes the domain of *noema*. The perceived as such refers to *noema* and its meaning, but it has a transcendent reference too, i.e., the material, physical, transcendent object. Gurwitsch's analyses and examples of *noema* demonstrate that the physical object is the transcendent reference of *noema*. Føllesdal on the other hand, refers to meanings as *noema*, and his notion of meaning has linguistic expressions as their transcendent reference. Thus, both Gurwitsch and Føllesdal accept a transcendent reference while discussing *noema*.

2. Let us consider the example of the chair referred to earlier. It is a material, transcendent object, perceived in various ways, all of which are *noemata*, obtain their meaning from me, the *noesis*, for I assign a particular meaning to a *noema* depending on the situation. Føllesdal also describes something similar; that which is perceived is linguistic expressions, and that which is grasped as such is their meaning. Consider the word perception itself, I assign meaning to it; it may be a sensorial perception at times, an intellectual grasp at certain others or intuition/ vision at other occasions. Such an assignment of meaning depends on me, the *noesis*, in which case, perception is the transcendent object to which a meaning, i.e., a *noema* is assigned by the *noesis*. From these examples, my question is, how can there be any major difference between the positions of Gurwitsch and Føllesdal? Both search for the meaning of a transcendent object, finding them in *noemata* from their own perspectives.

3. In discussing *noema*, Gurwitsch points towards a transcendent reference, i.e., the chair and its *noema*, the meaning, i.e., chair as a weapon. This sort of an analysis of *noema* leaves no room for abstract judgements or logical statements. It is common knowledge that Husserl was a mathematician who entered into

the domain of philosophy on account of his enormous interest in logic, ideal entities and necessary truths. He was also equally interested in epistemological issues and related problems. True, he spoke of perceptual *noema* in *Ideas I* (Husserl, 1976c, 1976f, 1976p), but his interest could not be confined to the problems of perception. Føllesdal realized the propensity of Husserl's thought and derived a strong push from *Ideas III* (Husserl, 1980a), though he did not cut himself off completely from *Ideas I*. His innumerable references to quotations from *Ideas I* demonstrate his awareness of continuity from *Ideas I* to *III*, implying that he also realized the continuity of Husserl's thought on *noema*. Therefore, I would say that Føllesdal's notion of *noema* as an intentional or conceptual entity is only a logical, nay, a phenomenological extension of Gurwitsch's perceptual *noema*. There is no incompatibility or incongruity between the two notions of *noemata*.

4. Why did Husserl introduce the notion of *noema* in the first place if his concerns were confined to Brentano's problem of intentional inexistence? Husserl's early notions of epoché and phenomenological reductions would have been sufficient to sort out the former. Husserl could have led a cosy intellectual life without having bothered so much about major issues such as *noema*. But he had different aims in life. Gurwitsch's approach does not concern such deeper and major issues of phenomenology. The importance of the concept of *noema* shines forth only when we turn away from the perceptual domain to the realms of *noema* at the abstract realms of judgement and logical disciplines. Hence the natural urge for fulfilment of Husserl's philosophy leads it from Gurwitsch to Føllesdal, from perceptual to conceptual *noema*. Gurwitsch's approach makes Husserl just a philosopher like many others, but Husserl's commitment to intentional *noema*, as elucidated in *Ideas III* (Husserl, 1980a), and as explained further by scholars like Føllesdal, make him an outstanding philosopher like Aristotle, Kant, and others. It is indeed true that Husserl's *Ideas I* contain a detailed analysis of the notion of perceptual *noema*, but even so, he devotes several passages for the elaboration of intentional, conceptual and judgemental *noema* in *Ideas III*. Though Husserl was initially interested in perceptual *noema*, it was the *noema* of judgement that brought his philosophy to fruition and perfection. In Thesis 1, Føllesdal writes, "the thesis and its consequences go against the usual interpretation of Husserl," by which he refers to the

interpretation of *noema* in terms of perception, for there was no other interpretation of *noema* available until then. It is very unfortunate that Føllesdal here uses the expression, 'against', which is not just inappropriate, but also indicates his lack of complete understanding of the full ramifications of his own notion of *noema* as a continuation of perceptual *noema*.

5.   To substantiate my views, I would like to add something based on Føllesdal's article (Føllesdal, 1969). In the introduction, he uses the word 'centaur', which can have only an intentional *noema*. However in Thesis 8, he refers to the perceptual *noema* of a tree (following Husserl). Does it not prove that Føllesdal himself was concerned with the perception of transcendent objects and therefore of perceptual *noema* as well, while simultaneously being concerned with conceptual *noema*? True, perceptual *noema* was not Follesdal's primary concern, but he did not ignore it completely. It may be kept in mind that, in and through the notion of perception, Gurwitsch points out that *noema* is irreal, not unreal or an imagination or a phantom. Føllesdal also arrives at the same conclusion like Gurwitsch that *noema* is meaning, and is irreal. Their conclusions are convergent, though the routes taken by them are divergent, one by way of perception, and the other by way of intentionality and judgement.

6.   There is a broad agreement between Gurwitsch and Føllesdal on a number of theses. Consider for example, Theses 3, 4 and 5. Husserl tells us that *noema* intends an object, yet *noema* is not an object in itself. To elucidate this, Gurwitsch would say that the chair is perceived from various perspectives, each giving rise to a *noema*. While one perspective gives rise to *noema* as a weapon, another gives rise to *noema* as an elevated platform. We see the richness of objects through these perspectives. Føllesdal's interpretation is based not on mundane perception, but on conceptual judgements that lead to *noema*. In other words, like Gurwitsch, Føllesdal also states in Thesis 3 that it is *noema* that allows consciousness to be directed to the object. Gurwitsch agrees with Føllesdal's Thesis 4, which states that *noema* is an act, and not the object of an act. Gurwitsch also agrees with Thesis 5 that points out that there is only one object per *noema*. Such agreements can also be found in Theses 7, 8 and 9.

7.   There is a need to distinguish between perception and abstraction, two terms crucially related to both Gurwitsch and Føllesdal. The

word, 'perception', originates from Latin, *percipere*, where, '*per*' means thoroughly, and '*capere*' means to take. Combining these two parts of meaning allows us to capture meanings thoroughly by way of sense organs, especially sight. Although this is the original etymological meaning, the word, 'perception' evolved with time, leading to developments, interpolations, insertions and amendments. It is now used in different senses only remotely associated with the original meaning. Instead of adhering to the original, etymological and pure meaning, scholars began to use it to refer to capture by intellect, i.e., intellectual vision or intuition, to attain awareness or understanding, etc. Hence one can perceive the chair (a transcendent material object) via sense organs and mental vision as well. Thus, in the course of time, both etymological and interpolated meaning were given equal value and identical worth, which may be one way to account for the growth and development of language.

8. Meaning is abstract. The word, 'abstract' originates from the Latin expression, '*abstrahere*', which means to draw away or disassociate from specific instances or insufficiently factual cases. The meaning of the chair, grasped by my mind is abstract, immanent, bereft of any reference to context. The chair, to be used as a weapon or as an elevated platform, is the meaning that I assign to the chair. The meaning to be assigned is in my thought, and therefore abstract. When meaning is materialized, contextualized or concretized, it can be noticed by sense organs. Meaning is not perceived by sense organs as such, but when actualized or concretized, this materialization can be perceived by sense organs. Thus, the word perception minimally has two senses, and both are valid uses of the expression from an etymological point of view. Hence, in Gurwitsch, there is a close connection between the material, transcendent object (here chair), and the meaning that I assign to it (weapon, elevated platform, etc.). In other words, Gurwitsch's notion of perception leads to abstraction, as stated by Føllesdal in Theses 8 and 9. This again demonstrates continuity from Gurwitsch to Føllesdal, a continuity from perceptual to conceptual judgement.

9. According to Kant, knowledge is possible only by way of judgement, since all the operations of understanding are reducible to acts of judging. Therefore acts of understanding can be represented by the power of judging. To judge is to think, to unify, to synthesize the manifold of appearance by means of

concepts to form cognition. It is understanding that judges. In the case of Gurwitsch, perceptual *noema* also needs to be judgemental to be an integral part of knowledge. Hence, to assume that perceptual knowledge remains exclusively in the domain of sense perception is to hold that it does not lead to judgement, and hence deny that it is knowledge at all. This is an injustice to Gurwitsch, for his notion of perceptual *noema* definitely leads to judgement and knowledge. Gurwitsch speaks of empirical knowledge on account of transcendent reference and perceptual *noema*, which leads to eidetic knowledge and finally to eidetic sciences. From all these, we need to conclude that Gurwitsch's notion of perception is not exclusively sensual, but eidetic as well. Hence, there is a certain continuity from Gurwitsch to Føllesdal.

10. An object is perceived through sense organs by way of perspectives, not so with *noema*. If we apply the perspectival approach to *noema* as well, we would definitely fall into infinite regress. In perception, the perspectival origin of *noema* is demonstrated by a sensory approach to the object, here the chair. But in the case of Føllesdal, perspectival character is brought about by sentences and expressions in language; we have observed the perspectival character of word perception and the various meanings of 'perception'. One can elicit several instances to demonstrate the perspectival character of words and expressions, i.e., language in general that we use in our daily life.

11. In the context of discussion of *noema*, we find that Husserl's writings progress from one book to another, from *Logical Investigations* to *Ideas I*, and further on to *Ideas II* and *III*. This is in fact, a general feature of Husserl's major writings. Gurwitsch holds on to *Ideas I* while, Føllesdal accepts *Ideas III* as the basis and foundation. Following in the footsteps of Husserl in achieving progress from one book to another, we can understand the progress which Føllesdal made from Gurwitsch, i.e., from perceptual *noema* to intentional *noema*. But Husserl did not stop with *Ideas III*, and goes on to speak of Life world, lived experiences and other such concepts in the books that follow. In and through these concepts, Husserl demands us to discover meanings in our experiences and in the context of our life-situations. Will Føllesdal, who speaks of *noema* as an abstract concept, have any objections to it? I assume not, since he ignored the rigorous distinctions between *Sinn* and *Bedeutung* and

upheld the primacy and primordially of *Sinn*, which refers to meaning in general (Table 6.1). From that perspective, inasmuch as *Sinn* refers not just to the meaning of language and expressions, it also refers to the meaning of life in general. By upholding the primacy and validity of *Sinn*, was Føllesdal not accounting for the meaning of life world as well as lived experiences?

12. Husserl was an excellent logician whose major contribution was towards transcendental logic and allied notions. In fact, logic was his stepping-stone to philosophy. Husserl's acumen as a logician can be observed in *Logical Investigations, Vol. 2* (Husserl, 1977t). However, his early disciples were not equally interested in logic. Although Heidegger was committed to ontology, he once remarked that his books could not be understood meaningfully without a rigorous grasp of logic. However, it may be noted that Heidegger, from 1919 onwards, i.e., during his pre-*Being and Time* period, delivered a number of lectures, and organized several seminars on logic. This absence of interest in logic in Husserl's major disciples was remedied by Føllesdal, a logician who worked on Frege's problem of *Sinn* under the supervision of another well-known logician (Willard Van Orman) Quine. Føllesdal, thus fills a void amongst Husserl's disciples. But one thing is to be kept in mind. Despite Husserl's commitment to logic, he devoted himself subsequently to philosophy, consciousness, intentionality, etc., and later on to life world and lived experiences. In other words, Husserl utilized logic as a launching pad for his philosophical explorations; but Føllesdal's paper does not exhibit any such directions and intentions.

13. I also wish to submit one another additional point for consideration. The example of the chair has been used extensively to illustrate the concept of perceptual *noema*, in addition to the elucidation of the problems of intentional, or conceptual treatment of *noema* to a certain extent. Does this not demonstrate that there is no hard and fast difference nor any uncompromising incompatibility between the positions of Gurwitsch and Føllesdal, who started his journey towards *noema* where the former stopped.

Husserl's thoughts and ideas find continuous growth and sustained development from *Logical Investigations* to *Ideas* (all three) to *Crisis of European Sciences*, with no apparent break or discontinuity in his thoughts. A similar evolution of concepts and thoughts is observed in the development of his notion of *noema* as well, through which, he emphasizes the notion of meaning in our lives. But his disciples go no further than the meaningfulness of perception, concepts, and judgements. Husserl, on the other hand, goes beyond them all, stressing the meaningfulness of human existence in general in terms of life world and lived experiences, all of which are a manifestation of an unending quest to discover the meaning of life.

6.5 References

de Boer, T. (1978). *The Development of Husserl's Thought* (T. Platinga, Trans.). Martinus Nijhoff Publishers, The Hague.

Dreyfus, H. L. (1972). The Perceptual Noema: Gurwitsch's Crucial Contribution. In L. E. Embree (Ed.), *In Life-World and Consciousness: Essays for Aron Gurwitsch* (pp. 135–170). Evanston: Northwestern University Press.

Føllesdal, D. (1969). Husserl's Notion of Noema: First delivered as a lecture in the 66th session of the Annual Meeting of the American Philosophical Association, Eastern Division, on 16 October, 1969. *The Journal of Philosophy*, 66(20), 680–687.

Gurwitsch, A. (2010). The Perpetual Noema. In R. M. Zaner & L. E. Embree (Eds.), *The Collected Works of Aron Gurwitsch (1901-73). Volume III: The Field of Consciousness: Phenomenology of Theme, Thematic Field, and Marginal Consciousness: Phaenomenologica 194* (pp. 167–176). Springer Science+Business Media.

Husserl, E. (1976a). Descriptive and Exact Sciences, Section 74. In W. R. B. Gibson (Trans.), *Ideas: General Introduction to Pure Phenomenology* (pp. 167–170). Humanities Press.

Husserl, E. (1976b). Noematic Meaning and Relation to the Object. In W. R. B. Gibson (Trans.), *Ideas: General Introduction to Pure Phenomenology* (pp. 365–370). Humanities Press.

Husserl, E. (1976c). Noematic statements and statements concerning reality. The noema in the psychological sphere, Section 89. In W. R. B. Gibson (Trans.), *Ideas: General Introduction to Pure Phenomenology* (p. 260). Humanities Press.

Husserl, E. (1976d). Noesis and Noema. In W. R. B. Gibson (Trans.), *Ideas: General Introduction to Pure Phenomenology* (pp. 255–281). Humanities Press.

Husserl, E. (1976e). Real (*reelle*) and intentional factors of experience. The noema, Section 88. In W. R. B. Gibson (Trans.), *Ideas: General Introduction to Pure Phenomenology* (pp. 257–259). Humanities Press.

Husserl, E. (1976f). Sections 74, 89, 131. In W. R. B. Gibson (Trans.), *Ideas: General Introduction to Pure Phenomenology* (pp. 207–208, 260, 365–367). Humanities Press.

Husserl, E. (1976g). The Analogous Distinctions in the Spheres of Sentiment and Will, Section 95. In W. R. B. Gibson (Trans.), *Ideas: General Introduction to Pure Phenomenology* (pp. 276–278). Humanities Press.

Husserl, E. (1976h). The hyletic and noetic phases as real (*reelle*). The noematic as non-real phases of experience, Section 97. In W. R. B. Gibson

(Trans.), *Ideas: General Introduction to Pure Phenomenology* (pp. 282–285). Humanities Press.

Husserl, E. (1976i). The 'noematic meaning' and the distinction between 'immanent' and 'real (*wirklichen)* objects', Section 90. In W. R. B. Gibson (Trans.), *Ideas: General Introduction to Pure Phenomenology* (pp. 261–264). Humanities Press.

Husserl, E. (1976j). The 'object', the 'determinable X in the noematic sense', Section 131. In W. R. B. Gibson (Trans.), *Ideas: General Introduction to Pure Phenomenology* (pp. 365–367). Humanities Press.

Husserl, E. (1976k). The transformations of Attention in regard both to noesis and noema, Section 92. In W. R. B. Gibson (Trans.), *Ideas: General Introduction to Pure Phenomenology* (pp. 267–270). Humanities Press.

Husserl, E. (1977a). Investigation V: Descriptive Characterization of 'Acts' as Intentional Experiences, Section 10. In J. N. Findlay (Trans.), *Logical Investigations Volume 2* (pp. 553–556). Routledge & Kegan Paul.

Husserl, E. (1977b). *Logical Investigations, Volume 2* (J. N. Findlay, Trans.). Routledge & Kegan Paul.

Husserl, E. (1980). Noema and Essence. In T. E. Klein & W. E. Pohl (Trans.), *Ideas Pertaining to a Pure Phenomenology and to a Phenomenological Philosophy, Third Book: Phenomenology and the Foundation of the Sciences* (pp. 73–76). Martinus Nijhoff Publishers.

Langsdorf, L. (1984). The Noema as Intentional Entity: A Critique of Føllesdal. *The Review of Metaphysics, 37*(4), 757–784.

Larrabee, M. J. (1986). The Noema in Husserl's Studies. *Husserl Studies, 3*, 209–230.

McIntyre, R., & Smith, D. W. (1975). Husserl's Identification of Meaning and Noema. *The Monist, 59*(1), 115–132.

Mckenna, W. (1982). *Husserl's Introductions to Phenomenology: Interpretation and Critique: Phaenomenologica 89.* Springer Netherlands.

Ryle, G. (2000). *The Concept of Mind.* University of Chicago Press.

Smith, D. W., & McIntyre, R. (1982). *Husserl and Intentionality: A Study of Mind, Meaning, and Language* (Vol. 154). Reidel Publishing Company, Dordercht-Holland.

Solomon, R. C. (1977). Husserl's Concept of Noema. In F. A. Elliston & P. McCormick (Eds.), *Husserl: Expositions and Appraisals* (pp. 168–181). University of Notre Dame Press.

Thomas, V. C. (1990). The Development of Time Consciousness from Husserl to Heidegger. In A.-T. Tymieniecka (Ed.), *The Moral Sense and Its Foundational Significance: Self, Person, Historicity, Community: Analecta Husserliana* (pp. 347–360). Springer, Dordrecht.

Chapter 7

Husserl's Examination of Lived Body

7.1 Introduction

Traditionally, the human body is not a topic of discussion in philosophy; it is studied mostly in physiology, biology and in other branches of medical science. Although Descartes dealt with it in his philosophy, it was not given due importance on account of his rationalist priorities, but not so with Husserl. He began his parley with the human body in 1907, early in his phenomenological career, in his lectures, *Thing and Space*. Our bodies are material, physical external objects, which is how a physician or a surgeon looks at them, but not so for us personally. Our external perception of it is bound to remain fixed and limited. We can spatially distance ourselves from every object, but not so from our bodies, for I am my body. I can move around things, part by part, by moving my body around them. But I cannot move around my own body. We need to move our bodies to move other things. Our body is a peculiar thing that can sense other objects, whereas an object cannot sense other things. Not only can we perceive our bodies externally, and witness its contact with the environment, we can also feel our bodily movements internally and immediately. Primarily, our body belongs to the constituted transcendent realm and not to the constituting realm, i.e., the transcendental domain. Our bodies are interpreted as something over and against consciousness, viz., as a thing in the empirical environment. Our bodies are in close contact with, and in immediate proximity to us, whereas all other things around us are at arm's length. They are to our right or left, either near or far away from us, implying that our spatial experience of the environment is oriented to a centre, i.e., my body. Moreover, our body is a constituted thing that we can manipulate and move around. This implies that the constitution of the environment as a horizon of all possible movements depends on the constitution of our own body as an immediately moveable thing. All these point us to a constituting consciousness that must already be embodied, but not in the same sense as a movable spatial object. Our body is constituted as a thing, in and on which sensations are localized. Our body can be constituted as constantly proximal, sensing and movable, in which our constituting consciousness is itself somehow embodied, which means that our body cannot be experienced as a mere physical thing. To put it in the language of Husserl, insofar as we have a *Körper* (a worldly, physical body), we are necessarily a *Leib* (a lived body), which is *a priori* necessary condition to have a *Körper.*

Possessing a body does not mean having an abstract thought about it, or a concrete sensation localized in the body, since embodiment is what makes possible the ascription of thought and sensation to the subject. Phenomenology of the human body opens up the possibility of considering embodiment in its constitutive significance. Originally, I do not experience my body as a thing in an objective space. The body is neither given speculatively, nor is it given to me hypothetically. I am not given for myself as belonging to any spatial object. Originally, I do possess consciousness of my body as an object. I do not perceive it, rather I live it, I am it. Primarily, my body is experienced as a unified field of activity and affectivity, with a volitional structure and a potentiality for mobility, an 'I do', and an 'I can' (Husserl, 1973c, 1976e, 2001c, 2005). When my body moves and acts, I am moving and acting (Husserl, 1973c). To put it differently, the constitution of the body is performed, not by the disincarnated functioning of the body, rather by an already existing bodily subject. Subsequently, the body is split up and apprehended as belonging to different body parts. It is only thereafter that sensing is localized, and we are confronted with an experiencing system of fingers, eyes, legs or any other body parts.

7.2 History of Husserl's Study of Body

Husserl began his long and distinguished inquiries into the notion of lived body and embodiment in 1907 while delivering lectures on *Thing and Space* during which, he studied primarily three things: 1) constitution of objective space and physical things, 2) spontaneously moving body-subject and the function of sense organs and, 3) sense-field and kinaesthetic system that operate with the notion of the body (Husserl, 1973e, 1973f). During the 1910-11 winter semester lectures on *The Basic Problems of Phenomenology*, he continued to examine the same concern regarding the body (Husserl, 2006h, 2006d, 2006c). However, in *Ideas I*, he shifted his focus from the notion of lived body, assuming that he must set aside everything bodily in order to enter into the phenomenological domain that would disclose the pure ego. In other words, in *Ideas I*, he dealt with disembodied consciousness, *noema* and phenomenology of reason, among other things, disregarding concepts such as body, intersubjectivity or temporality, which later became the fulcrum of his philosophy. However in *Ideas II*, which Husserl wrote immediately after *Ideas I*, i.e., the beginning of genetic phenomenology, his vision transformed, and he added a lot of material on lived body, including corporeal body within the domain of phenomenological attitude. Fundamentally, he considers the corporeal body as a psychological reality. To understand the depth of his concern with the lived body, one only needs refer *Ideas II* (Husserl, 1989e, 1989g, 1989d). In *Ideas III* however, Husserl speaks solely about the *noematic* sense of the body (Husserl, 1980c). There are hardly any discussions on human body in *Logical Investigations*, wherein his primary concern is epistemological. But his concern for the lived body reappeared in his 1919 lectures on *Nature and Spirit* (Husserl, 2002h), *Phenomenological Psychology* (Husserl, 1977b, 1977k, 1977l) and *Cartesian Meditations* (Husserl, 1960a, 1960c, 1960b). Furthermore, Husserl speaks of the lived body in his books, *Problems of Intersubjectivity* (Husserl, 1973h, 1973g), *Life world* (Husserl, 2002e) and his manuscripts on *Spatiality* (the "D" MSS in all eleven manuscripts) also contain a large amount of rich material on lived body.

7.3 The Distinction Between *Leib* and *Körper*

According to Spiegelberg (Spiegelberg, 1971), it was Max Scheler, who in all probability, originally made a distinction between *Leib* and *Körper*. Scheler was always in touch with Husserl's students in Gottingen University where Husserl taught for some time and delivered his ground-breaking synopsis of his future phenomenological works, *The Basic Problems of Phenomenology* in the winter semester of 1910-11. Interaction with his former students at Gottingen University must have led Husserl to discover Scheler's distinction between *Leib* and *Körper* that appealed to him very much, and therefore he decided to use them in his writings, since they express what he really wanted to say. One may not find such an articulated and complicated distinction in any ordinary dictionary. While *Körper* is the externally appearing, physical and material body, *Leib* refers to my unique, living or lived body. I have free reign over my body that governs all my sense organs. My perceptual acts are bodily as well, governed by *Leib*, which is my life; it is my living body. It is much more than a merely animal body; it is a body with spirit, the ego. While the physical body (*Körper*) is a thing of nature, *Leib* is much more than that; *Leib* belongs to my ego, it is I myself. *Leib* is I myself, inasmuch as I am my body. Bodily acts do not constitute the body, but instead, on account of the self-constitution of my body as *Leib*, my acts are constituted. The body itself is constituted intentionally only in reflective acts. The subject constituted as a counterpoint of nature (*Körper*) i.e., as an I, is that to which the body belongs, as a field of localized sensations. The entire consciousness of the human being is bound to its lived body. The *Leib* is not just the bearer of my consciousness, but also of my sensations; it is subjectivity. The expression, 'my' in this context points to subjectivity, which refers to my body as *Leib*, the subject's living organ. My lived body is the basis and foundation of my spiritual life (Husserl, 1989c, 2002a). Human body as the living organ, has two characteristics, sensibility and mobility. Sensibility demonstrates that my body is the bearer of sensations, and therefore is aesthological (Husserl, 2002e); aesthology is a Greek word meaning sensation or touch, while mobility demonstrates that body is an organ of movements. It is by virtue of my body's capacity for mobility that I move freely.

There is a clear distinction between moving a mere thing by mechanical devices, and in my saying, 'I move'. The 'I move' indicates the movement of a living or lived body. The 'I move' is the bridge between subjectivity (my being-in-the-world) and physical thinghood of the world. The bridge metaphor was used by Husserl in his 1919 lectures, *Nature and Spirit* (Husserl, 2002h), suggesting that body is the link between subjectivity and nature, and therefore shares characteristics of both regions. The bridge metaphor will be discussed further when we examine Husserl's notion of body as the in-between. However, body as *Körper*, is a thing among things (Husserl, 2002g); it is extended in time, it is enduring, with a place of its own in objective chronometric time. *Körper* means flesh, corpse, carcass, it is the body-thing. It is in space, possessing a certain shape, figure, volume, colour, given in perspectives. It interacts with things and can withstand or resist movements, pressure or deformation. Husserl discusses these concepts under naturalistic attitude.

How does *Körper* appear in our everyday experience? In this context, Husserl examines both transcendental and naturalistic standpoints. The latter focuses on natural things, highlighting propensities such as spatiality and (chronometric) time, while the former refers to meaning, value or purpose. These descriptions raise the query as to how these two regions are connected, which is where the treatment of the body comes in. Husserl voiced similar thoughts in his 1919 lectures, *Nature and Spirit*, where he speaks of the world of things and subjects (Husserl, 2002b). Natural things are real predicates founded on significance-predicates (Husserl, 2002c), whereas subjects are spirits. Husserl summarizes these in the following manner. Anything identified as *Körper* has three basic characteristics namely, 1) it is temporal or extended in time, it possesses duration within objective time that can be measured and calculated, 2) it is spatial, i.e., has a location in objective space and, 3) anything identified as a thing (*Körper*) has both substantiality and casualty. A natural object is not merely a *Körper*, some are animate, while others, inanimate. Animate organisms are living bodies with a soul or a principle of life (e.g., animals), but persons have an ego. In *Ideas II*, Husserl explains extensively on these topics, going even a step further, to point out that the constitution of ourselves as human beings involves the emergence of physical organisms, an animal living body as the sensory body and an animal soul, while the higher is the psychic ego.

7.4 Three Ways of Studying Human Body

Human body can be examined from a naturalistic standpoint, a personalistic attitude and a phenomenological attitude.

7.4.1 The Study of Body from Naturalistic Attitude

Naturalistic attitude, also called psycho-physical attitude, posits nature as the basis for all beings. From the naturalistic, scientific point, the human body is a spatio-temporal material, a physical object with intimate, inseparable psychic attachments in a mutually penetrating and reciprocative manner. In the early part of *Thing and Space*, while discussing spatiality, Husserl emphasizes that living bodies can be given to us as material things in an objective space, as a thing among other things. But later on, he points out that this kind of givenness depends on the more fundamental phenomenon of expressive bodies belonging to the domain of understanding, which would mean that the concrete living body is not merely a material thing with psychic capacities, but the basis for all that is material and naturalistic (Husserl, 1973e, 1973f).

7.4.2 The Study of Body from Personalistic Attitude

In *Ideas II*, Husserl commences from naturalistic attitude and moves on to personalistic, subjective attitude. He affirms that the former is subordinated to the latter, obtained by an abstraction from personalistic attitude. Husserl refuses to accept the primacy granted to the former by the scientific community, and subordinates it to personalistic attitude. He points out that persons are not two-layered as matter and spirit, i.e., realities with casual connections; instead, they are a unified phenomenon of expression, surrounded by friends, spouse, parents, brothers and sisters. These are not casual or functional dependencies, but expressive and motivational links. The personalistic attitude of human sciences thematizes human body as expressive wholes with motivational relations. Husserl's analysis of the constitution of living bodies is crucial to his notion of intersubjectivity. Personalistic attitude posits the spirit and spiritual unities as fundamental, being two different ways of studying and understanding human beings. In *Ideas II*, Husserl begins his study on naturalistic attitude, then proceeds to personalistic, subjective attitude, stating that latter has primacy over the former, i.e., naturalistic attitude is subordinated to personalistic attitude.

In personalistic attitude, the lived body is experienced differently compared to naturalistic attitude. In the former, lived body is not just a mere thing, but expressive of person and personhood, expressed by bodily gestures, movements, facial expressions and tones of voice (Husserl, 1989b). In natural attitude, a natural scientist considers my body to be a biological or physiological object, rather than its capacity for expressing and communicating with persons. In personalistic attitude, we are not just organisms reacting to external stimuli, but members of social communities, human beings grasped as spiritual bodied wholes. We form a complex relation of motivation in dealing with others and social institutions. We influence one another, which in turn influences our social institutions. Body expresses social, cultural, familial milieu that shapes persons, and to which persons contribute. This implies that Husserl's notion of society presupposes bodily intersubjectivity.

7.4.3 The Study of the Body from Phenomenological Attitude

This attitude is a step higher than personalistic attitude, and refers to the constitutional primacy of one's own living body, which means that my living body is essentially the first and the only one to be given. It is only when I have constituted my living body, can I constitute that of others. This constitutional primacy does not mean that my body is more important or valuable than those of others; the question is not about value or worth, but that of necessity, i.e., I cannot think of others' living bodies unless mine is constituted first. In other words, the constitution of my lived body is a necessary condition for the constitution of others' bodies. The phenomenological analysis of the human body implies the constitutional primacy of one's own living body. Husserl points out that the original givenness of the living or lived body, i.e., my lived body is essentially the first and the original one. Much of what Husserl says about lived body in *Ideas II* arises from his 1910-11 Winter semester lectures, published as *The Basic Problems of Phenomenology*. The phenomenologically thematized body enters into his writings prior to any scientific theorizing about nature.

7.4.4 The Five Characteristics of *Leib*

Phenomenological attitude to the body leads us to the five characteristics of the lived body, 1) kinaesthetic characteristics, 2) organ and field of freedom, 3) organ of perception, 4) bearer of zero point of orientation and, 5) the importance of touch.

7.4.4.1 Body as the Field of Localization for Kinaesthetic Sensation

Every appearance of the body is correlated to some kinaesthetic circumstance such as, moving eyes in a particular direction for better vision, moving arms, hands and fingers for touching, bringing the ear closer to the source of sound for better hearing, etc. Husserl makes the perceiving body as the main theme of phenomenological investigation, and what stands out is the freely movable body, whose characteristic is its natural ability to move immediately and spontaneously. Additionally, Husserl points out that one can constantly accomplish the same thing the same way, freely moving and returning to the same position, which holds good, not just for movements connected to perception, but also for the normal custom of holding and working on things around oneself. So, my bodily capacities function as practical possibilities of being able to do. These capacities are not fixed or static, but develop from infancy to youth to maturity until old age.

7.4.4.2 Body as the Organ and Field of Freedom

The contents of this heading can be summarized by 'I can', which on examination is referred to as freedom of subjectivity. However, all bodily movements are not necessarily an expression of freedom (e.g., the expansion and contraction of lungs). Similarly, I require no knowledge of certain other movements. However, I execute my free will in many conscious acts even if the area of operation of free will is limited. It is indeed true that Husserl has not developed this area beyond its initial stages. The essence of Husserl's teaching described a domain of voluntary action and free will, which he took note of, and was solicitous about.

7.4.4.3 Body as the Organ of Perception and as that which is Perceived

I can readily see my hand, but not my eyes. Similarly, there are other parts of my body which I can see only partially and perspectively. Husserl states that the same body that serves me in my perception of objects, obstructs me in perceiving something of itself. When I look at other things, I can change my position for a better vision. But unfortunately, I cannot gain enough distance from my body to do this with respect to myself, implying that I cannot get out of myself to have a good look at myself, i.e., my own body. Moreover, I can never fully see my own body directly from outside, in the same way that others see it.

Body contributes to the perception of reality, for perception presupposes a particular type of bodily sensitivity. What is that which enables us to perceive the same object in a series of changing appearances? One might say that perceptual intentionality presupposes a moving, and therefore, an incarnated subject, which implies that our perceptions presuppose movements. I can perceive the hardness, smoothness, extension or height of an object, say a table. It is also possible for me to shift my attention from being preoccupied with the perception of the table to becoming aware of my hand touching it, feeling the pressure of touch, including movements not apprehended, but nevertheless localized in the hand. This implies that the same sensation can be interpreted in two radically different ways, namely, perception of the appearance of an object experienced, and for localized sensing in the correlated experiencing bodily part.

7.4.4.4 Body as the Zero Point of Orientation

My body is the central point in terms of which everything else out 'there', namely near or far, above or below, right or left, in front of or behind, east or west, south or north. It is the body according to which things appear in a certain orientation relative to the perceiver; Husserl refers to this as the zero point of orientation or the zero position or posture. When I place myself in the centre of my lived space, all directions originate from it. It is from here that we can speak of a shared, spatial world, i.e., an intersubjective system of locations. Although I am always here, I can exchange standpoints with another person who is always there.

7.4.4.5 Body as the Organ of Touch and Primacy of Touch

This is an important direction of development in the context of the body as the organ of perception. Husserl's position regarding the sense of touch is as follows. My eyes see an object, but I cannot see the process of my seeing an object, i.e., I cannot see my seeing. Similarly, my ears can hear a sound, but my ears cannot hear the process of my hearing. But the situation is different with regard to the sense of touch. When I touch something with my hand, I can feel the object's qualities such as smoothness, hardness or roughness. Moreover, I can also feel and turn my sensing to tactile sensation localized in the hand, implying that the body can feel its sense of touch. More precisely, whereas I do not 'see' the visual sensation of my eyes, or 'hear' the auditory sensation of my ear, I do locate tactile sensations in my body while touching. According to Husserl, the ear cannot hear its own hearing, the eyes cannot see its own seeing, but the body can feel its own feeling of touch, which means that the body has the capacity for sensing the object, and also its own sensation of the object simultaneously, i.e., touch-sensation has a double aspect, that of external touch of an object, wherein I feel the objects' qualities and my tactile sensations localized in the hand (i.e., body) itself.

If I touch the table, I have a series of appearances apprehended as belonging to the table. When my hand slides over a table, I perceive its physical features such as hardness or smoothness. It is also possible to shift my attention to my touching hand and of touch itself. These are not apprehended as objective properties of the hand, but are nevertheless located in the hand that manifests its functioning as an experiencing organ. Therefore, the sensation of touch can be interpreted in two radically different ways, one, as the properties of an object experienced, and the other as localized sensations in the experiencing body. Husserl was well aware of the distinctions between the touched and the touching hand. Whereas the properties of the material object (i.e. the table) are constituted partially, it is not so with localized sensations, i.e., sensations of touch are not experienced at the skin-level, but deeper, as if they were parts of its organic tissue. Although body entails objectivation, it does not imply a complete suspension of subjectivity, because the touched hand feels the touch.

7.5 Problems of Primacy of Touch

All these explanations and elucidations do not mean that Husserl's emphasis on the primacy of touch is without problems and difficulties. I would say that there are mainly two problems.

1. It is not clear why the body's role should be any less towards its intentional constitution than its passive role as the bearer of tactile sensations. Why should my body appear to me as the site of localized sensations in order for me to experience my actions and perceptions as embodied? Husserl does not examine this issue.

2. If it is by virtue of my tactile sensations together with my free bodily movements that I comprehend possessing a body as Husserl suggests, this is possible only by a certain prior consciousness of myself or a distinct form of self-identification. In fact, Husserl himself points out that I do indeed possess such a sense of self, prior to and independent of any external object of consciousness, namely the awareness of myself as a transcendental ego, the fulcrum of all my intentional acts.

In conclusion, bodily intentionality is a kind of intermediary phenomenon, bridging the conceptual abyss separating consciousness from reality according to Husserl. Body is not a mere thing, a *Körper*, or just a discrete object of perception, but a kind of quasi-object that is essentially embodied, a transcendental self-possessing the locus of subjective sensations. The body does not constitute intentionality, but instead, the body is constituted by transcendental subjectivity.

7.6 Lived Body: The In-Between

Husserl's phenomenology, right from its beginning, was based on certain strict and categorical distinctions between different concepts, one of them being the distinction between the immanent sphere of consciousness (i.e., conscious experience) and the transcendent domain of external objects, popularly known as the distinction between being qua experience, and being-qua-being (external reality). Another distinction is between the real, concrete thing in space-and-time and the ideal of abstract entities. These are just limited examples; many such distinctions can be unearthed upon careful examination.

The question we need to answer is, where do we place the body? The discussions until now seems to designate the human lived body to be an anomaly, uncategorizable exclusively within the scope of both consciousness and the reach of things. This is because my body is neither internal to my consciousness nor external to me in the environment. Husserl in *Ideas II* (Husserl, 1989b) points out that the lived body is a thing inserted in-between the material world and the subjective sphere of consciousness. The body's go-between status is further discussed in *Nature and Spirit* (1919). One's own body cannot be a discrete object of perception, for Husserl goes on to say that, 'I do not have the possibility of distancing myself from my body, nor it from me, since the very same body serves as a means of all my perceptions' (Husserl, 1970g), which raises the question, is Husserl a dualist? The answer is a firm no. Husserl's ontological neutrality is praiseworthy. Yet, it allows for a ray of doubt to creep in. Husserl is not a dualist, like an empiricist or a rationalist; he takes no particular stand in the mind-body problem, nor is he worried about trends of dualism from the standpoint of empiricism or rationalism. He focuses on describing things as they appear to consciousness, rather than construct an explanatory device. He even refutes the mind-body issue and Cartesian dualism in *Crisis of European Sciences* (Husserl, 1970g) and earlier works. And, surely nobody can call him an empiricist; he is far distanced from it, though he held high respects for both Locke and Hume, considering them to be a sort of phenomenologists. According to Husserl, empiricism and rationalism failed due to their inability to raise themselves to the transcendental level and recognize pure consciousness as an autonomous region.

Yet, one cannot deny a ray of duality in Husserl and his phenomenology. This is because, intentionality, the root concept of phenomenology, implies a distinction between consciousness and reality. The notions of epoché, bracketing, reduction, etc., that form the corner stones of Husserl's phenomenology, demand the exclusion of transcendent objects from the realms of consciousness. This being the case, at the most, one can speak of 'conceptual dualism,' in Husserl, which refers to the fact that consciousness and reality are separated by an abyss of meaning. This implies that there is a strict distinction between being qua experience and being qua reality. This indicates the fundamental dichotomy between the sphere of consciousness, and the realm of things (reality). This contention that both are separated by the province of meaning assigned by consciousness is called conceptual dualism.

7.7 The Lived Body and Intentionality

In the early part of his phenomenology, i.e., in static phenomenology, Husserl refused to acknowledge the role of body in the context of intentionality, which changed radically as he progressed to genetic phenomenology. In the final stages of his philosophy, he regarded the intuitive identification of ourselves with our bodies, an accomplishment based on intentionality, in which we comprehend ourselves as embodied, transcendental egos in possession of subjective sensations. Husserl, in his later phenomenology, exclaims that sensing belongs to the soul, which was considered the transcendental ego of the earlier period. Husserl also states that it was not cognitive attitudes, but bodily skills that bridge the gap between the mind and world.

The expression, bodily intentionality, has been used on a few occasions so far. Such an expression would have been anathema during the earlier part of Husserl's phenomenology, but not so much during the later part. Bodily intentionality is the immediate sense of being embodied; it is an intermediary phenomenon bridging the conceptual abyss separating consciousness from reality. The body is not a mere thing, a *Körper*, but our essentially embodied transcendental ego, which is the locus of its subjective experiences. The body itself is not constitutive of intentionality, but it is indeed, intimately and inwardly connected to transcendental subjectivity.

7.8 Interiority and Exteriority of the Body

Husserl is anxious to emphasise the two sides of the body, its interiority and exteriority (Husserl, 1973b, 1973d, 1991a, 2001a). Volitional structure and dimensions of sensing demonstrate interiority, while visual and tactile appearance are indicative of the latter. To understand the relation between the two, consider our hands, if we examine the right hand touching the left, the touching hand feels the touched hand, but the act of touching is not simply given as a mere object, since it also feels the touching itself. The crucial difference between touching (one's own body) and being touched is that, the relation between the touching and the touched is reversible, since the touching is touched and the touched is touching. It is this reversibility that demonstrates that interiority and exteriority are different manifestations of the same (Husserl, 1973a, 2008). This phenomenology of double sensation consequently, presents us with an ambiguous setting in which the hand alternates between two roles, that of touching and being touched; it provides us with an experience of the dual nature of the body. It is the very same hand that can appear in two different fashions alternatively, as touching and being touched.

7.9 Lived Body and Perception

Body is the condition for the possibility of perception and interaction with transcendent objects (Husserl, 1973c). Every worldly experience is mediated by, and facilitated by our embodiment (Husserl, 1991c, 1997, 2001f). Perception presupposes bodily sensitivity. What is it that enables us to perceive the same object in a series of changing roles? One might say that perception presupposes a moving, and therefore the incarnated subject, the crucial point being that we can presuppose movements and not just perceive it.

In *Ideas II* (Husserl, 1989f), Husserl points out that our own body never appears to us as a discrete object of perception. Moreover, he writes that it is not feasible for oneself to distance onself from one's body, or the body from oneself, as it is the means for any perception. This means that the perception of an object excludes the perceiving organ, viz., the body from the domain of objects perceived. In other words, the body cannot see or touch itself in the same manner that it deals with an object, since it cannot step back and hold itself at arm's length. But with one of its parts, the body can see or touch them. So, what about the relation of perception to itself? Body is not merely an organ of perception, but also something that is perceived. I can see my hand, but my head and certain other parts can be perceived only partially. As a body that serves as a means of perception of external objects, it also obstructs me in the perception of itself. When I look at things, I freely change my position in relation to them, but unfortunately, this is not possible for perception of itself, as I cannot gain enough distance from my own body and perceive the same from different angles or perspectives.

7.10 Lived Body, Intersubjectivity and Empathy

Husserl points out that our understanding of the lived body transforms our approach to the environment, nature or culture. However, an important transformation takes place at the level of intersubjectivity. Husserl declares in his *Nature and Spirit* (1919) lectures that it is clear that the world receives its full sense only through relation to a plurality of subjects who enter into communion with us (Husserl, 2002f). This intersubjectivity creates an intersubjective world of experiences from amongst a particular world of individual subjects. For a multiplicity of subjects, the transcendent world is given only through empathy, for which a living body is necessary. This amounts to saying that the natural, cultural and spiritual world constituted by me in my primordial experience on account of intersubjectivity, become something for everybody, through empathetic communication. My lived body is mine by a relation of identity with me, for I am my body. However, the relation with another's lived body is by empathy, through which the other's body is first presented to me as a natural thing that I understand as a subject who feels, and governs that lived body due to apperception. Thus, the other's body is appresented in an analogy to mine. This understanding of the body leads me to grasp the significance of intersubjectivity comprehensively. Empathy is a faculty through which subjects of the same type understand the modes of existence of each other. It is based on the possibility of subjects being able to accomplish an analogizing apperception of others, dependent on one's ability to conceive of similar subjects, not identical, but analogous to itself. The other self can be conceived and represented as a possible modification of my body, for it is possible to conceive a lived body, not identical, but merely analogous to mine. My lived body is related to me by a relation of identity, for I am my body, whereas the relation of the other to me is by way of empathy.

Constitution of one's own body leads to subjective experience. However, against individual subjects, there are associations of subjects that perform social acts (Husserl, 2002d) leading to social communities, i.e., articulated subjective wholes and personalities of higher order, which could result either in temporary groups, e.g., a transitory association like a local sport club, or a permanent association like marriage, while the highest association is the state. The members of society acquire titles such as officials, employees and staff only functionally. These functional acts produce cultural acts that reflect the achievement of personalities that work together in higher order societies like parliament, judiciary or university faculties. They have convictions, their own points of view; they take their own decisions and form collective bodies. This level is intertwined with communication, wherein language comes into play.

Husserl's analysis of the constitution of living bodies are crucial for his notion of intersubjectivity and community. Since Husserl argued that all objectivity is grounded initially in subjectivity, and later on in intersubjectivity, embodiment is no more a minor, theoretical side issue, but a fundamental topic in rigorous philosophy. He finally returns to the topic of embodiment in his *Crisis of European Sciences*, where he explicates the relation between the objective world of science and Life world, shared by subjects in experience (Husserl, 1970g). Without the possibility of distinct spatio-temporally lived bodies, there would be no possibility of empathy, which is why Husserl conceives empathy as an analogizing apperception in which, I represent the other as a modification or representation of my lived body. Husserl is interested in disclosing the possibility of coexistence of subjects who can acknowledge the presence of each other, as well as corroborate their respective experiences to arrive at knowledge of the same nature.

7.11 The Body of Others

Husserl has been elucidating one's own lived body till now, but what about the lived body of others? Can phenomenology account for them? Husserl's notion of the lived body of the other rests on his notion of a transfer of sense. He points out that the experience of localized sensations and a primitive sense of living is transferred over from one's body to the other's, motivated by the similarity of perceived movements. I detect and observe certain things with regard to the other that resemble my own lived body. The other's body reacts to external stimulus, akin to my body shivering in the cold winter, and tremors due to fever at high temperatures. I have these experiences, and when I see the other person experiencing them as well, I have transferred my sense of experiencing from myself to the other. The other's body appears to have similar sensations as mine. If I cannot live without them, I believe that the other also cannot live without his own sensations. This empathetic transfer is not an inference or extrapolation from my experiences to the other. The other's lived body is not derived, deduced or induced from mine; it is always, already there. It is a new type of apprehension. I have mastered these experiences in my case, and on the basis of evidence available, I have now transferred my mastery from myself to the other on the basis of similarity of experiences. What is transferred to the other is not a psychic unit, but a reflective capacity.

7.12 Consequences of not having a Lived Body

A bodyless subject cannot empathize with other subjects, and therefore are inherently solipsistic. In the absence of a lived body, we would be doomed to a solipsistic existence, since there would be no way to distinguish the other and myself. It seems then that it is the physical separation amongst our bodies that motivates me to look at the other as an analogue to my lived body and therefor empathize with it. The thesis concerning worldless or bodyless subject is highly problematic. In *Ideas I*, Husserl, following Descartes, provides arguments for a bodyless subject, but goes on to argue against him and his own position of *Ideas II*. But from 1930 onwards, he no longer considered birth and death as empirical phenomenon. Now, he holds that birth, death, as well as generativity are all constitutions of an objective and historical world (Husserl, 2019).

7.13 Conclusions

Husserl's achievement in the study of the body indicates that constitutive awareness and movements have perception, spatiality and embodiment in relation to lived body. The crux of the issue of the study of lived body is the interpretation of the incarnated body in the world. The phenomenological approach to the body enables us to distinguish between different modes and layers of the body expressing and disclosing their interrelations, which makes possible an interpretation of the same, devoid of naturalistic interpretation and resistant to all forms of reduction. Finally, in our discussion on lived body, the following points can be reflected upon:

1.   Lived body is not an object, akin to a material, physical or mundane object. It is the medium through which, and by means

of which, I apprehend and interact with the world around me. I am engaged in the world through the medium of my body. Not only do I find myself engaged in the world, I also move towards it, and organize it through my projects. The surrounding world is grasped through my individual projects and concrete situations.

2. In all its worldly involvements, the lived body exhibits a bodily intentionality that reveals a dynamic relationship between the body and the world. It is the embodied consciousness that simultaneously engages and is engaged in the surrounding world. My living body, as my embodying organism, is always experienced as being in the midst of environing things, in a certain situation, i.e., some kind of being-in-the-world.

3. My body is not a self-enclosed object, but is always an open and an ever-incomplete entity. Sense organs reveal their openness and continuous growth due to their fundamental incompleteness.

4. The body-world relationship reflects the fact that the lived body represents, not just one's bodily being, but one's being-in-the-world.

5. In the body-world continuous interaction, lived-body synthesizes the various senses and movements into a unity of experiences.

6. As the means by which one interacts with or within the world, the lived body facilitates the existential project that expresses one's personhood. Consequently, the description of bodily capacities has a significance that far exceeds merely mechanical function.

7. Lived body is both the intentional and orientational locus of myself. It is both the spatial and temporal centre around which my world is arranged and organized. My body has several modes of givenness; that being the case, the surrounding space is intimately related to the position of my body, i.e., near or far, high or low, right or left, depending on my body position. I cannot distance myself from my body (although certain parts of can be separated, say by means of surgery), which also means that others and other things are located over *there* in relation to my body.

8. The term, 'embodied' refers to the unity of body and consciousness. The fact that I am embodied implies that the body is always with me. But this relationship to my body is not an ownership, in the sense that I own a pen. I am embodied, implying that I exist or live in my body, i.e., I am my body.

9. On certain occasions, I am aware of my alienation from my body
   when I feel that it is something other than me. This sense of
   bodily alienation is particularly profound during the experience
   of bodily illnesses, depression, bodily breakdown and the like.

10. As an embodied being, I have a certain corporeal style and bodily
    identity that is unique to me in my behaviour and in my gestures.
    They are identified as mine, but they also reflect my social and
    cultural identity. They somehow express myself and my personality.

7.14 References

Husserl, E. (1960a). Presumptive evidence of world-experience. World as an
idea correlative to a perfect experiential evidence: Section 28. In D. Cairns
(Trans.), *Cartesian Meditations: An Introduction to Phenomenology* (p. 61).
Martinus Nijhoff Publishers, The Hague.

Husserl, E. (1960b). Survey of our intentional explication of experiencing
someone else: Section 62. In D. Cairns (Trans.), *Cartesian Meditations: An
Introduction to Phenomenology* (pp. 148–150). Martinus Nijhoff Publishers,
The Hague.

Husserl, E. (1960c). The intentional object also belongs to the full monadic
concretion of ownness. Immanent transcendence and primordial world:
Section 47. In D. Cairns (Trans.), *Cartesian Meditations: An Introduction to
Phenomenology* (pp. 103–104). Martinus Nijhoff Publishers, The Hague.

Husserl, E. (1970). The Origin of Geometry. In D. Carr (Trans.), *The Crisis of
European Sciences and Transcendental Phenomenology* (pp. 353–378).
Northwestern University Press.

Husserl, E. (1973a). Beilage VI: Das Problem der Konstitution des Leibes als
eines physischen Dinges in der solipsistischen Erfahrung (1921 oder etwas
später). In I. Kern (Ed.), *Zur Phänomenologie der Intersubjektivität Zweiter
Teil: 1921-1928: Husserliana: Edmund Husserl-Gesammelte Werke Band XIV*
(p. 75). Martinus Nijhoff Publishers, The Hague.

Husserl, E. (1973b). Das Problem der Konstitution des psychophysischen
Einheit. Die reduzierte originale Erfahrung enthält keine Verknüpfung von
Leib und Seele. Die Apperzeption 'Ich-Mensch' durch die Einfühlung
vermittelt. Zur Lehre von der Einfühlung (17. Januar 1927). In I. Kern (Ed.), *Zur
Phänomenologie der Intersubjektivität Zweiter Teil: 1921-1928: Husserliana:
Edmund Husserl-Gesammelte Werke Band XIV* (p. 414). Martinus Nijhoff
Publishers, The Hague.

Husserl, E. (1973c). Die Konstitution des Raumes in der originalen
Erfahrungssphäre. Die Bezogenheit der Aussenbewegung auf die
Selbstbewegung und die dadurch ermöglichte Erfahrung eines Ichanalogons
(Februar 1927). In I. Kern (Trans.), *Zur Phänomenologie Der Intersubjektivität,
Zweiter Teil:1921-1928, Husserliana: Edmund Husserl-Gesammelte Werke Band
XIV* (p. 540). Martinus Nijhoff, The Hague, Netherlands.

Husserl, E. (1973d). Die Selbstapperzeption als Ich-Mensch und die originale
Selbsterfahrung. Übergang zur transzendentalen Reduktion (30. Januar
1927). In I. Kern (Ed.), *Zur Phänomenologie der Intersubjektivität Zweiter*

Teil: 1921-1928: Husserliana: Edmund Husserl-Gesammelte Werke Band XIV (p. 462). Martinus Nijhoff Publishers, The Hague.

Husserl, E. (1973e). Section 47: Einlegung der kinästhetischen Empfindungen in den Leib. In U. Claesges (Ed.), *Ding und Raum: Vorlesungen 1907: Husserliana: Edmund Husserl-Gesammelte Werke Band XVI* (pp. 161–163). Martinus Nijhoff Publishers, The Hague.

Husserl, E. (1973f). Section 83: Sich Bewegen und Bewegtwerden des Leibes. Grenzen der kinästhetischen Konstitution des Leibkörpers. In U. Claesges (Ed.), *Ding und Raum: Vorlesungen 1907: Husserliana: Edmund Husserl-Gesammelte Werke Band XVI* (pp. 278–284). Martinus Nijhoff Publishers, The Hague.

Husserl, E. (1973g). *Zur Phänomenologie der Intersubjektivität: Texte aus dem Nachlaß. Dritter Teil. 1929–1935: Husserliana: Edmund Husserl-Gesammelte Werke Band XV* (I. Kern, Ed.). Martinus Nijhoff Publishers, The Hague.

Husserl, E. (1973h). *Zur Phänomenologie der Intersubjektivität Zweiter Teil: 1921-1928: Husserliana: Edmund Husserl-Gesammelte Werke Band XIV* (I. Kern, Ed.). Martinus Nijhoff Publishers, The Hague.

Husserl, E. (1976). Noematic Meaning and Relation to the Object. In W. R. B. Gibson (Trans.), *Ideas: General Introduction to Pure Phenomenology* (pp. 365–370). Humanities Press.

Husserl, E. (1977a). Characterizing the psychophysical realities of the experiential world. Greater self-sufficiency of the corporeal vis-a-vis the psyche: Section 15. In J. Scanlon (Trans.), *Phenomenological Psychology, Lectures, Summer Semester, 1925* (pp. 79–82). Martinus Nijhoff Publishers, The Hague.

Husserl, E. (1977b). Hierarchical structure of the psychic: Section 21. In J. Scanlon (Trans.), *Phenomenological Psychology, Lectures, Summer Semester, 1925* (pp. 99–100). Martinus Nijhoff Publishers, The Hague.

Husserl, E. (1977c). Hyle-hyletic data as matter for intentional functions: Section 31. In J. Scanlon (Trans.), *Phenomenological Psychology, Lectures, Summer Semester, 1925* (p. 127). Martinus Nijhoff Publishers, The Hague.

Husserl, E. (1980). The Relations between Phenomenology and Psychology. In T. E. Klein & W. E. Pohl (Trans.), *Phenomenology and the Foundations of the Sciences: Third book, Ideas Pertaining to a Pure Phenomenology and to a Phenomenological Philosophy* (Vol. 1, pp. 19–64). Martinus Nijhoff Publishers, The Hague.

Husserl, E. (1989a). Character of the Body as Constituted Solipsistically, Section 42. In R. Rojcewicz & A. Schuwer (Trans.), *Ideas Pertaining to a Pure Phenomenology and to a Phenomenological Philosophy: Second Book Studies in the Phenomenology of Constitution* (pp. 168–169). Kluwer Academic Publishers.

Husserl, E. (1989b). *Ideas Pertaining to a Pure Phenomenology and to a Phenomenological Philosophy: Second Book: Studies in the Phenomenology of Constitution (Husserliana: Edmund Husserl-Collected Works, Vol. 3)* (R. Rojcewicz & A. Schuwer, Trans.). Martinus Nijhoff Publishers.

Husserl, E. (1989c). Motivation as the Fundamental Law of the Spiritual World, Section 59, 60a. In R. Rojcewicz & A. Schuwer (Trans.), *Ideas Pertaining to a Pure Phenomenology and to a Phenomenological Philosophy: Second Book,*

Studies in the Phenomenology of Constitution (pp. 266–276). Kluwer Academic Publishers.

Husserl, E. (1989d). The Aestheta in their Relation to the Aesthetic Body, Section 18 a & b. In R. Rojcewicz & A. Schuwer (Trans.), *Ideas Pertaining to a Pure Phenomenology and to a Phenomenological Philosophy: Second Book Studies in the Phenomenology of Constitution* (pp. 60–69). Kluwer Academic Publishers.

Husserl, E. (1989e). The Body as the Origin of the Will and as Seat of Free Movement. In R. Rojcewicz & A. Schuwer (Trans.), *Ideas Pertaining to a Pure Phenomenology and to a Phenomenological Philosophy: Second Book: Studies in the Phenomenology of Constitution* (p. 159). Kluwer Academic Publishers.

Husserl, E. (1989f). The Constitution of Psychic Reality Through the Body, Sections 36-42. In R. Rojcewicz & A. Schuwer (Trans.), *Ideas Pertaining to a Pure Phenomenology and to a Phenomenological Philosophy: Second Book, Studies in the Phenomenology of Constitution* (pp. 152–169). Kluwer Academic Publishers.

Husserl, E. (1991a). How Does the Unity of a Process of Change That Continues for an Extended Period of Time Come to be Represented? (Intuition and Representation). In R. Bernet (Ed.), & J. B. Brough (Trans.), *On the Phenomenology of the Consciousness of Internal Time (1893-1917): Husserliana: Edmund Husserl-Collected Works Volume 4* (p. 145). Kluwer Academic Publishers.

Husserl, E. (1991b). The Double Intentionality of Recollection. In J. B. Brough (Trans.), *On the Phenomenology of the Consciousness of Internal Time (1893-1917): Husserliana: Edmund Husserl-Collected Works Volume 4* (p. 56). Kluwer Academic Publishers.

Husserl, E. (1997). The Amsterdam Lectures on Phenomenological Psychology. In T. Sheehan (Ed.), & R. E. Palmer (Trans.), *Psychological And Transcendental Phenomenology And The Confrontation With Heidegger (1927-1931): Husserliana: Edmund Husserl-Collected Works Volume 6* (p. 220). Springer-Science+Business Media, B.V.

Husserl, E. (2001a). Affection as Effecting an Allure on the Ego, Contrast as its Fundamental Condition. In R. Bernet (Ed.), & A. J. Steinbock (Trans.), *Analyses Concerning Passive and Active Synthesis. Lectures on Transcendental Logic Husserliana: Edmund Husserl-Collected Works Volume 9* (pp. 196–197). Kluwer Academic Publishers.

Husserl, E. (2001b). Corroboration and Verification. In R. Bernet (Ed.), & A. J. Steinbock (Trans.), *Analyses Concerning Passive and Active Synthesis. Lectures on Transcendental Logic Husserliana: Edmund Husserl-Collected Works Volume 9* (p. 391). Kluwer Academic Publishers.

Husserl, E. (2001c). Picturing, Clarifying and Confirmation in the Synthesis of Bringing to Intuition. In R. Bernet (Ed.), & A. J. Steinbock (Trans.), *Analyses Concerning Passive and Active Synthesis: Lectures on Transcendental Logic: Husserliana: Edmund Husserl-Collected Works Volume 9* (p. 124). Kluwer Academic Publishers.

Husserl, E. (2002a). Die Gliederung in Dinge und Subjekte gemäß der Unterscheidung von Natur und Geist. In M. Weiler (Ed.), *Natur Und Geist,*

Vorlesungen Sommersemester 1919, Husserliana: Edmund Husserl-Materialien Band IV (p. 122). Springer Netherlands.

Husserl, E. (2002b). Die Gliederung in Dinge und Subjekte gemäß der Unterscheidung von Natur und Geist. In M. Weiler (Ed.), *Natur Und Geist, Vorlesungen Sommersemester 1919, Husserliana: Edmund Husserl-Materialien Band IV* (p. 118). Springer Netherlands.

Husserl, E. (2002c). Die Gliederung in Dinge und Subjekte gemäß der Unterscheidung von Natur und Geist. In M. Weiler (Ed.), *Natur Und Geist, Vorlesungen Sommersemester 1919, Husserliana: Edmund Husserl-Materialien Band IV* (p. 125). Springer Netherlands.

Husserl, E. (2002d). Die Gliederung in Dinge und Subjekte gemäß der Unterscheidung von Natur und Geist. In M. Weiler (Ed.), *Natur Und Geist, Vorlesungen Sommersemester 1919, Husserliana: Edmund Husserl-Materialien Band IV* (p. 134). Springer Netherlands.

Husserl, E. (2002e). *Die Lebenswelt Auslegungen Der Vorgegebenen Welt Und Ihrer Konstitution Texte Aus Dem Nachlass (1916–1937): Husserliana: Edmund Husserl-Gesammelte Werke Band XXXIX* (R. Sowa, Ed.). Springer, Dordrecht.

Husserl, E. (2002f). Die physische Natur als Gebiet von Wissenschaften und Wahrheiten. In M. Weiler (Ed.), *Natur Und Geist, Vorlesungen Sommersemester 1919, Husserliana: Edmund Husserl-Materialien Band IV* (p. 195). Springer Netherlands.

Husserl, E. (2002g). Grundlinien einer Ontologie und Phänomenologie der physischen Natur. In M. Weiler (Ed.), *Natur Und Geist, Vorlesungen Sommersemester 1919, Husserliana: Edmund Husserl-Materialien Band IV* (p. 182). Springer Netherlands.

Husserl, E. (2002h). *Natur Und Geist, Vorlesungen Sommersemester 1919, Husserliana: Edmund Husserl-Materialien Band IV* (M. Weiler, Ed.). Springer Netherlands.

Husserl, E. (2005). Critical Discussion of the Differences Between Perception and Phantasy put Forward by the Psychologists. In R. Bernet (Ed.), & J. B. Brough (Trans.), *Phantasy, Image Consciousness and Memory (1898-1925): Husserliana: Edmund Husserl-Collected Works: Volume 9* (p. 14). Springer Netherlands.

Husserl, E. (2006a). Considerations about the Ideas of the Phenomenological Reduction, as well as the Autonomy and the Connection of Monads in the Lecture Course 'The Basic Problems of Phenomenology' (1910-1911) (probably from 1921), Appendix IX (XXX). In R. Bernet (Ed.), & I. Farin & J. Hart (Trans.), *The Basic Problems of Phenomenology* (pp. 159–164). Springer Netherlands.

Husserl, E. (2006b). Empathy of the Other Consciousness and Divine All-Consciousness (1908), Appendix XIII (IV of No. 1). In R. Bernet (Ed.), & I. Farin & J. Hart (Trans.), *The Basic Problems of Phenomenology* (pp. 177–178). Springer Netherlands.

Husserl, E. (2006c). The Localization of Lived Experiences in the Lived Body. In G. H. James & I. Farin (Trans.), *The Basic Problems of Phenomenology* (p. 4). Springer Netherlands.

Husserl, E. (2008). Time Consciousness and Constitution of Time. In U. Melle (Ed.), & C. O. Hill (Trans.), *Introduction to Logic and Theory of Knowledge:*

Lectures 1906/07: Husserliana: Edmund Husserl-Collected Works Volume 13 (p. 263). Springer-Science+Business Media, B.V.

Husserl, E. (2019). The Indefiniteness of the Left-Open Continuation of Connections Lying in the "And So Forth". The Origin of the Concept of Set. In C. O. Hill (Trans.), *Logic and General Theory of Science: Husserliana: Edmund Husserl-Collected Works: Volume 15* (pp. 171–172). Springer Nature Switzerland.

Spiegelberg, H. (1971). The Phenomenological Circles. In *The Phenomenological Movement: A Historical Introduction: Phaenomenologica 5* (p. 168). Martinus Nijhoff Publishers, The Hague.

Chapter 8

Life world: A Conceptual Overview

8.1 Introduction

Husserl's notion of life world did not spring up overnight. I am of the opinion that Husserl obtained his initial insights into this notion of life world from Richard Avenarius' concept of the human world, and goes on to quote him extensively during his 1910-11 winter semester lectures, published as *The Basic Problems of Phenomenology* (Husserl, 2006f). However, Husserl uses the term, 'world' as early as in *Logical Investigations*, wherein he writes, 'the world is merely the unified objective totality corresponding to and inseparable from the idea/system of all factual truth' (Husserl, 1977d, 1977a). Unfortunately, this notion of the world as an objective totality is completely different from the kind of world described in *Crisis of European Sciences* (Husserl, 1970f). It means that Husserl, in the course of his phenomenological career, enriched and developed his notion of world, transforming it from a mere objective, physical reality to a later form, which is the basis for all human dealings and sciences. Husserl, while discussing the same in *Ideas I* speaks of two different kinds of world, 'I am aware of a world spread out endlessly, and in time, becoming and become without end' (Husserl, 1976r). Immediately thereafter, he describes yet another world that is a correlate of consciousness, adding that such a world is not merely one of facts and affairs, rather one of values and goods, a practical world. Husserl goes on to describe the general theses regarding the world viz., that it exists by itself, independent of consciousness; it has a prior and independent reality. Though Husserl discovered a new world, namely the life world, a world linked to consciousness, i.e., the human world, Husserl does not reject, deny or refute the material, physical, empirical world. This phenomenological world from *Ideas I* evolved further in *Ideas II* (Husserl, 1989a), christened the spiritual world, and reached its culmination in the understanding of life world in *Crisis of European Sciences* (Husserl, 1970d). A comparative reading of *Ideas II* and *Crisis of European Sciences* demonstrates that several notions from *Ideas II* do appear repeatedly in the latter. Husserl begins by highlighting the drawbacks of the Galilean mathematical world and the notion of pure geometry (Husserl, 1970c) before moving onto the concepts of life world in detail (Husserl, 1970c). Life world is culturally defined as the spatio-temporal horizon of every-day life. Scientific procedures that separate the subject and object, thought and action, people and environment are inadequate to discuss the notion of life world. It is strictly a human world with strong cultural moorings.

In the book of Genesis (of the Bible), it is stated (English Standard Version Bible, 2001, Genesis 1:26) that God granted man dominion over everything, and that man exercised it by naming all things and animals (English Standard Version Bible, 2001, Genesis 2:19). Instead of listening to these attentively in a sympathetic manner, he dictates the manner and the mode of their existence, and in doing so, he loses direct, immediate and personal contact with them, for he perceives them through his own constructions, i.e., through the prism of abstraction and representation. He approaches them through the lens of master and lord, or in other words, prohibits them from speaking their own language, unwilling to listen to them in a solicitous manner, and is disinclined to pay attention to them in an empathetic manner. He thereby becomes their ruler, failing to be their shepherd (Heidegger). He instead should have been a shepherd to the folk as was the Lord (English Standard Version Bible, 2001, Genesis 2:19). According to Husserl and also from a general phenomenological perspective, man's 'Crisis' consists in the fact that he forgot his assigned role to be a guide to creation, he ignored his entrusted responsibility of being a guru, and instead assumed the mantle of a dictator. Right from the beginning of his phenomenological enterprise, Husserl demanded a return to things, i.e., to let a thing speak for itself, whence man shall listen to them empathetically, with an open heart and a liberal attitude. Unfortunately, man began to interfere in the affairs of things and animals since creation, assuming himself superior, and interpreting them using his own perspective of cause and effect, language, from a mathematical standpoint and several other such constructs. In fact, many in the western civilization and the Christian world claim divine sanction to man, considering him to be bestowed with authority to be the lord of things by the creator. They erringly interpret the initial chapters of the Bible for their selfish motives, thereby imposing himself upon fellow creatures. This resulted in the loss of his innocence regrettably, thus diminishing his simplicity and weakened his ties to things and animals. Hence the 'Crisis' is for all who accept the primordiality and primacy of representation and abstraction, no matter his race or creed.

Galileo Galilei (1564-1642), an eminent scientist and a great mathematician, articulated the abstract and representational point of view most emphatically in modern times. He was awestruck by the Greek notion of pure geometry, a science of exact and objectively valid knowledge of objects that enabled him to overcome the subjective relativity of the appearance of experience for *me*. True, for the Greeks, geometry was not an abstraction, not unrelated to their ordinary, everyday life. For them, it arose from the practical needs of measuring and surveying their land exactly. The very word geometry etymologically indicates it.

The terrible and the dreadful conclusion that Galileo arrived at was, "the exact and objectively valid knowledge of the real world can be attained by treating everything about the world as an example of geometrical relation or geometrical object" (Husserl, 1970a). Thus, he made a paradigm shift from the ordinary, everyday understanding of geometry to the scientific and objectively valid notion of objects. This can be translated into the following. Physical shape, mass, length (i.e., primary qualities in general) are seen after being measured as accurately as possible. Geometrical figures or mathematical statements about properties and other relationships will provide information about nature, which shares the exactness and universality of pure geometry.

Galileo had no difficulty explaining secondary qualities such as smell, colour, taste, etc.; the Greeks themselves pointed out that the pitch of a tone emitted by a vibrating string (in a musical instrument) is dependent on the length, thickness or tension of the string itself. Thus, Galileo could account for the entire universe, (i.e., both primary and secondary qualities) in pure mathematical, measurable, calculable, quantifiable and objectively valid terms. This is Galileo's mathematization of nature. Thus, nature translates itself into a domain of mathematical entities and/or techniques. Philosophically understood, Galileo's fundamental claim is to be is to be measurable and calculable, which is his metaphysical claim. Natural scientists followed in his footsteps and claimed that he dominated the entire human realm in and through his mathematical procedures. Husserl's strong criticism against Galileo was directed, not so much against Galileo's mathematical procedure, but against his mathematically rooted metaphysical claims.

Against Galileo's mathematical/geometrical abstraction of the world, Husserl, a mathematician himself, boldly points out that the intuitively given world is a world of sense-experience, the pre-scientific world. Science makes abstractions and generalizations from this concrete world, consisting of both primary and secondary qualities. It is the real world of human existence, in contrast to Galileo's abstract, objective, mathematical world. It is subjective, but not in the sense of being mind or consciousness dependent; it is subjective in the sense that it is the source of my meaningfulness, for it is consciousness that assigns meanings. The problem with the mathematico-scientific abstract approach to the world is that such a world loses its pristine purity and originality, bereft of its character of being, in which man always and already lives. It becomes an artificial world projected by science. Man's reason is no longer a faculty that searches for truths about the world, or an aptitude that assigns meaning, but a propensity conceived in terms of instrumental significance, which according to Husserl, is the deprivation of the meaning character of modern, mathematical and objective, natural sciences. The fact is that the objective, mathematical, scientific explanation is only one kind of contact with things, and it is in no way the most fundamental either. Hence, Husserl points out that science fails to grasp itself, lacking self-understanding and self-consciousness. Under the influence of Galileo, modern science affirms the objectivity of the world of science. The universe of science proves to be a network of ideal, theoretico-mathematical super structure, similar in concepts and standards as mathematical sciences.

When confronted with the problem of the mathematico-logico-objectivist point of view of the world, Husserl's solution consists in the description of man's pre-scientific experiences by minute analysis of life, as it exists prior to objectification and abstraction. Therefore, by means of the accurate examination of his daily pre-scientific experiences, Husserl demonstrates the irrelevance of the objectivistic, mathematical mode of existence in human affairs. According to life world, the world of our immediate experiences and things appear according to their colours, on the basis of their sensible qualities, and in terms of their practical meanings. Life world is a vast domain of subjective phenomena, comprising things as immediately experienced. It is subjective, practical and eternally relative, with each thing being individual and independent to each person. Scientists aim to conquer the subjective and eliminate the practical, getting rid of the relative, terminating the mythical, eradicating the magical, thereby destroying the ritualistic aspects of life world. Science appears to transcend life world, but conceals this aspect of its character, since it unknowingly lapses into objectivism in an attempt to overcome the subjectivity of the world. Science does not understand that its own origin is found only in life world. The truth is this: the foundations of science require subjective interpretation rooted in life world.

A return to the world of immediate experience does not exhaust itself in the naïve descriptions of what is experienced, but requires a reflection on that which is experienced. This is a reflection on the subjective achievement of experiencing itself, or on the condition of the possibility of experience, insofar as these are found in the experiencing subject. Man's self-understanding and self-interpretation with reference to the world is lost on account of abstraction and mathematization, due to which he is unable to guide the world. This breakdown that exhibits man's failure, is not limited to theoretico-scientifico-mathematical explanations, but extends to every practical orientation to the world. This breakdown is described by Husserl as objectivism, which states that the claim to the truth of the world consists in what is expressible only in objective, scientific, mathematical and calculable statements. The underlying assumption of such a statement is that, neither man's knowledge, nor his praxis, nor his technology will be left to incomprehensible and subjective factors, as a consequence of which objectivism has eliminated the mystery-component from the world. Objectivism considers the world to be problem that can be solved, whereas Husserl beholds the world as a mystery, to be approached reverentially.

8.2 From the World of Science to Life world

Husserl's treatment of life world is the logical culmination of his investigations into the notion of world, which began around 1900, while he was working on *Logical Investigations*. During these investigations, he concentrated on the notion of the world as given to us from our immediate experiences and surroundings. They are not an isolated phenomena; every material thing manifesting itself in experience reveals a horizon, spatially and temporally extended. World is the horizon of all our perceptions and attitudes; things experienced manifest themselves in a certain horizon, with the basic contention that the known guides us to the unknown, which will in turn reveal and manifest itself as something valuable and useful, provided we try to discover it. We commence our pilgrimage towards the unknown from the already known, for the unknown constitutes the horizon of the known. For example, for centuries, scientists believed that atom was the final point of matter, beyond which no further division was possible. Phenomenologically, this implies that the atom has no further horizon. But towards the end of 19th century, scientists discovered that the atom could be broken down into electrons, protons and neutrons, for which J. J. Thompson was awarded the Nobel Prize in 1897. Phenomenologically, the atom has revealed its horizon. This was considered the end of the story for several years, until sub-atomic particles known as quarks were discovered. This was proceeded by the discovery of six different kinds of quarks, a feat achieved by the Large Hadron Collider experiment. Therefore, newer horizons revealed themselves at each discovery. Sartre's notion of the trans-phenomenality of phenomenon refers precisely to this aspect of the horizon. Consider another example, I stand at the entrance of the college from where its facade is visible. On further exploration, I come across students, the principal's office, classrooms, the teachers' rooms and so on. As I stand at the façade of the building, its horizons are presently unknown to me, and reveal themselves when I strive to discover them by further exploration of the campus. Husserl's contention is that everything is given with its horizon, nothing is given devoid of it. The world is the horizon of everything experienced and experienceable, and cannot be perceived unless experienced. In other words, the world cannot be experienced in the same way as things; only in and through the experience of things can the world be perceived. This implies that the world cannot be an object of our everyday experience. Instead, it is the horizon of all things that I experience. In the experience of individual things, the world as horizon is co-present, for the world is co-perceived as the horizon of things that I experience. This contention enables Husserl to remark that the world (as the horizon) is pre-given, which means that unless the world already exists, an object of experience cannot exist, or cannot be given. And, from that perspective, as Heidegger puts it, the world is *a priori* as well. We find ourselves amongst things described by their colour, size, shape, functions, such as tools, instruments, books, buildings, objects of art, all of which have human meanings, serve human purposes, human aims, human desires, any of which can appear as, or provide horizons for man. They provide a framework within which humans live. They constitute the components of life world.

According to Husserl, life world is the foundation upon which the world of science rests as a super-structure. All theoretical truths, be it logical, mathematical or scientific, have their roots and justifications in the same, implying a privileged status over the scientific, objective world. This makes it imperative for us to return to life world, so that science can achieve self-consciousness. At every moment of our life, we are concerned with things, we are interested in our pets, friendships and feelings for people; we are simultaneously involved in several things. We view ourselves as an integral part of the world. None of these appear in isolation, each being a framework into which it is inserted and manifested, within the all-encompassing world-horizon. The world presents itself to us continuously, as the universal field of all actual and possible activities. If the world always exists as a pre-given, it is because it proclaims itself simultaneously with the appearance of every mundane being, with which we are involved. This implicit and vague awareness of the world permeates all our movements and integrates itself into our existence. Therefore, the world is the foundational network of all our meaningful relations, implying that life world is the milieu of lived experiences.

We live in a common world, with different attitudes to different people, disinterestedness towards some, or mutual friendship and cooperation with others. Our relationship with our family members is of a deeper kind. We work together to actualize our potentialities, living together in the world. The process with which we interact with others indicate that none of us are isolated individuals, we are all members of a historical family. In other words, the world thus constituted has a historical and social implication, suggesting that life world is relative to a given society and its history. Life world is the basis of our life, a foundation existing prior to, and independent of all our individual and collective activities. life world is inter-subjective, on account of which, we are simultaneously, both subjects and objects in relation to the same.

After having constructed a very clear and distinct elucidation of the notion of life world, Husserl courts controversy and confusion yet again by bringing up a new position regarding the same. One can surely blame Husserl for having ignored his original and pristine insight, but he always had his own reasons and justifications for further developments; otherwise, he would not have been an all-inclusive philosopher. As discussed, life world is the world of all humans; this includes science, scientists and scientific theories as cultural facts, implying that they are cultural facts, and part of life world. This means that science and scientists arise and flow into life world, adding themselves to its composition. Does this mean that Husserl retracts his earlier professed statement that life world exists in contrast to scientific theories and mathematical calculations? Previously, he distinguished life world from the world of science, going on to later include science, scientists, and scientific theories into life world as its components.

Husserl clarifies the apparent contradiction as follows. Science and scientists are spiritual components and intellectual accomplishments of the human existence. Scientific theories are logical constructs, unlike monuments, houses or trees; they are human formulations related to human activities and potentialities, belonging to the concrete unity of life world, whose concreteness extends beyond the concreteness of things. Remember, scientists are human beings, and as humans, they are components of life world. All claims to objectivity are in fact an inter-subjective agreement on scientific interpretations, whose purpose is to overcome subjectivity. But what does objectivity mean to scientists? Objectivity is established neither outside nor in opposition to subjectivity, but within the very heart of subjectivity. This means that scientists are merely shifting their perspectives. In light of these, we can further expand the scope of life world to include institutions (like university, state, religion), literature, language, etc. The original understanding of life world was the world of immediate experience, i.e., the pre-predicative, and the immediately given. How can we understand the extended notion of life world in terms of the concepts of immediate experience? Husserl goes on to add that, when life world is described as a cultural phenomenon including the above-mentioned components, they indicate historical or sociological relativity, over and above the subjective relativity of life world. Utilizing the phenomenological notion of reduction, Husserl discovers a general structure in all relative features of life world, which however is not relative, but represents essential features common to all relative structures. This is *a priori* of life world and the essence shared by all life worlds.

From the Husserlian perspective, there are differences between life world as the world of immediate experience, and as the cultural world incorporating science and scientific theories. They are:

1. The ontological status of the community practising a particular culture and the status of institutions such as state, religion, literature, customs, etc.

2. The cultural sense of the community can change historically, leading to a plurality of cultures. Husserl strove to determine the eidetic structure of such changes, i.e., the essential condition of such cultural transformations.

3. The structure and role of language upon which communication is based.

These are not problems when life world is considered as a world of immediate experience. But this does not mean that life world, as the world of immediate experience, and as a cultural fact, are totally unrelated to, or incompatible with each other. The cultural world is a dependent world. The cultural community is not an island, unrelated and isolated. We are a part of the cultural community; we perceive the community, and are active practitioners along with people known to us; The cultural community depends on the perceived world, though both are unidentical and irreducible to one another. Like the scientific world, the cultural world has its meaning in the world of perception. I wish to conclude by comparing the scientific world and Life world.

Table 8.1 Comparison of the world of Science and Life world

No.	World of Science	Life world
1.	Science operates on with abstraction	Life world is the concrete-fullness from where/which abstraction is derived. It is primordially a world of percieved bodies, in which things perceived have their perspectival character with both inner and outer horizons
2.	Science constructs superstructures	Life world provides the matrix from which construction originates
3.	Scientific constructions preclude sense-intuition	Life world is a field of intuition; it is the universe of what is intuitable in principle. It is the domain of original self-evidence (to which the scientists must return to verify their theories)
4.	Science explains what is given	Life world is the locus of all givenness
5.	Scientific entities possess mediated character	Life world exhibits the character of immediacy
6.	World of science is founded on Life world	Life world is prior to all science and theories, not just historically, but also epistemologically

Husserl conceives life world as a totality of life in its multitudinous facets. It is the field wherein life occurs on a daily basis. Husserl's treatment of life world indicates the correlational *a priori* in its most fundamental and universal form. It indicates the essential relatedness of conscious life and the world, although the primordiality of consciousness cannot be denied. Life world has two divergent or even conflicting strands of thoughts, one prior to scientific domain, which is the world of immediate experience, and the other, falling into the scientific domain. Despite these disparities, how did Husserl go about combining both? Or in other words, do both worlds share anything in common? Had there been nothing in common between the two, Husserl would not have linked them together. The intertwining threads are as follows.

1. Life world is a conglomeration of several varying concepts and notions, linked together and mutually associated with each other, some of them being, Husserl's assumption about the theoretical science of nature, his reflection on linguistic developments of the community, his notion of the human world, his understanding of culture, his views on experience, his ideas of the pre-given, his apprehension about the pre-theoretical, etc. The analysis of life world involves a plurality of major concepts elaborated by Husserl in phenomenology during the course of development, implying that the notion of life world cannot be developed as a single concept, since each requires elaboration and enunciation of their meaning in life world.

2. Husserl speaks of two different kinds of worlds, one of which is foundational to the other. The first is the world of modern mathematical, physical or natural science, i.e., the problem of theoretical sciences of nature, though Husserl claims that mathematical and theoretical science is facilitated through the world of immediate and perceptual experience that Husserl considers to be the world of culture and linguistic community. The cultural world is world a of immediate experience. Science must possess at its disposal, a linguistic world or community, constituting and imposing pre-conditions for the world of science.

3. Pre-given is another concept in close association with the notion of life world. It refers to the already existing, the foundation of that which is yet to come. It is that which is taken for granted in all our dealings; it is that which is received. The scientific world, i.e., the cultural world is built upon life world, and it is only because life world is always already given, that the scientific

world is built. This implies that life world is the *a priori* necessary condition for the existence of a scientific world.

4. Along with the notion of the pre-given, another important basis for life world is the understanding of the pre-theoretical, in developing which, Husserl roots himself in the elucidation of consciousness, since consciousness at this level, is the domain of ends to be attained and projects to be carried out. Life world, as we know, is the world of immediate experience, and the milieu in which the pre-theoretical, practical life is lived, and runs its course. Moreover, we need to keep in mind that culture does not speak primarily of theory, but only of a mode of living that Husserl considers pre-theoretical.

To conclude, the cultural world and the world of immediate experience together form the horizon of primordial consciousness with pre-theoretical attitude. Husserl lays the foundation for science, which is part of our cultural ethos upon life world.

8.3 References

Husserl, E. (1970a). Berkeley. David Hume's psychology as fictionalistic theory of knowledge: The 'bankruptcy' of philosophy and science. In D. Carr (Trans.), *The Crisis of European Sciences and Transcendental Phenomenology* (pp. 86–87). Northwestern University Press.

Husserl, E. (1970b). The clarification of the origin of the modern opposition between physicalistic objectivism and transcendental subjectivism, Sections 8-27. In D. Carr (Trans.), *The Crisis of European Sciences and Transcendental Phenomenology* (pp. 8–102). Northwestern University Press.

Husserl, E. (1970c). The clarification of the transcendental problem and the related function of psychology, Sections 28-55. In D. Carr (Trans.), *The Crisis of European Sciences and Transcendental Phenomenology* (pp. 103–190). Northwestern University Press.

Husserl, E. (1970d). The Crisis of the sciences as expression of the radical life-crisis of European humanity. In D. Carr (Trans.), *The Crisis of European Sciences and Transcendental Phenomenology* (pp. 1–20). Northwestern University Press.

Husserl, E. (1976). The World at the Natural Standpoint: I and my World about me, Section 27. In W. R. B. Gibson (Trans.), *Ideas: General Introduction to Pure Phenomenology* (pp. 101–102). Humanities Press.

Husserl, E. (1977a). Appendix: References to F. A. Lange and B. Bolzano. In J. N. Findlay (Trans.), *Logical Investigations Volume 2* (pp. 141–143). Routledge & Kegan Paul.

Husserl, E. (1977b). Critique of specific relativism and, in particular, of anthropologism. In J. N. Findlay (Trans.), *Logical Investigations Volume 2* (pp. 78–81). Routledge & Kegan Paul.

Husserl, E. (1989). Analysis of the Theoretical Attitude, of the Theoretical Interest, Section 3. In R. Rojcewicz & A. Schuwer (Trans.), *Ideas Pertaining to a Pure Phenomenology and to a Phenomenological Philosophy: Second Book Studies in the Phenomenology of Constitution* (p. 5). Kluwer Academic Publishers.

Husserl, E. (2006). The A Priori of Nature, the Natural World-Concept, and the Natural Sciences. Avenarius' "Critique of Pure Experience". In R. Bernet (Ed.), & I. Farin & J. Hart (Trans.), *The Basic Problems of Phenomenology* (pp. 22–28). Springer Netherlands.

Chapter 9

Husserl's Notion of The Other and Intersubjectivity

9.1 Introduction

The notion of the other, also called social philosophy or intersubjectivity is a difficult problem to examine. For an empiricist, the notion of the other is a non-issue, for he commences with a plurality of existents. However, for any philosophy that affirms the superiority and supremacy of consciousness over the mundane realm and material existence, this is a serious problem, all the more so for phenomenology, since it affirms the primacy and primordiality of consciousness, in the sense that consciousness not only assigns meaning to experiences, but also gives them their being or mode of existence. Consciousness is the fulcrum around which phenomenology turns. Phenomenology insists on the primacy of consciousness, which being the case, it is a serious problem to speak of an alter ego. It is all the more so when Husserl speaks of a solitary, absolute wordless, transcendental ego in *Ideas I.*

To elucidate the formation and development of a community is not an easy task. There are two elements within each person, 1) the body presented and perceived directly, identifying him as this individual and, 2) the consciousness appresented and apperceived pointing towards self. When I perceive the body, I can only have an apperception of his consciousness. Inasmuch as the other person has his body and consciousness, I also have the same, which implies that all of us, be it the other or myself, confront the same situation. If consciousness and body remain two distinct elements, we are said to suffer from a psychological problem. But consciousness and the body constituting the very same reality also lead to serious and unending problems, reflected upon by Husserl, in the V Meditation of *Cartesian Meditations* (CM) (Husserl, 1977f), discussed below.

Consciousness announces itself through the body, and while the two are not identical, they are inseparable. There is unity in multiplicity here, maybe a contingent unity that lasts until the death of the individual. The issue is not the unity of body and consciousness, but instead, as to how the other, who has unity of body and consciousness, appear to me? Husserl continues his discussions on the other, post-publication of *Cartesian Meditations*, some of which include horizontal intentionality, open intersubjectivity, concrete experiences of the embodied other, *a priori*, and *a posteriori* consideration of transcendental intersubjectivity, etc. He wrote a great deal on the subject in his post-Crisis manuscripts, which he did not publish during his lifetime. Husserl's winter semester lectures of 1910-11, published as *The Basic Problems of Phenomenology*, discussed the issue of the other in some detail (Husserl, 2006g).

   This chapter has three parts; in the first, I elucidate the notion of the other, from the point of view of *CM*, followed by examination of the notion of intersubjectivity based on post-*CM* writings, and finally draw out my conclusions from Husserl's writings.

9.2 Part 1: The treatment of intersubjectivity in CM (V Meditation)

Husserl gives a transcendental phenomenological treatment of the other in the V Meditation of *CM*, the longest of them all and almost as long as all other four put together. The V Meditation is the culmination and the touchstone of transcendental intersubjective phenomenology. There are five points that stand out in the same, namely,

1.   Solipsism and transcendental phenomenology (CM 42-43) (Husserl, 1977g).

2.   Sphere of ownness (CM 44-47) (Husserl, 1977h).

3.   The other from an analogical angle (CM 48-54) (Husserl, 1977i).

4.   The other and myself (CM 55) (Husserl, 1977e).

5.   The individual and the community (CM 56-58) (Husserl, 1977j).

9.2.1 Solipsism and Transcendental Phenomenology

Solipsism, from Husserl's *Ideas I*, exemplified the culmination of transcendental phenomenology. It is an integral part of idealistic philosophies, inviting common sense objections. Common sense conceives a plurality of egos; the others are distinct from me; they are other egos. Husserl's transcendental philosophy accepts a certain kind of solipsism. Here Husserl's phenomenology is confronted with two problems, the first, *CM*, being an integral part of transcendental phenomenology, must follow reduction to the end. The second problem is that constituting the other from perspective consciousness, and precisely as the other without inconsistencies is a major task. Constitution refers to the constitution of a thing, and here, it refers to the constitution of another human being, i.e., the difference between the modes of givenness versus experience of the other. In other words, it means that givenness of the other cannot be reduced to the level of givenness of a thing. This paradox has three levels; at the first level, I alone am the subject, while I am with the other. But the other is neither a psycho-physical object nor a thing, but in himself, a subject of experience like me. In the second layer, the world is not private, but instead a phenomenon experienced, the world within the domain of experience of a subject. In the third level, the world is not just a physical phenomenon, but a cultural object, referring not just to my constitutive capabilities, but in addition to those of a community constituting us all.

9.2.2 Sphere of Ownness (CM 44-47)

The domain of ownness also involves two major difficulties. To elucidate the notion of the other, we subject him to a special kind of reduction that is similar yet different from eidetic reduction, namely, the reduction to the sphere of ownness. In the ordinary, non-phenomenological sense, the other exists as an ordinary human person or being. but in the present case, I take into consideration only that which is my own. But one can question this sense of ownness. Everything in the world speaks of the other; the world is one of culture, it is for everybody to share, and hence a world of the other as well. One can then assume that there is a world prior to intersubjectivity, or in other words, the world is an *a priori* necessary condition for intersubjectivity. Insofar this is the case, the genesis of the other cannot be myself. The sense of the other, however, arises from me, since I first assign a sense to myself, only after which can I bestow a sense to the other and the world at large. This constitutes the other as a phenomenon. But caution needs to be exercised, as the other as a phenomenon is very different from things as phenomena. Although Husserl does not surrender himself to the temptations of ontology, one cannot ignore the ontological differences present in his philosophy between a chair, a material physical object, and a human, a living meaning-giving person, though they are both merely phenomena from the perspective of phenomenology. The sense of the ego is transferred from myself to the other, which is *a priori* for the other to be an alter-ego. This reduction to the sphere of ownness in no way constitutes a dissolution of the other into me, rather the other remains a distinct entity, which implies that there is another constituted ego, unidentical to me, mirroring and reflecting my ego.

Husserl uses the expression 'going beyond' (encroaches on) and 'mirroring' as two terms to explain the constitution of the other. They imply that 'I go beyond myself to the other,' or to use Husserl's term, 'I encroach into the other', which may be an imperfect way to explain the expression. It would imply that I transcend myself to go to the other in the context of intersubjectivity. The second term, 'mirroring' is the act of viewing myself reflected on, or going beyond myself to the other in the context of intersubjectivity. In the natural sphere, devoid of reduction, I am as I am. The world is also real. But everything transforms in the phenomenological attitude; the world becomes the world for *me*, with a sphere of ownness. But this own sphere is one of abstraction, and poses a serious difficulty. While I am concrete, the other is also concrete, then where does abstraction occur? According to Husserl, abstraction does not have an Aristotelian meaning or a Lockean sense, rather, it is the commencement of methodological separation, i.e., abstraction is an isolable totality. The world as a phenomenon is abstracted from, or separated from the world as a spatio-temporal existent. From this perspective, the notion of abstraction does not create any contradiction. This isolable totality is the lived body (*Leib*) that is mine, the body that facilitates my movement and perception, and facilitates the expression of myself; it serves as a referent pole for all other physical bodies (*Körper*). Hence *Leib* is also abstracted from *Körper*. *Leib* indicates a primordial nature, an owned nature from where ownness arises. With reference to *Leib*, Husserl states that this reduction is to my transcendental sphere of peculiar ownness (Husserl, 1977v). The own sphere is autonomous and a positive totality, furnishing the other with an antecedent foundation.

9.2.3 The Other from an Analogical Angle (CM 48-54)

How can the sphere of ownness go beyond oneself to the domain of the other? It is here that Husserl introduces the most important theme of analogy, namely the analogical grasping of the other as the other ego, which also forms the core of the V Meditation. Three key points that stand out in the V meditation are the following.

1.   Respect for the other and his otherness.

2.   Transcending the sphere of ownness, and

3.   Rooting my experience of the other in my primordial transcendental self.

Due to the analogical apprehension of the other, I overcome solipsism without sacrificing my ego. In my experience of the other, the other announces himself as a person in flesh and blood. But what about his life? What about himself as a person? On account of his flesh and blood, i.e., in the light of what he presents himself to me, I apprehend his life, I apprehend him as a person, I perceive his body and blood, thereby perceiving his life and himself as a person. But do I perceive his life, perceive him as a person in the same way that I perceive his body and blood? The answer is no. I perceive that which is directly and immediately given to me, i.e., his body and blood. His life and himself as a person cannot be directly and immediately perceived. Husserl goes on to say that, while I have perception of his body and blood, I have apperception of him a person. His body and blood are rooted in his life, in himself as a person, on account of which, I have apperception of him as a person and as a self. So, how can I relate my perception of his body, flesh and blood, with the apperception of him as a person, or in other words, how are perception and apperception related to each other, and used to identify the presented with apresented? Husserl's answer to this query comes in terms of the development of the notion of analogy in three stages. I develop only the first two stages since the third stage is only hypothetical, with a lot of ifs and buts.

9.2.3.1 The First Stage

By virtue of analogy, the sense of the other moves from me to the other, i.e., the sense of the ego is transferred from myself to the other. Husserl's text in *CM* can be summarized as follows. Someone enters my perceptual domain; as such, it (nay he) is a *Körper*, but I am a *Leib*; but for the world around me and the other, I am also a *Körper* constituted as an organism. Therefore, it is clear that only a resemblance connecting the other's body with mine can provide foundation and motive to conceive by analogy that the other's body is also a *Leib*, like mine. If this is the case with me, so is the case with the other, implying that I attribute to the other, what I have, i.e., making it impossible to reject the same to the other. The following are certain characteristics of analogy, according to Husserl:

1. Analogy is pre-reflective, moving from one object to another in the normal course. For example, God is faithful, husband is faithful, wife is faithful, a dog is faithful. God, husband, wife, dog, etc., are those in which faithfulness is rooted, and this analogy moves from one object to another, i.e., from God to husband to wife to dog. But Husserl's analogy differs from the above in that, analogy moves from subject to subject (i.e., from myself, a subject, to another person who is also a subject from his own perspective).

2. In every analogy, there is a pairing, i.e., God's faithfulness is compared with or paired with that of the husband's or wife's or dog's faithfulness, providing associative support to analogy.

3. In the bodily presence of the other, I recognize my reflection in the other, extending my sense of ego to the other, i.e., akin to a transfer taking place. In terms of analogy, I anticipate the other, I presume the presence of somebody else out there. But this transfer needs to be confirmed by signs that confer fulfilment and being-status from the other. In other words, I behave in a certain manner expecting a response or communication from the other.

9.2.3.2 The Second Stage

I am aware of myself as a *Leib*, a lived body. I am also aware of my body as a *Körper*. However, I am also aware that there is an identity between my *Leib* and my *Körper*, for it is I myself as a subject (*Leib*) with a body (*Körper*). Inasmuch as I perceive my physical body (*Körper*), I apperceive my lived body (*Leib*), acquainting me (by way of apperception) of my own subjectivity. My *Leib* is one with my *Körper*. But how do I verify his subjectivity, his *Leib*, from the experience of his *Körper*? Or in other words, how do I identify his *Leib* with his *Körper* merely by experiencing his *Körper*? I am aware that my physical, bodily (*Körper*) experiences are expressions emanating from my *Leib*. I experience his bodily experiences or expressions in my personal domain. But these spring, not from my *Körper*, but from my *Leib*. Therefore, analogically, insofar as my bodily expressions originate, not from my *Körper* but from my *Leib*, his bodily expressions also originate, not from his *Körper*, but from his *Leib*, i.e., if mine is like this, then his cannot be different from mine; I cannot deny what I have to the other. I grasp expressions of his *Körper*, knowing fully well that they originate from his *Leib*. This understanding is as a result of the analogical knowledge that expressions of my *Körper* cannot exist unless they originate from my *Leib*. Analogy certifies that the other is an ego, like me. All that belongs to my ego is grasped by myself, having a privileged access to myself, so is the case with him as well.

9.3 The Other and Myself (CM 55)

Husserl is well aware of the fact that he has not been able to demonstrate conclusively the existence of the other, for various reasons, namely,

1. The analogical grasping of the other does not account for reciprocity amongst egos.

2. The other is a projected and modified ego, which implies that there is no symmetrical relation between the other and me.

3. Pairing is unidirectional, from myself to the other; there is no reverse pairing, i.e., from the other to me. Consequently, the apodicity of existence of the other remains derivative from mine.

To solve this problem, Husserl suggests that we need to coordinate empirical realism (where everybody is a real person) with transcendental idealism (where everything has a meaning assigned by me). The fulcrum of the problem is the human body. How is the body of the other the same for him, who lives it here and now, and for me who perceives it as my there? Note: everybody has a body. Remember what Gabriel Marcel said: "I am my body.

Devoid of body, there is nobody." I call out the name of a student, 'Suresh'. The boy lifts his hand up and responds: "I am here." The hand is a part of the body, and the body (hand, here) stands out for the self. The name reflects the self, which means that there is an identity between the body and self. A few things need to be clarified here.

1. Initially at least, there is a chasm between the other and me.

2. There are many worlds corresponding to each subjectivity, for the world is dependent on it.

3. As I am a subjectivity in myself, the other is also a subjectivity in himself.

4. How do two subjectivities intend the same object in the very same way (e.g., this is a chair both for the other and me) i.e., how can an object be the same for a plurality of subjectivities? It all boils down to this, how can a body perceived by me over there, be apperceived by him, the other, as his own? My experience tells me that the body over there indicates another subjective life. This implies that it is apperception that brings about the identification of what is over there, with that is here; apperception refers to the subjective life of the other (as grasped by me).

Perception refers to grasping of his body (by me), while apperception refers to grasping aspects such as person, subject, subjectivity, etc., aspects not directly and immediately perceivable. However, perception is grasping the externals, like the body grasping what is directly and immediately perceivable. Similar notes can be attached to presentation and appresentation. Now the question is, can we overcome the distance between perceived and apperceived to arrive at their identity? This division exists, not just in me, but also in the other. I know for sure that, despite this division within me, I am not a divided self, there is intimate personal unity in me; this is my experience. I also attribute the same to the other, for analogically, it must be the same with the other as well. Consider the example of a magnet; while we speak of separation and distinction, the south and north poles of a magnet cannot be separated, although there is a distinction between the two, and similarly with either sides of the palm. In such cases, if one is given, the other must definitely accompany it; one cannot exist without the other, there being an *a priori* necessary requirement for the other to be present when the first is present. Similarly, so is the case with the presented and appresented and the perceived and apperceived.

This implies not just a reciprocity of consciousness, but also a synthesis of association, and the identification of both presented and appresented, perceived and apperceived. From my perspective of the other, there is synthesis of association between his body and subjectivity. But from his perspective, there is synthesis of identity between his body and subjectivity. So is the case with me, from his perspective. To grasp the other phenomenologically, the synthesis of association and identity must be recognised as one and the same.

9.3.1 The Individual and the Community (CM 56-58)

Communities are made up of persons. It is in the nature of persons to work towards the formation of a community. Formation of a community, i.e., a common world is the first step towards the formation of intersubjective or intentional communities. Sociology originates from a group. Unlike sociologists, Husserl grounds the possibility of human relationships upon intentional creative community. In connection with community, Husserl speaks of two different notions, reciprocity of stand points and objectifying equations. What do they mean? For transcendental phenomenology, I am I, while all others are others. But by way of objectifying equations, I become the other; I am another amongst others. Then we have equalization by way of reciprocity, abolishing the privileges of the (single) I, the ego. Objectifying equation with reciprocity lets us understand that there are only others, i.e., I am another amongst others. Thus, equation in conjunction with reciprocity makes possible a community. Husserl also speaks of psychic communities brought about by psychic constitution. This implies that ego must appear in the world, not merely constituting flesh and blood, but by way of psychic characteristics. Intersubjectivity has psychic character. This means that my friendship with the other is not a bodily relation, but a mental or psychic one, a relationship of love and friendship, a bond of concern and solicitude. And this psychic relation, friendship and care, is much more than every other kind of relationship. Psychic relationship is a relationship of heart, mind and spirit. Had it been a relation of mind alone, it would have been a simple Platonic relation. Husserl also speaks of higher levels of communities, a community that can be considered personalities of higher order, and higher-level people corresponding to the cultural world.

9.4 The Treatment of Intersubjectivity after CM

Husserl's examination of intersubjectivity, post-*CM*, is treated at three levels: 1) the *a priori* level, 2) the *a posteriori* level and, 3) the pre-theoretical or pre-reflective or the pre-active or instinctual level. The *a priori* consideration consists of two notions namely, 1a) the horizontal notion of intersubjectivity and, 1b) open intersubjectivity, while *a posteriori* level consists of 2a) generatively handed down by normality, 2b) conventionality and, 2c) tradition. And, finally, intersubjectivity based on the pre-theoretical or instinctive level is much more primordial and fundamental in comparison to *a posteriori* level. I shall combine together 1a) & 1b) of *a priori* consideration. I do not deal with 2) *a posterori* consideration, but I have a few words for 3) the pre-theoretical or instinctual consideration.

Husserl's transcendental phenomenology of reduction and constitution in *Ideas I* led to the problem of solipsism, for which he proposes a solution in *CM*. Husserl overestimated the constitutive powers of transcendental ego in *Ideas I*, though he was aware of the notions of intersubjectivity, empathy, etc., long before *Ideas I* (1913) and *CM* (1936), already during the 1910-11 Winter semester lectures. The major issues of these lectures, along with the results of *Ideas I*, disturbed Husserl so much that, after the publication of *CM*, Husserl worked on solutions to those issues at a higher level, published in his post-1936 writings. They are examined here.

9.4.1 A priori Capacity

Husserl begins his new consideration of intersubjectivity by stating that the potentiality to constitute intersubjectivity within me is *a priori*, implying that the constitution of the other is possible only if a certain kind of constitutive capacity for intersubjectivity already exists in me. My experience of the other does not make him an object of intentional experience, but instead, the other is already present in my horizontal intentionality. And, this horizontal openness is the condition for the possibility of my concrete experience of the other. Since the other is constituted, that kind of constitutive power of intersubjectivity must definitely exist. This is not to presuppose the existence of the other dogmatically. According to Husserl, my capacity or potentiality for intersubjectivity is prior to my encounter with the other, implying that intersubjectivity is not a contingent relation, but which occurs due to the capacity already existing or present in me. Therefore, intersubjectivity belongs to the very *a priori* structure of the constituting subjectivity.

9.4.2 Horizon of Perception

The analysis of the notion of temporality (*vide* Chapter 10) reveals the role of the horizon with respect to perception. Present profiles have an intimate relation to absent profiles, i.e., relation between the past and the one about to occur. This implies that no perceptual awareness of the object (i.e., the present) is possible without an intuitive grasp of past and future profiles. So, for a perception to be the perception of the present object, it must be permeated by the horizon of the past and future. Husserl goes on to state that absent profiles (of the past and future) are *noematic* correlates of my present perception. In other words, at any given moment, the object possesses a plurality of coexisting profiles. Although the past and future are as such absent, they would appear to be intentionally present, since the temporal dimensions of the object (the primal impression, retention and protention) are a unified whole. In other words, the past and future, though presently absent, are conjointly given with the present horizon; the reality of absent horizons are determined by the present perception.

9.4.3 Present Perception and Correlative Apperceptions

Perception of the object implies that we have perception of its present (the now phase) and apperception of its past and future. The latter is not an imaginative or fictitious act, but an intentional perception. This apperception is a correlative of perception (of the present), compatible with actual perception.

9.4.4 From the Perception of Objects to Persons

Inasmuch as the object is given in perception with its horizons or profiles, the other person is also given to me with horizons of his past and future. To clarify his position further, Husserl brings in the notion of open intersubjectivity.

9.4.5 Open Intersubjectivity

Every object of perception (of present profiles) implies a reference to the co-perceived past and future profiles. Husserl transfers it from the realm of objects to that of subjects. The analysis of horizons seems to refer to the perception of a plurality of possible subjects, from which Husserl derives the notion of open intersubjectivity, which he explains as follows. The transcendent perception (of an object) is permeated with reference to absent profiles; these perceptions are of other people as well (inasmuch as we speak of perceptions of objects). This being the case, every perception, due to its horizontness, presupposes a reference to open intersubjectivity.

9.4.6 Human Compatibility

According to Husserl, perception and apperception are co-relative; apperception is compatible with actual perception. Similarly, a human being is said to be compatible with or co-related to another human being. I perceive an object; it is compatible with another object. Traditional epistemology describes compatibility between a human being and a thing/object. Correspondence theory speaks about the compatibility between the human being (mind) and the object. In contrast, Husserl's notion of compatibility, which is strictly phenomenological, is not between human beings and things, but amongst human beings.

9.4.7 Any Contradictions between 1913 & 1936 and post-1936 writings?

Transcendental phenomenology establishes the exclusive existence of I (transcendental ego), whereas, open intersubjectivity (post-1936 writings) proposes a plurality of subjects. Though apparently contradictory, they are not so in fact, because they are statements of two different periods, one from the transcendental, static phenomenological period, while the other is from the genetic phenomenological period. One should keep in mind that Husserl covered a lot of intellectual miles in formulating these two phases, and these two statements are indicative of Husserl's journey through his phenomenological expedition rather than contradictions.

9.4.8 Objectivity in the very Heart of Subjectivity

Husserl firmly considers our concrete bodily experience of the other to be the foundation of the constitution of open intersubjectivity. This is emphasized by his detailed account of empathy in considering the concrete bodily experience of the other, a constitutive condition for the possibility of our reference to open intersubjectivity. In addition, this experience of the other furnishes our life with a universal intersubjective horizon. On account of open intersubjective experience, I am given to the other, as the other is given to me. I myself am the other with respect to the perception of an alter ego; I realize that I am only one among others. This realization dethrones my ego pole, implying that objectivity can be constituted only when the ego perceives itself to be one among others. Therefore, constitution of objectivity becomes a collaborative activity, wherein objectivity attains a subjective agreement amongst multiple egos.

Consider, for example, the well known equation, $E=MC^2$. There is universal agreement amongst physicists regarding its validity, implying that objectivity is constituted, not outside, not besides, but within the very heart of several subjectivities. What it means is this: several physicists, individually and personally, i.e., subjectively considered and examined the validity of the said equation before arriving at a common, i.e., objective and universal agreement regarding its validity and truth. What follows from this consideration is that it is subjectivity that constitutes objectivity; subjectivity is the foundation of objectivity. To put it simply, I can constitute objectivity only when I have constituted myself as one among others, integrating myself with them. Constitution therefore, is not an individual activity, but a collaborative one. From a phenomenological standpoint, this implies that objectivity refers to the practical world that I engage with, before theoretical understanding of things and people. In this world, others are subjects like me. Inasmuch as I share a relationship with my surroundings, they share the same relationship. Despite the different lenses with which we view the world, with differing perspectives and varied experiences, we end up in the same objective world, which according to Husserl, is made possible by empathy, the primordial experience of participation in the other person's actions and feelings without actually becoming another person. Empathy, thus, is the non-relational, non-cognitive understanding of the other.

Husserl also speaks of intersubjectivity, prior to any bodily experience of the other, operating at the pre-theoretical, pre-predicative, pre-active level, active, even at the instinctual level. Consider a new-born baby searching for the mother to suckle. How does the baby *know* that there is a mother next to her, willing to feed her; is the knowledge that milk is available to the baby, at the level of instinct?

9.5 Conclusions

Intersubjective transformation of transcendental phenomenology indicates a decisive transition of phenomenology from the strict egological, static concept of apodictic certainty of *Ideas I* towards a phenomenology of the other. The explication of the transcendental horizon leads to the actual co-present other and their horizon, making it clear that every ego is characterized by an apodictic universal structure of intersubjectivity. In *Conversations with Husserl and Fink* (Cairns, 1976), Husserl tells Cairns something as follows, apodictic transcendental subjectivity constitutes the world as intersubjective; the other self is necessarily and intentionally co-equal with myself. My transcendental self perceives itself without superiority (or even inferiority) over itself and the other. This follows from the fact that I do intend a world that is necessarily intersubjective. This implies that an analysis of transcendental subjectivity leads to transcendental intersubjectivity. The following are a few salient features from Husserl's treatment of transcendental intersubjectivity.

9.5.1 Intersubjectivity is more than Shared Mutual Understanding

A mere psychological interpretation of intersubjectivity is problematic, since it is not a mental state, but a person-to-person relation, and therefore, more than mutual understanding. Unfortunately, many commentators interpret intersubjectivity as a transition in our understanding on account of inaccurate translations of Husserl's expressions *Wechelverstandnis* and *Wechelverstandung*, derived from *Wechel*, that refer to change, succession or alteration. This translation, as pointed out by several commentators, is inadequate and unfair to Husserl. The meaning assigned by Husserl to 'intersubjectivity' goes far beyond the scope of the etymology of *Verstandnis* or *Verstandung*, wherein, understanding is used as a mental or cognitive process, a kind of knowing. Consider the Biblical excerpt, 'Adam knew his wife…' (English Standard Version Bible, 2001, Genesis 4:1). Is this knowing a cognitive act or a mental process? Neither, as it is a very personal, unique, intimate, distinct way of knowing that involves personal concern, intimate solicitude and deep personal interest. It is a kind of knowing with no reference to mental processes or cognitive attitude. This is referred to as my being for the other, being involved in the affairs of the other and accepting responsibility for the other. Husserl's answer to Cain (English Standard Version Bible, 2001, Genesis 4:8-10). is: 'yes, I am my brother's keeper'. This is the sum and substance of Husserl's genetic phenomenological ethics as well, which he developed in the 1920s. Hence intersubjectivity in Husserl involves a sense of sharing, a recognition of participation, an awareness of appropriation, a sense of being responsible for the other. From this perspective, his is the antithesis of Sartre's position regarding the other in *Being and Nothingness* (Sartre, 1992). Concern for each other is much more than mutual understanding. It has a unique reference to empathy. To conclude, intersubjectivity, according to Husserl, is an understanding, furthermore, an agreement amongst people of mutual concern, including solicitude for each other, both of which amount to much more than mere mutual understanding.

9.5.2 Intersubjectivity is Possible only by Exchanging Places and Positions

In intersubjectivity, I become the other, and the other becomes me. It is the condition through which I maintain the assumption that the world, as it presents itself to me, is the same as the one presented to the other, for I assume that if you were in my place, you would see the world the same way I see it, akin to trading places or exchanging positions, which is possible only by empathy. Empathy is *me* looking at the world from the point of view of the other, which is accepting the feeling of the other as mine, or me assuming the feelings of the other. Intersubjectivity is the existential condition that can lead to a shared understanding, in the light of which, Husserl goes on to say that nature itself is an intersubjective reality. This does not mean that we share a mutual understanding with nature, but that we share the same with other people and the world at large.

9.5.3 Intersubjectivity is the Source of Objectivity

Objectivity characterizes the world of natural attitude in which I engage myself before phenomenological procedures, at the onset of which everything transforms. Therefore, I experience others as subjects like me, who have similar relationships with their surrounding world, namely, the common world, facilitated via empathy, or in other words, participation in the actions and feelings of another person, without actually becoming the other. Empathy is a non-rational, non-cognitive understanding, originating from our experience of their bodies, such as moving and acting in ways similar to our own under similar circumstances. Husserl writes that it is clear that the apprehension of the body plays a special role for intersubjectivity in which all objects are apprehended. Objectively, things are in one objective space, time and world. In every case, exhibition of objectivity requires a relation to the apprehension of a multiplicity of subjects, sharing mutual understanding.

Let me elucidate a little more on intersubjectivity as the source of objectivity, with an example. Consider for example, Einstein's well-known equation, E=MC^2. Those unfamiliar with Einsteinian physics would make offhand comments about it, disregarding it, unlike scholars well versed in the same. As laymen, we accept the objectivity and truth validity of Einstein's equation based on the knowledge and authority of such scholars. It is the agreement amongst these scholars that gives us firm conviction about the truth, validity and objectivity of Einstein's position. Therefore, objectivity is an intersubjective agreement or, according to Husserl, constituted in the very heart of subjectivity.

9.5.4 Intersubjectivity and Social Sciences

Husserl's work on the notion of intersubjectivity and its implications inspired and paved the way for the development of several related branches in social sciences. Albert Schütz, whom Husserl characterized as a 'banker by day and a phenomenologist by night', realized the significance of his work, and went on to adopt and expand Husserl's views on the centrality of intersubjectivity, referring to it as 'we-relationships', and in doing so, transforming it into the corner-stone of interpretative social sciences. Schütz understood that intersubjectivity was a universal condition for human existence, *sine-qua-non* for humanity through which the world is experienced and derives meaning. Intersubjectivity, or we-relationships, according to Schütz, is the foundational ontological category of human existence in the world. The possibility of self, the discovery of the ego, the capacity to perform epoché, the possibility of communication and establishing communicative surroundings are all founded on the primordial experience of we-relationships. Intersubjectivity is not a product of or an effect of communication, but a necessary condition for the possibility of communication. It is the basis for the use of language and communicative resources, being fundamentally social and collective. It is the achievement of mindfulness for others, and the reason for our daily rituals, activities, encounters, seeking clarifications, initiating or even terminating communication, dealing with children, providing instruction, etc. For Husserl, intersubjectivity is predominantly a theoretical, rather than a practical problem. He wanted to reconcile the intersubjective quality of human experience with subjective foundation, i.e., we all start from individuals. But for Schütz, it was no more a theoretical issue, but a practical programme for everyday life.

Husserl may not have resolved the problem of intersubjectivity to the satisfaction of all phenomenologists (e.g., Sartre), but paved us a path for its resolution. Intersubjectivity is an existential condition for being human, or being-in-the-world, as Heidegger puts it. It is this condition that informs us of the presence of others even before the commencement of communications. There is intersubjectivity even in the absence of others, for it is *a priori*, or the potentiality present in all human beings for communication. And as Schütz points out, it is already present in Husserl's notion of natural standpoint. A man experiences his neighbours, despite them being not present bodily. Consider the way we ponder the presence of our departed forefathers. Man is surrounded by objects produced by others, not just material in nature, but linguistic, cultural, aesthetic objects, artefacts, systems of signs, etc., all indicative of the close and immediate presence of the other.

9.5.5 Intersubjectivity, Temporal Structure and the Other

First, I must be able to extend my consciousness beyond myself, implying that I must have a consciousness that goes beyond the momentary present. We find this in consciousness as a living, gnawing or extended present. It is due to the protention-retention-structure of consciousness that I am capable of apperception. Secondly, my experience of the other cannot simply be the experience of the ontological other, i.e., if our analysis remains within the bounds of Husserlian phenomenology, the other cannot be foreign to my consciousness; this is unimaginable. There must be some analogy between myself and the other. It is here that Husserl speaks of the similarities between our bodies, leading to similarities of consciousness. However, it may be noticed that the experience of my body from within is completely different from the same from without. But I know the existence of another consciousness immediately, without reflection, without any originary experience, without any prior learning. I must already be open to the other, who is already a subject, which in turn would imply the recognition of intersubjectivity. In other words, intersubjectivity is the recognition of the existence of transcendental egos before I encounter some individual subject's body. It must already be a part of my consciousness, for me to apprehend the other individual subjects. Since we find such an openness already in my temporal structure established primarily in my living, primordial present, this is my sphere of ownness; it is I myself. Thus, this link to intersubjectivity rests somehow on myself as temporality. In other words, there must be some kind of intersubjective structure as part of my temporal consciousness that allows me to apprehend the other subject. In fact, Husserl writes that the other is co-present in me.

The absolute ego, as living, streaming, existing, concrete present, as appresentatively manifesting itself in me, is also manifesting in the other as an ego, who has constituted me in the co-presence of its living present. In other words, there must be an open intersubjective structure associated with my personal temporal structure that allows my immediate appresentation of another subject's consciousness. This intersubjective structure is actually a part of my personal temporal consciousness, taking my consciousness beyond myself. In other words, inasmuch as temporality carries me beyond myself, intersubjectivity takes me beyond my primordial presence, to the horizon of the co-present other.

This move towards the other is a move away from solipsism, towards the apprehension of another subject, which is direct and immediate, i.e., the other subject is already present in our subjectivity as our open possibility exceeding our own temporal consciousness. This implies that Husserl realizes that earlier attempts at reduction in *Ideas I* were never completely possible. Intersubjectivity is a requirement for my experience; my own consciousness extends beyond myself to the other. The absolute transcendental ego is never solipsistic, it is both I and we together. For this reason, we find the absolute temporal ego both a primordial sphere of ownness and an openness to the other (by way of apperception), which can be understood, not only as an openness to new objects and experiences, but also to intersubjectivity that allows me to know the other subjects immediately as other absolute consciousness.

Husserl's post-1936 elucidation of intersubjectivity definitely goes far beyond *CM*. It culminates in the understanding that subjectivity requires intersubjectivity to complete it, to fulfil it. The other is the fulfilment of my subjectivity. Temporality, yet again, proves to be the most fundamental concept in phenomenology, for intersubjectivity is an achievement of a deeper understanding of temporality.

To summarise, it should be kept in mind that Husserl was a path finder. He does not claim to have solved all philosophical problems connected with intersubjectivity to the total satisfaction of all and sundry. However, he has indicated the path towards possible solutions. Intersubjectivity is the capacity inherent in all human beings, enabling them to deal with the other. It can be interpreted now that Husserl's position regarding natural standpoint (*vide Ideas I*) has reference to transcendental intersubjectivity, which appears much later in his philosophy. In this context, Schütz writes that, even from a natural standpoint, a man experiences his neighbour. He is surrounded by objects that inform him as to where it was produced (work place or factory), who produced it (workers), how it reached the current place (transport), etc., all of which imply that man, money and other materials were involved. In other words, what is available to us is not merely material things, but they constitute furniture, artefacts, etc., summarized as cultural, aesthetic, linguistic objects, all of which have reference to the other. This indicates that Husserl's concern for the other commenced at the very beginning of his phenomenological career, and not at a later stage, as often some scholars believe.

To conclude, Husserl realized the limitations of his static phenomenology by the time he completed *Ideas I*. His attention thereafter focused on ways and means to overcome these limitations. It took him over two decades (from 1913-post 1936) to formulate and formalize his thoughts and reflections, ever-growing in his mind over that period, the result being the ground-breaking notion of transcendental intersubjectivity. This chapter traces the path by which he arrived at the notion of transcendental intersubjectivity.

9.6 References

Cairns, D. (1976). *Conversations with Husserl and Fink: Phaenomenologica 66.* The Hague: Martinus Nijhoff.

Husserl, E. (1977a). Establishment of the Community of Monads. The First Form of Objectivity: Intersubjective Nature: V Meditation. In D. Cairns (Trans.), *Cartesian meditations: An Introduction to Phenomenology* (pp. 120–127). Martinus Nijhoff Publishers, The Hague.

Husserl, E. (1977b). Fifth meditation. Uncovering of the sphere of Transcendental being as Monadological Intersubjectivity. In D. Cairns (Trans.), *Cartesian Meditations: An Introduction to Phenomenology* (pp. 89–150). Martinus Nijhoff Publishers, The Hague.

Husserl, E. (1977c). Fifth Meditation, Uncovering of the Sphere of Transcendental Being as Monadological Inter-Subjectivity, Sections 42, 43. In D. Cairns (Trans.), *Cartesian Meditations: An Introduction to Phenomenology* (pp. 89–91). Martinus Nijhoff Publishers, The Hague.

Husserl, E. (1977d). Fifth Meditation, Uncovering of the Sphere of Transcendental Being as Monadological Inter-Subjectivity, Sections 44-47. In D. Cairns (Trans.), *Cartesian Meditations: An Introduction to Phenomenology* (pp. 92–102). Martinus Nijhoff Publishers, The Hague.

Husserl, E. (1977e). Fifth Meditation, Uncovering of the Sphere of Transcendental Being as Monadological Inter-Subjectivity, Sections 48-54. In D. Cairns (Trans.), *Cartesian Meditations: An Introduction to Phenomenology* (pp. 105–119). Martinus Nijhoff Publishers, The Hague.

Husserl, E. (1977f). Fifth Meditation, Uncovering of the Sphere of Transcendental Being as Monadological Inter-Subjectivity, Sections 56-58. In D. Cairns (Trans.), *Cartesian Meditations: An Introduction to Phenomenology* (pp. 128–135). Martinus Nijhoff Publishers, The Hague.

Husserl, E. (1977g). Reduction of transcendental experience to the sphere of ownness. Fifth Meditation, Section 44. In D. Cairns (Trans.), *Cartesian Meditations: An Introduction to Phenomenology* (pp. 120–127). Martinus Nijhoff Publishers, The Hague.

152   *Chapter 9*

Husserl, E. (2006). *The Basic Problems of Phenomenology* (F. Ingo & G. H. James, Trans.). Springer Netherlands.

Sartre, J.-P. (1992). *Being and Nothingness.* Simon and Schuster.

Chapter 10

Husserl's Understanding of Lived Time

10.1 Introduction

Husserl commenced his inquiries into time-consciousness in 1893, a few years prior to the start of his career in phenomenology, analyzing the human awareness of time. He considers time-consciousness to be a miracle, rich in marvels, and one of the most cumbersome of all phenomenological problems. He also remarked that the problem of time-consciousness was crucial and essential, as it involves an intricate examination of the inherent mysteries of the structure of consciousness, time being omnipresent in all aspects and dimensions of human existence. Yet, there can be no one single definition of time, acceptable to all who work on it. It is such a puzzle that it breaks down into a large number of associated problems on further analysis.

One fascinating facet of time is that, time analysis can be contemplated only in accompaniment with objects in time and our experiences of the same. However, Husserl points out that time itself is a form, and our consciousness of time is formal, since time has a formal structure. And since time analysis can be undertaken only with the objects in time, the form of time is only a form of individual objects. Therefore, phenomenological analysis of time consciousness cannot be undertaken without examining the constitution of temporal objects. All empirical objects are in time. Events occur in time, processes open up in time and are related to one another in terms of a before and after, or in terms of simultaneity, all temporal in character. Experiences divulge themselves in time. Consciousness, being inherently temporal, forces everything else to be temporal. Husserl considered our consciousness of time and the awareness of the temporal character of consciousness, the most fundamental of all human accomplishments. Husserl remarked that the consciousness of time requires time, while the consciousness of duration requires duration, implying that each perceptual encounter has an intentional reference to an object in time, which means that all our experiences themselves are temporal.

Husserl's basis for the analysis of temporality can be summarized as follows. The perception of a temporal object, succession and change would be impossible if perception consisted of consciousness of that which is exclusively in the present. That our consciousness is capable of perceiving succession and duration implies that we can perceive not just the present, but also that which is beyond the present, i.e., those past, and those yet to come. Therefore, while we are conscious of the present, we can be co-conscious of the just-been, and the yet-to-occur. Then the question of paramount importance is this, how can one be conscious of the past, i.e., no longer present and the future, the not-yet-present, while being conscious of the present? How can present apprehensions provide us with an intuitive awareness of something just-past or something just about to occur? Following in the footsteps of William James, a philosopher whom Husserl greatly admired, Husserl explains this in his notion of width of presence, or gnawing presence. In other words, Husserl holds that the present is not a thin-edged, blade-edged, knife-edged present, but a duration-block, implying that it consists of temporal dimensions, with three temporal modes of the present, past and future. Husserl's terminologies, we shall see in the course of time, are very different from usual ones while elucidating these notions. What this means is that the present gnaws the past and future, and this gnawing present is truly the present.

To elucidate the notion of temporality, Husserl makes a pre-eminent distinction among three concepts: primal impression, retention and protention. Husserl is of the firm conviction that the perception of an object, its change and succession would be impossible if consciousness were merely givenness of a pure, just now-phase of the object, and a series of unconnected points of experiencing, like the beads of a rosary. Primal impression (present phase according to Husserl) is accompanied by two horizons, namely retention and protention. Retention provides us with the consciousness of the just-past or just-having-been, allowing us realize the phase as it sinks into the past. Protention refers to the immediate future, an indeterminate and anticipatory phase, yet to occur; it is a phase about to be concretised. In other words, while retention retains our consciousness of the object of our experiences directly, promptly and immediately, protention is the direct and immediate expectation of something yet to occur. Our perceptual objects are intentional and temporal. But what about our perceptions of these very objects? Are they also temporal unities that arise, endure and eventually perish? It may be noted that Husserl no longer talks about fixed objects like tables and chairs, but about objects involving succession and change, like melody. Husserl often speaks of the acts themselves being constituted in the structure of primal impression, retention and protention, given within this temporal framework.

Husserl's elucidation of time consciousness springs from two great men, Aristotle and St. Augustine. While Aristotle's reflections on time can be found in *Book IV, Physics* (Aristotle, 1996), the latter's meditations on time can be found in *Book XI, Confessions* (St Augustine, 1997). Aristotle, in his book, points out that movement is the most essential ingredient of time, which in turn is inseparably bound with movement; it is a definite formal moment of movement. Moreover, Aristotle's *Physics* itself is a kind of metaphysical justification for movement, to define which, he holds that time is several movements in respect of, before and after, i.e., time is inseparably linked to movement. It appears Aristotle was the first person who attempted to give a definition of movement. He also pointed out that now is identical to itself and is also invariable. But on the other hand, now must be understood as a universal form of boundary limit.

St. Augustine had an introspective approach to time, grasping it as a response of our mind. His elucidation of time finds its echo in Husserl's treatment of time. His contention that temporality is an essential property of human mind reverberates in Husserl, when the latter raises queries regarding the origin, conclusion and completion of time. It is worthwhile to note that Husserl's phenomenological description of inner-time consciousness was inspired by Augustine's elucidation of time. Husserl investigates not just the human ability to grasp something that is present-now, but also his ability to remember the past phase, while anticipating the future phase. In this manner, the remembered past phase is always understood as a past consciousness, while the expected future phase as a future consciousness. The phenomenological elucidation of different dimensions of time consciousness appears to be confirmed by psychic inwardness.

Time consciousness arises in relation to perception of objects in time. Consequently, time always refers to the time of conscious perceptions, it is a conscious act. Time is not a closed totality, but an open-ended phenomenon, since it implies the present with indefinite horizons opening forward and backward. Consciousness, thus, reveals itself through the horizon structure. The analysis of time consciousness is one of the most important aspects of Husserl's *Logical Investigations*. At least three reasons can be adduced to defend this claim, namely,

1. Husserl's phenomenological inquiries were the result of investigations of intentional acts and intended objects. However, such an inquiry will remain incomplete if their temporal dimensions are ignored.

2. Perception, constitution, synthesis of identity, etc., will remain incomprehensible from a phenomenological perspective unless their temporal dimensions are examined. For example, I see an elephant. I move towards it for a closer look. I synthesize my perception of the elephant, which is organizing our various acts and aspects of perception. Perception of the elephant does not

reveal itself as an unconnected and fractured event, but a synthetically organic moment. No further explanation is required to exemplify the temporal character of phenomena such as synthesis or constitution.

3. The transcendent object is perceived as a constituted object as in the case of the elephant, which is definitely temporal, implying that temporality is a formal condition for the possibility of constitution of an object, since it is the bed rock of phenomenology.

10.2 Husserl's Study of Time-Consciousness at Different Periods

Husserl delivered a series of lectures on time consciousness during the winter session of 1904-05, which were revised and edited by his personal assistant, Ms Edith Stein between 1916-18. Husserl, who was on a holiday in Bernau, was already in the process of editing his manuscripts with the intent of publication. But when Ms. Stein approached him with the proposal to revise the same, the latter started afresh with his meditations and reflections on an entirely new branch of thoughts, now known as *Bernau Manuscripts*, dedicated entirely to reflections on time consciousness, entitled *Time and Individuation*. In fact, on 28th March 1918, Husserl wrote to Heidegger, and later to Roman Ingarden, on 5th April 1918 that he was working on a new, great work on *Time and Individuation*. However, the manuscript was not published during his lifetime.

In 1926, Husserl was on another holiday with Heidegger, during which time, the latter showed Husserl his manuscript on *Being and Time*. Husserl was very interested in it, since it was mainly on time. Subsequently, Husserl requested Heidegger to publish his own lectures on time consciousness, which Heidegger readily agreed to, on condition that he would do it after publishing his own *Being and Time* (Heidegger, 1962), which Heidegger eventually did in 1927. As promised, Heidegger reviewed Husserl's typescripts on time-consciousness lectures in April 1928, and published it under the title, *On the Phenomenology of the Consciousness of Internal Time* (Husserl, 1991b). It may be noted that Heidegger acknowledged Ms Stein's contributions, exclaiming that she was the actual editor of the time-consciousness lectures. Heidegger also added an introductory remark referring to a later publication on continuing studies on time consciousness in connection with the problem of Individuation (undertaken since 1917). But he did not include any part of it in his edited work, since he did not wish to get involved in editing Husserl's Gabelsberger stenographic manuscripts. However, he included Husserl's writings on time from 1905-10 in his edited work. This means that Husserl's time-consciousness writings in *Husserliana X* is much more than the time-consciousness lectures of Husserl edited by Heidegger, and published entitled, *On the Phenomenology of the Consciousness of Internal Time*. This is just one part of *Husserliana X*. Heidegger's edited work also includes I Part, Sections 1-45, the II Part, entitled *Addenda and Supplements of the Analysis of Time-Consciousness from 1905-10*, consisting of 13 appendixes from 1905-10. Later in 1966, Husserl Archives, Leuven University, discovered a large amount of material on time-consciousness in Husserl's personal collection, which was later appended to *Husserliana X* by its editor, Rudolf Boehm. The Husserl Archives publication of *Husserliana X* includes Heidegger's edited works, supplementary texts, i.e., appendices from 1893-1901, 1904-05, 1905-07 and 1909-11. It may have been the case that, by the time Husserl requested Heidegger to edit and publish his lectures on time consciousness, he may have even forgotten that he had himself written a number of sections on time consciousness during that period. Luckily for us, The Husserl Archives discovered all material connected to Husserl's writings on time-consciousness, and published them in *Husserliana X*.

Table 10.1 Categorization of various sections of Husserliana X (1966): On the Phenomenology of the Consciousness of Internal Time (1893-1917)

On the Phenomenology of Consciousness of Internal Time		Portions of Hua. X, then unknown to Heidegger
First part	**Second Part**	Supplementary texts setting forth the development of the problem, consisting of Husserl's writings on time consciousness from 1893-1901, 1904-05, 1905-07, 1907-09, 1909-11. All these texts were in Husserl's library
Husserl's Lectures on the Consciousness of Internal Time: Husserl's lectures (1904-05) edited and published by Heidegger in 1928	13 Appendices written by Husserl between 1905-10, added to the book by Heidegger, while editing it	

The second part of Husserl's writings on time consciousness was the *Bernau Manuscripts*. Husserl stayed in Bernau for four months during August-September 1917 and February-March 1918 along with Ms Stein, who reminded him to revise and edit the former's lectures. Instead of jointly revising the lectures, the occasion prompted him to start contemplation on time consciousness afresh, which he wrote under the title, *Time and Individuation*, about which he later wrote to Heidegger and Ingarden. Since Heidegger was unwilling to publish the stenographic manuscripts, Husserl requested his then-assistant, Eugen Fink to publish the *Bernau Manuscripts* in 1928; Fink also could not do it. Finally, a large part of it was published as Volumes 23, 33 and 34 of *Husserliana*.

Husserl's reflections on time consciousness did not stop with *Bernau Manuscripts*. He contemplated on the same from 1929-30 till 1934, later published as *C-Manuscripts* by Husserl Archives. Husserl's early static stage examination of time consciousness was dominated by transcendental principles, abstract concepts and theoretical notions. But Husserl's discovery of genetic phenomenology made a world of difference to his phenomenology, now linked to the context of concrete living and Life world. These transformations also reflected on his on-going writings on time. We find Husserl discussing the relationship of time consciousness to the pre-given of *hyletic data*. The genesis of his present writings is the living present, or the lived present. He held that a return to this realm of experience was via a reductive method, similar to the transcendental method of reduction (1913). His later writings pursue the egological analysis of constitution with concrete individual objects and perspectives over a world of objects, including subjectivity, historicity, etc., and certain central themes of *Bernau Manuscripts*.

C-Manuscripts examine the self-constitution of transcendental ego, the notion of embodiment, and becoming a part of the world. It also examines instinct, pleasure, displeasure, illness, old age, birth and death, genesis and limits of subjective experiences. Thus, Husserl's preoccupation with time took a radical turn. This reflection on time consciousness, which started in 1929-30 was published in *C-Manuscripts*, and can be found in *Husserliana VIII*. Despite divergences between topics in *Bernau Manuscripts* and *C-Manuscripts*, Husserl believed that the latter was definitely a continuation of the former; yet, he did not want them to be published in a single volume. It may also be noted that the time consciousness lectures edited by Heidegger and *Bernau Manuscripts* were very close to each other due to their theoretical concerns and transcendental analysis. *C-Manuscripts* was concerned with living contexts and Life world, originating from his genetic phenomenology, taking transcendental phenomenology to its culmination and fulfilment.

In the time consciousness lectures of 1904-05, Husserl focused exclusively on constituted experiences, referring to immanent unities. Shortly thereafter, when he discovered absolute time constituting flow, he felt compelled to re-examine his lectures in this new light and its role in the constitution of experiences in immanent time. Although Husserl realized absolute time constituting flow in 1907-09, he made no references to it in *Ideas I* (1913), confining himself exclusively to immanent unities of the 1904-05 lectures. The second major set of texts devoted to the elucidation of time consciousness is *Bernau Manuscripts* (1917-18). In *Ideas I*, Husserl spoke about three modes of time consciousness, also mentioned in *Bernau Manuscripts*, though it is in the latter that Husserl draws a sharp demarcation between immanent temporal objectivity, constituted in internal time consciousness and absolute flow. Husserl's third and the final reflections on time consciousness appear in *C-Manuscripts* (1929-30 to 1934), which also speak about the above-mentioned modes, albeit with a slight change in terminologies and concepts. He adds that primal or experiencing flow is of a deeper level in comparison to the three kinds of constitutions. It may be noted that the three levels of time consciousness are not three different kinds of consciousness, but instead, they are different modes of one and the same consciousness, to understand what it means is to live as a conscious human being. Husserl speaks about time consciousness in *Ideas I* (Husserl, 1976i, 1976b, 1976a), in *Cartesian Meditations*, in *Crisis of European Sciences*, and in *Phenomenological Psychology* (Husserl, 1977u) as well.

In the concluding part of this introduction, I wish to make the following submission. It is true that Husserl made invaluable contributions in the study of time-consciousness in three distinct phases; but I do not wish to describe three separate sections representing each. It can be observed that there was constant growth and continuous development in Husserl's lectures on Time-Consciousness from *Bernau Manuscripts* to *C-Manuscripts*, which is just an indication of Husserl's development from realist phenomenology of *Logical Investigations*, to transcendental phenomenology of Ideas, to genetic phenomenology of *Crisis of European Sciences* and beyond. Therefore, I put forth an integrative approach to Husserl's entire work. There is close similarity and homogeneity amongst various themes discussed in the Time-Consciousness Lectures and the *Bernau Manuscripts*; and the position of *C-Manuscripts* is in no way opposed to the earlier two phases, if Husserl's growth from static to genetic phenomenology is rightly understood. Different phases highlighted different aspects and introduced new terminologies, but none contradict each other; I can only find a stream of flowing discussions on temporality, ranging from 1893-94. No other philosopher has studied and analyzed the phenomenon of temporal consciousness to the extent and depth as has Husserl, resulting in several massive, original volumes of *Husserliana*. As the stream progresses, it only gains depth and width, as is the case with Husserl's philosophy in general on inculcation of new insights, fresh ideas and clear options.

10.3 Basic Notions in the Study of Time-Consciousness

Husserl's examination of time-consciousness consists in the elaborate study of three basic concepts, namely, primal impression, retention and protention. Though Husserl rarely changes the usage of retention and protention, he constantly rechristens primal impressions with new expressions and novel terminologies. In fact, he is unwilling to use the expression now, on account of its Aristotelian connotation, preferring instead to use expressions like the now-phase, the living-present, standing-streaming present, primal impression, *Nunc stans*, etc. I shall briefly dwell upon each of these three concepts.

10.3.1 Primal Impression

Primal Impression is the now-phase, the direct and immediate consciousness of the immanent object. It is the standing-streaming living present. It is not an unconscious moment, but the consciousness of the present, including its horizons of retention and protention. The living present is not separated from retention and protention, but is continuous with them, and is inseparable from its horizons of retention and protention; this is described as the landscape understanding of the present, according to Professor John Brough.

Figure 10.1 Relation among Retention, Protention and Prime impression

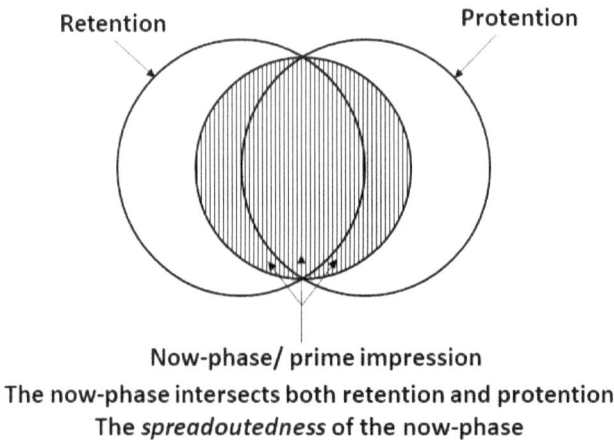

Now-phase/ prime impression
The now-phase intersects both retention and protention
The *spreadoutedness* of the now-phase

Husserl would claim that the foundation of self-awareness is the framework of primal impression-retention-protention. This is so because consciousness is a unity. The now-phase is not a location in time, but a point from which we move towards both retention and protention. The living present, or the now-phase is essentially flowing, since it is a stream. It is not entirely different from retention and protention, for it is continuously mediated with them. Every present-phase is necessarily the filling of the past, or more precisely, it is the immediately elapsed present gradually sinking into the past. We are familiar with datable, measurable, chronometric, historical, objective time in our everyday lives. Husserl's analysis is not concerned with any of these kinds of time, though he does not deny or reject them. He is concerned with the living present, a present which is lived through. He tells us that we need to apply phenomenological reduction to our naïve beliefs regarding the existence of objective time, and concentrate on lived time, as we are directly and constantly acquainted with it; he demands our return to our experience of lived time.

In order to examine the structure and role of the streaming-living-present, Husserl abandons his familiar examples of tables, chairs, trees, etc. (of *Ideas I*) in favour of objects with temporal extensions, i.e., objects whose different facets cannot appear simultaneously but emerge only in succession over a period of time, e.g., a melody implies change and succession. So how can I experience such objects that have change and succession inbuilt in them? The experience of such objects (melody, for example) would have been impossible if our consciousness were of the punctual now, allowing us to experience just the now points, and not temporal extensions or duration. But our consciousness always encompasses something that is given now and beyond now, i.e., the no longer-now and yet-to-be-present. It means that while we are conscious of the now-phase, we are also co-conscious of the no-longer and not-yet. But how so?

According to Brentano, our imagination enables us to transcend the punctual now, i.e., we perceive the now, and imagine the no-longer and the yet-to occur. But Husserl rejects this contention stating that we hear (i.e. perceive that which occurs now) rather than imagine music in its past and future, since we possess width of presence. Consider the instance when we listen to (Indian) music; the notes sā, rē, gā, mā, pā, etc., are played. Say we focus now on gā. Though we focus on gā right now, our consciousness still lingers on notes already sung, namely rē, sā. We do not imagine hearing rē and sā, rather these notes that have already been sung by the musician and heard by me, are simultaneous with gā, the notation that I hear now. This does not mean that there is no difference between our consciousness of the present hearing of gā and our awareness of rē and sā, the already heard notations. It implies the consciousness of temporal duration and not just the awareness of an isolated now, when we hear the now notes gā, rē and sā. We do not merely perceive the now-phase, but hear music that involves the present notation, the just-past, as well as future notations about to be sung. Husserl's most frequently-used term for the now-phase is primal impression. It never appears in isolation, and is always accompanied by its horizons, retentions and protentions.

Figure 10.2 Primal Impression and its Horizons

Primal impression is Husserl's term for the consciousness of the now-phase of an object. However, the now-phase is not just a now-point or a pluck, but instead it is the primal impression with its horizons towards the just-been (retention) and yet-to-come (protention). Hence primal impression is a unity of the now-phase, retention and protention. Retention and protention are not any kind of past or future with respect to primal impression, but instead, they are horizons of the former, implying that the now-phase, along with retention and protention, in their unity, constitute primal impression. Every actual phase of consciousness constitutes the primal impression-retention-protention structure. However, the now-phase, the primal impression, occupies a privileged status. It is the moment of genesis, the source of all orientations. It is the point of reference for all my temporal experiences. It is in relation to the now-phase that one can speak of past-phase (retention), or the future-phase (protention). Past-phase is something that was once a now-phase, while the future-phase is that which will become a now-phase later on.

It may be noted that the now-phase and the object given in the now-phase (for example a melody) are two distinct entities. The now-phase is the temporal moment in which the object is given. As time flows, the actual now-phase becomes a past-now. The now-phase, as a mode of temporal appearance, does not really become the past, but what was now at one time. It is not capable of independent existence and is always accompanied by its horizons, retentions and protentions. In other words, though the past-phase, future-phase and the now-phase are interdependent and distinct, they are inseparable. Husserl goes on to add that if one were aware of just the now-phase, one cannot experience temporality, for time implies a stream, a flow and not just a punctual, now moment. And, in that eventuality, one would not experience even the now-phase, for the now-phase is what it is, only in relation to its horizons, viz., retentions and protentions.

To conclude, an examination of inner time consciousness exemplifies Husserl's most profound investigations into self-awareness. He claims that self-awareness has a temporal structure, consisting of primal impression, retention and protention. It is not just the consciousness of the tone retained, but also primal impression, as it becomes the just-past. Each retention, not only retains the preceding tone, but also the preceding primal impression, i.e., the actual phase of flowing, retaining not just the tone of the just-been, but the elapsing phase of the flow as well. In short, retentional modification not only permits us to experience an enduring temporal object, it also provides us with temporal self-awareness.

10.3.2 Retention

Retention is an expression used by Husserl to designate the intentional relation of the phases of consciousness, namely, the just-past to the now-phase and to protention. Retention is not an entity we own in consciousness;

for example, we hear the just-past tone as it is retained, it does not remain existent in consciousness, like an echo, but is presented to consciousness as the just-past. It means that retention does not bring forward to consciousness what is absent, but manifests the absent as absent. Retention does not possess the real contents, i.e., the just-past tone is not actually present, but consciousness preserves it as an intentional content. It maintains the sense of what has consciously just passed. Retention is the direct and immediate consciousness of the just-past as it sinks. Retention re-presents what has previously been intended in the primal impression. The retentional moment is not directly conscious of my elapsed phases of the object; but it is directly aware of the just-elapsed phases of the temporal flow. Retention, according to Husserl, is an expression used to designate the intentional relation of the phases of consciousness to primal impression. Furthermore, more and more retentions occur when we have a phase called retention of retentions.

Retention is a particular kind of intentionality. It intends a past that has just-been. As Husserl writes, "retention is not a modification in which primal impressional data are really preserved. On the contrary, it is an intentionality with a specific characteristic of its own" (Husserl, 1969). Being retentionally aware of the just-past phase of the object does not mean that it is sensuously co-present. Retention provides us with an intuition of the just-past, retaining the sense of the just-past experience; whatever is intentionally perceived now will necessarily be what moves ahead, but still be intentionally present. This is precisely what is required if perception of succession is to be possible. The experiences in primal impression will be perceived in the next phase as the just-past, viz., retention. Sometimes Husserl calls retention as fresh memory, primary memory, short-term memory, etc. Just as primal impression is the original consciousness of the now-phase, retention is the original consciousness of the just-past phase. Only in primary memory do we see the just-past. That elapsed is still present in the primary memory as the just-past, in the sense that its being-past occurred just now. In that sense, it is not a past as such, but a presently-past, i.e., a past with intimate association with the present, implying that primary memory presents the past as just-past; it is the immediate consciousness of just having been.

The present always originates from the past. The appearance of any present phase is immediately preceded by another phase, slipping into the past simultaneously. Retention is our attitude to the present as it slips into the past. It is not an effect, but a process, bringing about continuous intentional modification to an actual present, as it falls into the just-past. Husserl explicitly insists that retentional modification presupposes an original self-manifestation, not just because consciousness is given as such, but also because retention of an unconscious content is impossible. Retention retains that which has appeared, and if nothing has appeared, there is nothing to retain. Thus, retention presupposes self-awareness. It is this modification that is intentionally modified when primal impression is transformed into self-awareness. From the example of tone and melody, tone is not only given as having just-been, but as having just-been experienced. Each phase of the flow may be said to possess three intentional moments of prime impression, retention and protention, with the retentional moment being directly aware of the just-elapsed phases of the flow. Retention retains the just-elapsed phases of the object co-related with it. The retained phases of the flow possess retentional consciousness preserved in it, through which earlier phases of the flow are preserved. Thus, we have retention of retentions.

Husserl developed his renowned theory of double intentionality while elaborating this theory of self-awareness. The theory of double intentionality is explicated in his notion of longitudinal (horizontal) and transverse intentionality; these are two intentionalities of retention that are the two sides of a single consciousness, working together, hand in glove. There is a unique flow of consciousness, in which both the unity of immanent time and the flow of consciousness itself becomes constituted. Thus, while it is possible to distinguish the directions of the flow of intentionality, it is impossible to separate them. It was the notion of absolute flow with its double intentionality that firmly established Husserl to explain how each phase of consciousness is intentionally related to the phases preceding it and following it, and through them, to the phases of the temporal object. Through its double intentionality, the flow as a succession, is at once consciousness of its own succession and of the object.

To explain retention and its double intentionality with an example, I make use of a river flowing downstream. Imagine that the river is not very clean, with things floating in it. Figure 10.3 shows A, B, C etc., depicting objects floating in the water, represented by the arrow. Flowing downstream, A pushes B, that in turn pushes C, and so on. This is a lengthwise push, and in the context of consciousness and intentionalities, it is longitudinal intentionality. Apart from the lengthwise push, there is also another push that is sidewise. A pushes X on both sides, similarly, B & Y, C & Z on both sides, etc. It is a sidewise push in the context of the flowing river, and in the context of intentionality, it is transverse intentionality. Both these intentionalities together are referred to as double intentionality by Husserl.

Figure 10.3 Relation between Retention and Double Intentionality. The arrow represents the flow of a river, while its contents, X, Y, A, B, C, etc., represent the objects floating in it

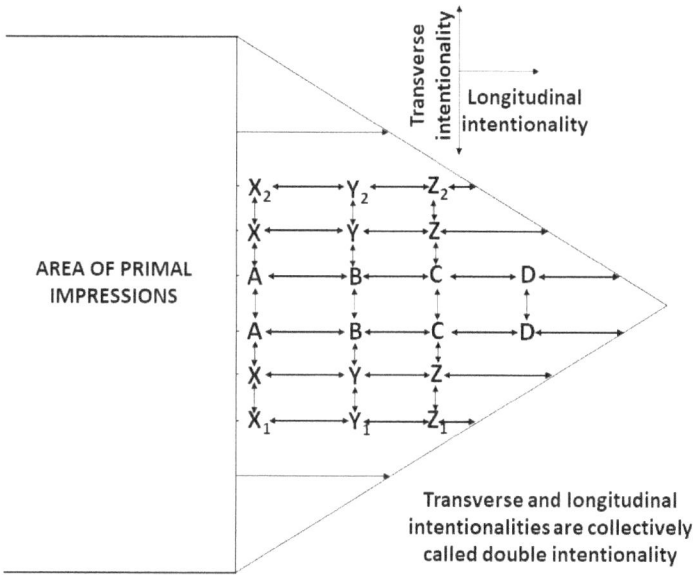

1. Primary memory or retention is not an act in itself, but a process. It is dependent on triple intentionality (the others being primal impression and protention). But recollection is also an act in successive phases. However, they can be differentiated by the various ways in which they intend their objects, i.e., retention admits only the just-past, whereas recollection does not have any such restriction or specification regarding the past.

2. Intentionality of retention represents the past, directly and immediately, as the just-past, whereas, the intentionality of recollection represents the object as such.

3. The originality of the past, arising from primary impression is retained in retention. However, recollection does not have that characteristic, since recollection can originate from the remote past as well. This means that the originality of the past is absent in the case of recollection.

4. Retention is the consciousness of the just-past. One cannot interfere in the relationship between primal impression and the just-past; one does not have the freedom to do so. In other words,

one does not have the freedom to review what has gone by. On the other hand, recollection creates a past, and my creativity comes into play in the context of recollection, in which I have freedom to intervene. Retention and recollection are essentially two different modes of temporality, but the modes of relationship of the present consciousness to retention, and to recollection are very different. In retention, the past is given immediately as a horizon; not so in recollection. Moreover, retention is related, not just to the just-past, but also to protention. As for recollection, one cannot determine the distance between primal impression and the remembered past. The distance between the primal impression and retention is that of the just-past, but there can be recollection of the recent and remote past.

10.3.3 Protention

Apart from retention, every now-phase of consciousness, i.e., primal impression, also has another horizon, namely, protention, due to which, we have a sense of the immanent future-phase of experience, i.e., the phase yet to occur. This is not expectation in the usual sense, but instead, protention is a window to a new potential now. Protentions are intentions of the phase of the object, just about to occur, which means that we always anticipate that which is about to occur. Our sense of surprise, expression wonder, awe, etc., reveal this anticipation. Since we can be surprised at any time, we always live in an anticipatory mode, i.e. we always have protentions.

Protention is a continuous opening to the new-now, because of which, 'waking life is living toward, a living that goes from now, towards the new-now.' What is protended is determined by what we have experienced immediately in retention projected into the future. Husserl in *Analyses Concerning Passive and Active Synthesis* (Husserl, 2001b) points out that protention is the shadow cast ahead. We can also say that for every primal impression, there is a backward-looking dimension. i.e., retention, as well as a forward-facing feature, as horizons of the present-phase. This forward-facing dimension is called protention.

Protention is an important aspect of temporality providing an opening towards the new and unknown, an aspect integral to intentionality. Protention is the future aspect of temporality. Husserl always conceived protention to be fundamental to intentional relation, as intentionality has a forward thrust, and protention is rooted in the forward movement of intentionality. Moreover, protention originates from primal impression as one of its horizons. This means that there is a relation between my momentary actualized intuition and my future. By moving to the future, I am able to fulfil my intuition. The moment of intuition, i.e., the present phase, extends beyond itself. Otherwise we would never strive towards a future. Striving implies intention, a forward thrust; intention cannot exist without the grasp of a future aspect of temporality. That time moves in a forward direction implies a futural dimension. My temporality has a futural direction, originating from my living present.

Husserl speaks of intentionality and its fulfilment, which can occur in the future, in the context of protention. However, fulfilment may be very indefinite. For example, I wish to go home in the evening after office hours, so I cross the road to take the bus home. The following possibilities can occur while doing so, 1) I successfully cross the road and wait for the bus to arrive; 2) the bus is late on account of a strike by the bus staff; 3) the bus arrives, but is overcrowded, which forces me to wait for the next bus; 4) I get hit by a vehicle as I cross the road, I am injured and taken to the hospital for first aid and treatment; 5) I cross the road, but notice that a vehicle hits another person, so I join the others to take him to the clinic for treatment and first aid; 6) I get into the bus, after moving a little, the bus breaks down, and I am unable to go home immediately; 8) while the bus moves ahead, someone cries out aloud saying that he has been pickpocketed, or a lady complains that someone has misbehaved with her. The driver, instead of proceeding to the destination, drives the bus to the next police station to get the criminal arrested; 9) the bus meets with an accident shortly after leaving the previous stop, and it cannot proceed any further without complying with subsequent legal formalities; 10) on the way home, I change my mind, and instead of going home, I go elsewhere, 11) and finally, I reach home. All these and several more are possibilities and instances of protention, indicative of some sort of fulfilment of intentionality. Protention is the awareness or openness to what is yet to come immediately. Retention is definite, for it refers to that which has already occurred, but protention is indefinite and empty. I expect something will unfold in it, but I am not sure about its timing, content or nature; I have no control over it. The definite thing about protention is that one of more possibilities will come to be. Hence protention is a primitive awareness of the future; in protention, I anticipate something. But how does the anticipated occur? It is anybody's guess. I listen to a wonderful piece of music, which I expect to reach its culmination and fulfilment. But the musician takes a different and unexpected course and stops it suddenly. What follows is utter silence and a great surprise. Husserl goes on to say that even complete quietude is a kind of protention of music.

10.3.4 Relationship between Retention and Protention

Retention and protention need to be distinguished from recollection and expectation. The difference between retaining a tone that has just been-sung (retention), and its recollection is something like this. For example, remembering a past holiday and looking forward to the next holiday are two different conscious acts, and therefore, intentional. However, protention and retention are dependent on events occurring now, i.e., primal impression. They do not provide us with new intended objects; they are merely horizons of primal impressions. A protention cannot have another protention as its horizon; the transcendental ego, subjectivity, alone can have a horizon. Otherwise the whole process will lead to infinite regress; so is the case with retention. On comparing retention and recollection, retention is an intuition of something just-past, whereas recollection re-presents an intentional act of a past occurrence. Retentional modification is a passive process that occurs due to the flow of consciousness, whereas recollection is an act that we actively initiate.

Husserl establishes an intimate relation between retention and protention. Primal impression stretches out to a before and after, i.e., to the past-phase and future-phase viz., to retention and protention respectively. In other words, primal impression finds its fulfilment both in retention and protention. Husserl also goes on to explain that which is anticipated is founded on the just-experienced. In other words, my participation in the present-phase anticipates my immediate future; my future is based on my current experience; my future is rooted in that which has already transpired. Each protention has a direct relationship with its fulfilment. A protention, as a fulfilled moment, passes on to retention; it is the retention of a fulfilled protention, without which there is no fulfilment, and consequently, no recognition of this achievement either. This implies that retention and protention overlap each other to some extent. Since they are integrated into one another and influence each other, they provide meaning and direction to each other in their unity. The fulfilment of an intuition is in the very living present. Retention and protention intersect the living present (*vide* Figure 10.2). However, their difference lies in the mode of their fulfilment. It is true that retentions and protentions modify each other, and their mutual modification is brought about through fulfilment.

Retention cannot be the last spoken word or the just-uttered sound; grasping a melody does not imply merely holding on to the last tone. Similarly, protention is not solely the expectation of the next word to be uttered. While retentions are made up of the totality of words already spoken (and that is how we exclaim a beautiful melody), protention is directed towards the completion of sentence or an idea. Thus, Husserl describes retentional-protentional consciousness as climbing up and sinking down, with relation to their fulfilment.

Figure 10.4 The temporal nature of Protention, Primal impression and Retention

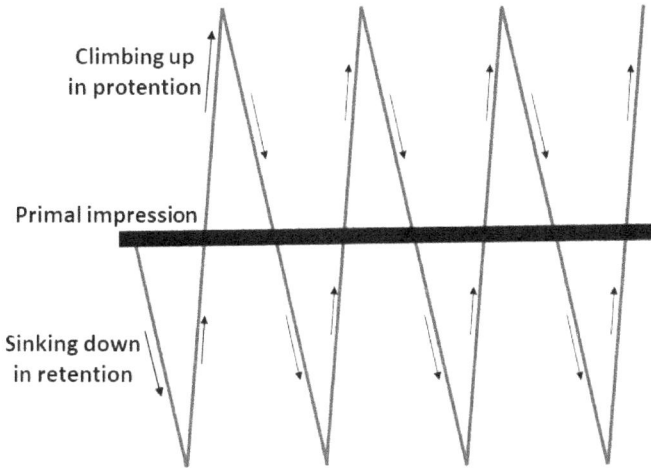

Climbing up in protention

Primal impression

Sinking down in retention

Sinking down and climbing up, i.e., retention and protention respectively, are what proffers meaning to the moment of fulfilment. What brings about retention and protention? The answer consists in establishing a relation between intentionality and its horizon, since protention and retention constitute the horizons of intentionality. The inter-relationship between consciousness and protention is explained as follows: 1) consciousness is temporal, it flows like a stream and is not empty; 2) the flow is a series of experiences and events; the flow is in terms of protention and retentions, i.e., the immediate past and immanent future; 3) protention and retention arise through the flow of consciousness, in other words, 4) protentional and retentional flow arise through the primordial flow of consciousness. Therefore, the structure of temporality exists in the very flow of consciousness, giving rise to both retention and protention.

Protention is the immediate awareness of the future. But can we actually perceive the future in protention? According to Husserl, the perception of the future, along with prime impression and retention, is forward-looking and future-oriented. He explains that it is essential for an intuition to be directed towards what is to come in perception of a temporal object. All experiences occur within the temporal domain of primal impressions, retentions and protentions, together constituting the living present, or *Nunc stans*, integral to consciousness. Both retentions and protentions emerge continuously from prime impressions, insofar as they are horizons of the latter. The present grasping of the present is prime impression, my present grasping of the past is retention, while my present grasping of the future is protention. So, what is the source of primal impression, retention and protention? They arise from the absolute flow of consciousness.

10.3.5 Absolute Consciousness

All acts of consciousness are experienced. Unlike external transcendent objects that can exist irrespective of whether one is conscious of them or not, the being of experience can exist only if it is perceived and experienced. This implies that to be conscious is to be self- conscious. My awareness of a tree includes not just my awareness of the same, but also my act of being aware of it, implying that I am not just conscious, but also self-conscious. Self-consciousness is embedded in the very act of consciousness (of an object). Experiencing is a non-objectifying self-awareness that Husserl refers to when he describes the deepest level of time consciousness, viz., the absolute flow of consciousness. Time originates from temporalization, which in turn gives rise to this absolute flow. In other words, experiencing is the primal temporalization from which all time consciousness arises.

Husserl speaks of three different modes of the same consciousness. The first mode is the consciousness of the object, i.e., intentional consciousness constituting objective time. To elaborate further, a specific tone is present in my perceptual domain now, and then sinks into the just-past. The temporal order of the tone does not totally vanish or disappear, but is retained in my consciousness. One can say that despite the fact that the tone has disappeared from the present phase of my consciousness, it is located at a certain point in time. The fact that the tone that is pinpointed at a particular location in the temporal order with a certain structure, can be remembered repeatedly, and identified with the temporal order with a certain structure that can be remembered, recalled and identified, is for Husserl, the first step toward the constitution of objective or chronometric time. This intentional act is conscious, and directed to the consciousness of the intended object. But in the intentional act, when we are aware of the intended object, the act manifests itself, i.e., the object is given through the act, and if there were no awareness of the act, the object would not be able to manifest itself. Therefore, the act, apart from being intentional (i.e., revealing the object), also characterizes an impressional consciousness.

The second mode of consciousness is subjective time, constituted in experiences, i.e., lived time. Since 1904, Husserl had the insight that the question of time would provide unity to phenomenological notions. He never doubted the veracity of this idea at any point in his philosophical career, though he questioned, and repeatedly revised several other notions that constituted the core of phenomenology. This implies that Husserl was absolutely sure about the validity and rationale of his initial insight into time. Time is the very basis of consciousness, for all conscious experiences are temporal. The most profound and essential assertion of Husserl in the elucidation of time is that, temporality is grounded in intentionality. Initially, he raises the question of objective time, but gradually moves on to the question of the difference between objective time and constituting subjective time, eventually gravitating towards consciousness constituting time or subjective time, and bracketing and reducing objective time. Husserl's primordial contention with time is that, lived time is subjective time. This is, strictly speaking, the domain of lived experiences. Bracketing of objective time and phenomenological reduction are used to reveal subjective time, i.e., the temporality of time within subjectivity. It is only when phenomenological reduction is applied to objective time that pre-empirical or subjective or constituting time appears within the flow of consciousness. Since transcendental ego constitutes time, it is said to be absolute, i.e., it transcends time. This implies that subjective time is constituted in absolute consciousness. This contention of Husserl is very controversial. But what is absolute consciousness?

The third mode of consciousness is absolute time consciousness, constituting not just subjective time, but also itself, temporally. This absolute time consciousness is unaffected by changes occurring in objective time; it does not arise or perish like intentional, objective time. Its temporality is also different from the subjective time of experiences; although absolute-time is subjective, it is self-temporalizing. In other words, it is different from the subjective time of constituted experiences, and therefore described as absolute-time; it is self-constituting time. He also goes on to say that absolute time is a-temporal or supra-temporal, to distinguish it from the temporality of objective and subjective time. This is inner-time-consciousness.

Therefore, Husserl operates on three different modes of time, namely,

1. The objective time of the intentional object, which is the temporizing of an intentional object.

2. Subjective time is the time of acts and experiences; it is the time of a melody, for example. It is the temporality constituted in our experiences.

3. Absolute time consciousness or inner-time consciousness, which is temporality temporalizing itself. This self-temporalisation of the transcendental ego gives rise to primal impression, retention or protention, implying that these three, in their unity, constitute absolute consciousness, as consciousness cannot but be temporal.

Absolute or inner-time consciousness creates three constitutive elements. As absolute time consciousness, I am my experiences; there is an identity between myself and my experiences, cemented by my self-temporalization of myself. Inner time consciousness is pre-reflective. This means that the non-thematic awareness of the act of consciousness and the act itself, is constituted in inner time consciousness, and brought to awareness via self-awareness. It is also called inner-time consciousness, as it belongs to the inner-most consciousness manifested in terms of primal impression, retention and protention.

Inner-time consciousness involves the following three points simultaneously,

1. Inner-time consciousness is the self-awareness of the stream of consciousness. It is absolute consciousness or pre-reflective self-awareness. It is not an intentional act in itself, but an intrinsic feature of our consciousness.

2. Awareness of temporal objects in one's own subjectivity, i.e., subjective, reflective consciousness.

3. Intentional consciousness of transcendent objects or objective time.

If acts of consciousness are temporally constituted, then are the acts temporal as well? This question leads to an infinite regress, as it leads to the question of whether these temporally constituted acts are further constituted, i.e., every act is constituted by a further act, or infinite regress. According to Husserl, time consciousness is inseparable from self-awareness. It is pre-reflective; it is a mode of awareness, without being explicitly reflective; this pre-reflective mode of self-awareness and time consciousness are inseparably and structurally joined together in such a way that they are one and the same, and cannot exist without the other. They are two modes of one and the same consciousness. For example, my awareness of hearing a melody, now gradually elapsing, is inseparable from my awareness of myself as hearing the melody, gradually elapsing into retention. This implies that both occur simultaneously, 1) the melody I hear elapses gently into retention, and 2) my awareness of myself as the hearer of the melody. These two modes of awareness merge into one single awareness, my awareness of myself, and of hearing the melody, like the two sides of a coin. It implies that my awareness of myself is through my awareness of my experiences, and therefore my self-awareness and my awareness of experiences are two sides, or two modes of the same awareness. I have distinguished them from one another, but they cannot be separated from each other. To summarize, both the object, i.e., melody, and the act of consciousness (of the object) elapse together; though both are distinguishable, they are inseparable. They are the two modes of the same consciousness of elapsing.

Since *Logical Investigations*, or even before that, since 1893, Husserl was aware that the perceptual act is temporal. Accordingly, Husserl remarked that it belongs to the essence of perception of a temporal object, that the object itself is temporal. It demonstrates that while Husserl acknowledges the act of perception of an object as temporal, he does not make any attempt to examine the nature and structure of that awareness until he introduces, at a later stage, the theory of absolute consciousness. In this context, he writes the following in his *Time Consciousness Lectures*. Perception is immanent to consciousness. This perceptual awareness belongs to a deeper level of immanence, i.e., to the foundational or absolute level, beyond which one can go no further. It is this dimension, understood as the consciousness of an immanent, temporal object that Husserl examines in the text to grasp absolute consciousness. This means that our usual, ordinary perception has a double implication. The perception of the transcendent object (e.g., the melody) will be followed by an immanent perception (of the melody) in consciousness, which is the rationale of the apprehension of melody. The content and the apprehension that constitute the perception of the immanent temporal object are not identical with the object itself.

Husserl also discusses the nature and structure of awareness that characterizes absolute flow. Absolute flow has three phases of temporality, prime impression, retention and protention; only one among them is actual, while the others are either elapsed or yet-to-come. The actual phase of the absolute flow has triple intentionalities with respect to the three phases of temporal moments. In the case of perception, a transcendent object is perceived through the perceptual act. I am aware of it, it is experienced or intended. This experiencing of the act is immanent and extended in immanent or subjective time, and brought about as an accomplishment of absolute consciousness, through retention, primal impression and protention, that constitute absolute flow. The absolute flow, as such, does not have content. And, each phase of the flow is purely and simply the consciousness of the immanent object. The content of the absolute flow provides the consciousness of primal impression, retention and protention of the immanent temporal objects.

There is one unique flow of consciousness in which both unity of the immanent object, and the unity of flow of consciousness are constituted into one. Thus, while it is possible to distinguish between the two different kinds of consciousness, it is impossible to separate them. It was the notion of absolute flow that enabled Husserl to explain how each phase of consciousness, primal impression, retention and protention, was intentionally related to the phases preceding and following it. Husserl also points out that, in using the word flow in absolute flow, he employs a metaphor from William James. The metaphor is useful since it conveys the fact that absolute flow is constant and continuous, and not still at any moment. Husserl also thinks that we are aware of the flow in its flowing character.

It is important to stress that the original time constituting process operating through absolute flow is nothing more than absolute temporalization. This means that primal impression, retention and protention do not belong to the flow as properties, but instead, these three, in their unity, constitute absolute flow. They embody primal flow in the various ways of constituting. Retention, for example, is absolute flow expressing what has just elapsed, while protention is absolute flow experiencing what is just about to occur. Therefore absolute flow is the way in which consciousness constitutes time at the primordial level.

The flow is absolute subjectivity. Husserl writes (Husserl, 1966), 'the flow is the primal flowing. It is in fact pre-time, for it generates temporality without itself being a temporal flow.' To characterize primal flow, Husserl uses expressions such as pre, quasi, primal, original, etc., to differentiate this change from every other change. In other words, the originating change, being absolute, being ultimate, is different from every other change. Elsewhere, Husserl points out (Husserl, 2001e) that primal flow is pre-being, pre-temporal. It is the absolute, timeless consciousness whose moments are beyond the ordinary notions of temporality, in the sense that all temporality originates from it. And, hence, it is not like ordinary temporality. The three moments, primal impression, retention and protention escape time and constitute subjective time as experiences. But are they temporal? The absolute flow is self-constituting and self-temporalizing. On closer look, it appears to be a dangerous position, for it suggests that it is no more temporal. Then one can ask: how can non-temporal flow give rise to temporal flow? Simultaneously, it needs to be pointed out that Husserl is ambivalent about the temporality or non-temporality of primal impression, retention and protention. Husserl's phenomenology originated with the assertion that consciousness is primarily and fundamentally temporal. And now, he speaks of the original or primal flow of consciousness as non-temporal, while, its moments, primal impression, retention and protention are temporal.

Whatever be the case, one thing is certain, flow cannot exist independently of the experiencing; it constitutes three moments. In the other way around, the experiencing exists only within the framework of flow. However, the flow and what it represents, viz., the experienced, cannot be identical, but are distinguishable. The flow is my subjectivity and what is experienced is due to the intentional character of the subjectivity, i.e., the consciousness that I am, constitutes my experiences.

"The living present, i.e., my life," writes Husserl (Husserl, 1999) "is an unbroken unity of primal flowing temporalisation". This means that Husserl's phenomenology of time consciousness is an attempt to understand conscious life in its identity with my temporal awareness. In *C-Manuscripts*, Husserl characterizes my living present as the standing flowing present. The present, here, represents absolute temporalizing flow, implying that the living present signifies the actual phase of flowing consciousness. It is the phase that indicates my existence. The living present is where I always stand, i.e., exist or remain. It is the standing, living present, or *Nunc stans*, namely, the moment from which consciousness reaches out to what is, what has been, and what will be. Therefore, *Nunc stans* is not static, but moves out from itself to retention and protention. It is the constantly present, where I live. It is the fullness of time, it is the moment, as Kierkegaard would put it. It is my concrete being, it is my concrete presence, my concrete flowing (Husserl, 1999). Since *Nunc stans* is the living moment of absolute flow possessing the three-fold structure of primal impression, retention and protention, it reaches out beyond itself to what has been, and to what will be. It also means I transcend my enduring present in each moment of my existence.

Right from the beginning of phenomenology, Husserl insisted that consciousness must transcend itself, and it is precisely here that we can find this occurring. *Nunc stans* is the gateway to what exists, what existed, and what will exist. Husserl describes *Nunc stans* as both flowing and abiding. Nothing remains static in the flow, which is originally a time constituting process. Yet it is not a process, in the sense that individual events are flowing or in the process of flowing. Individual events, whether transcendent or immanent, can begin, accelerate or slow down and finally end; not so in primal process. It exists with consciousness, and neither does it slow down nor quicken. It flows and flows, constantly and continuously.

10.4 Conclusions

Husserl has never claimed to have solved the cumbersome problem of time once and for all. He just wishes to lift the veil of the mystery of our consciousness of time so that the human experience of time can be articulated a little more clearly. It is with this intention that he writes that there is no beginning or end to conscious life, in the sense of one being aware of a beginning or an end. Consciousness, in the fundamental sense, is something deeper than having particular acts of consciousness that begin or end. My life as a conscious individual, an ego, is continuous all the time, ever open to new possibilities and experiences. The fundamental sense of protention is that, I am not identical to any acts of my past or present experiences. I stand beyond them. I exist as the flowing present, while my acts are caught in the flowing temporalization. They begin and end, whereas the flowing consciousness does not have a beginning or an end; it flows continuously. Death signals the end of conscious life. But in the absence of consciousness, one could never be aware that conscious life has ended. I can voluntarily undertake an act. However, I cannot voluntarily be conscious of the end of consciousness, i.e., death. Hence the final assertion of time consciousness is the sense of ourselves being aware of a sort of continuity of existence, i.e., a consciousness of continuity of self in the face of the relentless flow of time. I am living through a particular experience; it will eventually cease. But as long as we experience anything at all, we will be aware of ourselves, continuing ourselves.

This can be understood with the help of the metaphor of a river flowing downstream. Let us assume that we are unaware of its point of origin or its demise. It flows on, running its course constantly, continuously and unceasingly. This, from Heidegger's point of view, would mean that the flow is from nothingness to nothingness. One throws an object into the river. That which is thrown is a conscious individual human being, i.e., a transcendental self. Heidegger points out that *Dasein* is thrown into an existence. The object floats and flows along with several others in the river, subsequently sinking into its bottom. Sinking signals the death of the self (*Dasein*). Just because the self ("object," *Dasein*) sinks to the bottom of the river, nobody assumes that the river has stopped flowing. It flows and runs endlessly. The ever-flowing river signifies absolute flow. All that Husserl has accomplished is to substitute absolute consciousness for the constantly flowing river of consciousness, and subjectivity or (transcendental) ego for the object.

Before we conclude, I wish to bring up two points. It appears that for Husserl, absolute flow is both temporal and a-temporal; he has a lot of ambiguities regarding the same. If subjectivity is temporal, no doubt, it is finite. But if it is non-temporal or a-temporal, does it mean that it is eternal? When subjectivity is both temporal and a-temporal, it does not imply a contradiction. From my perspective, contradictions occur only in the domain of logic (Kierkegaard) and not in the domain of absolute living realities like subjectivity. As certain early Hindu and Christian mystics pointed out, when we deal with a reality that combines in itself the opposites, we are not in the domain of contradictions, but rather, in the domain of mysticism. Does this mean that Husserl became a mystic of subjectivity while engaging in the final analysis of temporality? True, Husserl does not claim it anywhere. Husserl has not raised any such issues, and therefore, we cannot expect any answer from his writings. But in the light of his writings, such a hypothesis cannot be ruled out; we can only raise the question and speculate over it endlessly.

Transcendental ego, in the final analysis, is a creature beyond creatureliness in the sense that, it is its own creator and preserver. It accounts for its own presence. In the Christian conception of God, God, who is his own creator, has eternal presence, devoid of a past and future, or in other words, the past and future have been absorbed into the eternal presence, similar to a sublimated version of the gnawing present. i.e., a presence that encapsulates the past (retention) and future (protention). Is the eternal self-presence of God comparable to the non-temporal presence of subjectivity? I would put it like this, in his mystical journey, Husserl has covered a lot of ground to envisage a non-temporal presence of subjectivity, comparable to the eternal presence of God. What kind of mysticism can we attribute to Husserl, if at all we accept Husserl to be a kind of mystic? Well, there are various kind of mysticisms depending on religious traditions or one's philosophical commitments. I would suggest Husserl's kind to be a transcendental mysticism of subjectivity, in lieu of his transcendental philosophy.

10.5 References

Aristotle. (1996). *Physics: Book IV* (D. Bostock, Ed.; R. Waterfield, Trans.). Oxford University Press, USA.

Heidegger, M. (1962). *Being and Time* (J. Macquarrie & E. Robinson, Trans.). Harper & Row, Publishers, New York.

Husserl, E. (1966). Der Zeitkonstituierende Fluβ Als Absolute Subjektivität. In *Vorlesungen zur Phänomenologie des inneren Zeitbewusstseins: Edmund Husserl-Gesammelte Werke Band-X* (p. 75). Martinus Nijhoff Publishers, The Hague.

Husserl, E. (1969). Einheit des Zeitdinges als Identischen der Veränderung oder Unveränderung. (Sommerferien 1905). In R. Bernet (Ed.), *Texte zur Phänomenologie des inneren Zeitbewusstseins (1893-1917), Husserliana: Edmund Husserl-Gesammelte Werke Band X* (p. 118). Springer.

Husserl, E. (1976a). Continuation. The three-fold horizon of mental processes as at the same time the horizon of reflection on mental processes, Section 82. In W. R. B. Gibson (Trans.), *Ideas: General Introduction to Pure Phenomenology* (pp. 195–196). Humanities Press.

Husserl, E. (1976b). Reflection as a fundamental peculiarity of the sphere of mental processes. Studies in reflection, Section 77. In W. R. B. Gibson (Trans.), *Ideas: General Introduction to Pure Phenomenology* (pp. 174–176). Humanities Press.

Husserl, E. (1976c). Seizing upon the unitary stream of mental processes as 'Idea', Section 83. In W. R. B. Gibson (Trans.), *Ideas: General Introduction to Pure Phenomenology* (pp. 199–202). Humanities Press.

Husserl, E. (1977). *Phenomenological Psychology, Lectures, Summer Semester, 1925* (J. Scanlon, Trans.). Springer Netherlands.

Husserl, E. (1991). *On the Phenomenology of the Consciousness of Internal Time (1893-1917): Husserliana: Edmund Husserl-Collected Works, Volume 4* (J. B. Brough, Trans.). Springer Netherlands.

Husserl, E. (1999). *The Idea of Phenomenology: Husserliana: Edmund Husserl-Collected Works, Volume 8* (L. Hardy & R. Bernet, Trans.). Kluwer Academic Publishers.

Husserl, E. (2001b). Cognitive interest and striving for knowledge, Section 52. In A. J. Steinbock (Trans.), *Analyses Concerning Passive and Active Synthesis, Lectures on Transcendental Logic: Husserliana: Edmund Husserl-Collected Works: Volume 9* (pp. 288–289). Kluwer Academic Publishers.

Husserl, E. (2001e). Hat der Bezug des zeitkonstituierenden Flusses auf die Kerndaten noch die Form einer Auffassung von einem reellen lnhalt? In R. Bernet & D. Lohmar (Eds.), *Die Bernauer Manuskripte über das Zeitbewusstsein (1917/18): Husserliana: Edmund Husserl-Gesammelte Werke Band XXXIII* (p. 179). Kluwer Academic Publishers, Dordrecht, The Netherlands; Boston.

St Augustine. (1997). Book IX: Death and Rebirth. In J. E. Rotelle (Ed.), & M. Boulding (Trans.), *The Confessions: The works of St. Augustine, A Translation for the 21st century.* New City Press.

10.6 Further reading

Bernet, R. (2009). Husserl's Early Time-Analysis in Historical Context. *Journal of the British Society for Phenomenology, 40*(2), 117–154.

Bernet, R. (2010). Husserl's new Phenomenology of Time consciousness in the Bernau Manuscripts. In D. Lohmar & Y. Ichiro (Eds.), *On Time-New Contributions to the Husserlian Phenomenology of Time: Phaenomenologica 197* (pp. 1–19). Springer.

Brough, J. B. (2010). Notes on the Absolute Time-Constituting Flow of Consciousness. In D. Lohmar & Y. Ichiro (Eds.), *On Time-New Contributions to the Husserlian Phenomenology of Time: Phaenomenologica 197* (pp. 21–49). Springer.

Chernyakov, A. (2002). *The Ontology of Time: Being and Time in the Philosophies of Aristotle, Husserl and Heidegger.* Springer-Science+Business Media, B.V.

De Warren, N. (2014). Time. In S. Luft & S. Overgaard (Eds.), *The Routledge Companion to Phenomenology* (pp. 190–201). Routledge (Taylor & Francis), London and New York.

Heidegger, M. (1978). The Concept of Time in the Science of History. *Journal of the British Society for Phenomenology, 9*(1), 3–10.

Husserl, E. (1970). The clarification of the transcendental problem and the related function of psychology, Sections 28-55. In D. Carr (Trans.), *The Crisis of European Sciences and Transcendental Phenomenology* (pp. 103–190). Northwestern University Press.

Husserl, E. (1976a). Apprehension of the unitary stream of experience as 'Idea', Section 83. In W. R. B. Gibson (Trans.), *Ideas: General Introduction to Pure Phenomenology* (pp. 239–240). Humanities Press.

Husserl, E. (1976b). Continuation. The three-fold limit of experience, as at once the limit of reflexion upon experience, Section 82. In W. R. B. Gibson (Trans.), *Ideas: General Introduction to Pure Phenomenology* (p. 238). Humanities Press.

Husserl, E. (1976c). Reflexion as a fundamental peculiarity of the sphere of mental processes. Studies in reflection, Section 77. In W. R. B. Gibson (Trans.), *Ideas: General Introduction to Pure Phenomenology* (pp. 212–214). Humanities Press.

Husserl, E. (1977). Development of the Constitutional Problems Pertaining to the Transcendental Ego Himself, Sections 37-39: IV Meditation. In D. Cairns (Trans.), *Cartesian meditations: An Introduction to Phenomenology* (pp. 72–80). Martinus Nijhoff Publishers, The Hague.

Husserl, E. (1991). *On the Phenomenology of the Consciousness of Internal Time (1893-1917): Husserliana: Edmund Husserl-Collected Works, Volume 4* (J. B. Brough, Trans.). Springer Netherlands.

Liangkang, N. (2010). Horizontal-Intention: Time, Genesis, History-Husserl's Understanding of Their Immanent Relationship. In D. Lohmar & Y. Ichiro (Eds.), *On Time-New Contributions to the Husserlian Phenomenology of Time: Phaenomenologica 197* (pp. 187–211). Springer.

Lohmar, D. (2010). On the Constitution of the Time of the World: The Emergence of Objective Time on the Ground of Subjective Time. In D. Lohmar & Y. Ichiro (Eds.), *On Time-New Contributions to the Husserlian Phenomenology of Time: Phaenomenologica 197* (pp. 115–136). Springer.

Luis, N. (2010). Temporality, Stream of Consciousness and the I in The Bernau Manuscripts. In D. Lohmar & I. Yamaguchi (Eds.), *On Time-New Contributions to the Husserlian Phenomenology of Time: Phaenomenologica 197* (pp. 213–230). Springer Netherlands.

Morrison, R. P. (1978). Kant, Husserl, and Heidegger on Time and the Unity of 'Consciousness'. *Philosophy and Phenomenological Research, 39*(2), 182–198.

Rodemeyer, L. (2003). Developments in the Theory of Time-Consciousness: An Analysis of Protention. In D. Welton (Ed.), *The New Husserl: A Critical Reader* (pp. 125–156). Indiana University Press.

Rodemeyer, L. M. (2010). A Return to Retention and Recollection: An Analysis of the Possible Mutual Influence of Consciousness and its Content. In D. Lohmar & Y. Ichiro (Eds.), *On Time-New Contributions to the Husserlian Phenomenology of Time: Phaenomenologica 197* (pp. 231–249). Springer.

Sakakibara, T. (2010). Reflection Upon the Living Present and the Primal Consciousness in Husserl's Phenomenology. In D. Lohmar & Y. Ichiro (Eds.), *On Time-New Contributions to the Husserlian Phenomenology of Time: Phaenomenologica 197* (pp. 251–271). Springer.

Smith, D. A. (2003). Second Meditation. In *Husserl and the Cartesian Meditations* (pp. 60–107). Routledge (Taylor & Francis), London and New York.

Stefano, M. (2010). The Temporalizations of the Absolute Flow of Time-Consciousness. In D. Lohmar & I. Yamaguchi (Eds.), *On Time-New Contributions to the Husserlian Phenomenology of Time: Phaenomenologica 197* (pp. 169–185). Springer Netherlands.

Thomas, V. C. (1990). The Development of Time Consciousness from Husserl to Heidegger. In A.-T. Tymieniecka (Ed.), *The Moral Sense and Its Foundational Significance: Self, Person, Historicity, Community: Analecta Husserliana* (pp. 347–360). Springer, Dordrecht.

Thomas, V. C. (1997). Lived Time: Some Reflections. In S. J. Kozhamthadam (Ed.), *Interrelations and Interpretations* (pp. 246–264). Intercultural Publications, New Delhi.

Chapter 11

Conclusions

This concluding chapter has two parts. Part one brings to a close my discussions on Husserl's phenomenology, summarizing the chapters in the simplest possible manner, with minimal phenomenological jargon and complicated idioms. Part two is a brief assessment of the book, a comparison, if you will, wherein I wish to highlight how this book is different from others that I have studied on Husserl's philosophy in the recent past.

Phenomenology: A Study of Self and Beyond (Chapter 2), describes the fundamental aspects of phenomenology. Phenomenology, be it of Husserl, Heidegger, Sartre, Merleau-Ponty, or for that matter of anybody else, in the final analysis, is to a great extent, a study of self. However, every phenomenologist interprets self in his own way, differing from others in several ways. For Husserl, self is the transcendental ego, whereas for Heidegger, it is *Dasein*. Sartre would consider being for-it-self as the self. True, each one understands self in his own way. Each one has a different approach to, or a dissimilar perspective of self, interpreting it differently depending on each one's ingenuity. The common, connecting thread amongst them is their capacity to assign meaning to situations that they confront, which is arrived at by various processes and methods. While Husserl suggests phenomenological reduction, Heidegger suggests something else, viz., hermeneutic phenomenology to assign meaning. Due to Heidegger's, Sartre's and Kierkegaard's preeminent turn towards ontology and existential characteristics of the self, all of them speak of assigning meaning to the existential situation of the self. On the other hand, Husserl, due to his epistemological prerogatives, speaks about attributing meaning to objects, although this trend undergoes changes, both in his genetic phase and post-*Crisis* period. This may be because Husserl realized that there was a need to humanize transcendental philosophy in general, and transcendental ego in particular.

Temporality is another common characteristic that forms the core of self. Husserl wrote about time even before the commencement of his formal phenomenology period. He considered his insight into time to be ever valid, and while he continued working upon, revising several other phenomenological notions, he never altered his basic insights on time, believing that it unified all the other notions of phenomenology. Heidegger's magnum opus, *Being and Time* considers time to be the horizon for the revelation of Being. Time links Being and *Dasein*, and this link, as Heidegger points out, is the *'da'* (there) of

'Sein' (Being), where Being reveals itself in the most appropriate manner. Not only in his major work *Being and Nothingness*, but throughout his existential works, be it philosophy, novels, short stories, one-act plays, essays or interviews, Sartre's major concern was time and temporality. The discussion of time and finitude brings forth its various common characteristics such as being born at a particular time and place, living a particular kind of life, death as the end of life, etc., to be considered. These two notions are discussed in detail in this book (*vide* Chapters 3 and 10). Since this book is devoted exclusively to Husserl, Heidegger, Sartre and Kierkegaard are beyond the scope of this study. Certain other points of discussion in this chapter are: phenomenology as a descriptive and transcendental science, a rigorous, though not an exact science, devoid of (certain kinds) of presuppositions. This is followed by the origin and use of the term phenomenon, along with a working definition of phenomenology. Though Husserl never defined phenomenology, it is important for students being initiated into the same.

Consciousness and Intentionality: The Perspective of Husserl (Chapter 3) examines intentionality as the primary feature of consciousness. What is the nature of these entities? Are they the same, or two different entities? Scholars vary in their opinions, some holding them as a unified entity, while others consider them to be different. In my opinion, they are not two entities that are inseparable, but distinguishable. This is followed by an investigation of Brentano's theory of intentionality, differentiating object and relational theories of intentionality, Several serious flaws of the former are discussed, which can be sorted out only by means of Husserl's relational theory of intentionality. Object and content are distinguished using an example. Content gives meaning and direction to the object. It is the implicit object, conferring it with meaning. In the final analysis, Husserl identifies content as *noema*, pointing out that richer the content, richer the object. Content also constitutes the horizon of the object. Several prominent characteristics of intentionality are posited, along with an enumeration of intentionality in the context of human body, referring to Mohanty's essay dealing with twenty theses on intentionality. Chapters 2 & 3 are pretty generalistic, not based on any particular phase of Husserl's philosophy; they have an overarching scope. They study the fulcrum or crux of phenomenology, for these notions of consciousness and intentionality form the basis for a deeper understanding into the study of phenomenology.

Husserl's Investigation into Meaning (Chapter 4) is the start of a textual study of the different phases in Husserl's phenomenology. Phenomenology, be it Husserl's transcendental phenomenology, or Heidegger's hermeneutic phenomenology, or Sartre's descriptive phenomenology, Merleau-Ponty's existential phenomenology, is a search for meaning, not of meaning of expressions, sentences or idioms, but a search for meanings that are strictly personal and absolutely subjective, which can be summarized as, the question is not what it means, rather what it means *to me*. Husserl looks for meaning by examination of the issues of generalities and universalities, pointing out that meaning is the meaning of an act; it is an ideal entity. No other claim of Husserl has been subjected to so much of unfavourable criticism as this. Husserl also describes the objectivity of meaning in terms of identity, communicability and repeatability. He initially speaks about the meaning of linguistic expressions, and subsequently moves on to monologue, soliloquy and silent, inner dialogue, an important transition from communicative to confirmative speech, sowing the seeds of eidetic reduction already in *Logical Investigations*. This transition also strives to demonstrate that meanings have reference only in living contexts of humans. This chapter also includes certain theoretical discussions on meaning and essence, meaning and reference, etc. Another major point of discussion is whether Husserl was dependent on Frege to correct his pre-phenomenological leanings towards psychologism. My answer, based on the authoritative study of Mohanty, is that Husserl realized his erroneous position about the same, long before he came to know about Frege's position. In fact, Husserl realized his mistake while reviewing Schröder's book, shortly after publishing *Philosophy of Arithmetic*. It was more of a self-realization, helped by Lotze, that enabled Husserl to overcome psychologism. Does Husserl lean towards Plato while speaking of ontology of meaning? Though Husserl uses the expression, ontology of meaning, he goes far beyond Plato with respect to meaning, while using the expression, and it is due to lack of a better terminology, that he uses the same. The chapter concludes with a discussion on meaning intuition and meaning fulfilment.

Natural Attitude, Epoché and Reductions: Transcendental Phenomenological Method of Husserl (Chapter 5) is very crucial in Husserl's phenomenology, as he always held it impossible to do proper phenomenology without reductions. As far back in 1931, when Husserl wrote the Author's Preface to the English edition of *Ideas I*, he insisted on the absolute necessity to perform reductions in phenomenological procedure. The lack of phenomenological reductions in Heidegger's *Being and Time* was the primary reason as to why Husserl considered it a work in 'phenomenological anthropology'. This insistence on reductions also lost him most of his followers. Heidegger and the other followers considered Husserl the founder of phenomenology, but found their own paths later on due to the latter's restrictions imposed via reductions. They instead followed a method of philosophizing derived from Husserl's article for *Encyclopaedia Britannica*, declaring themselves to be phenomenologists of their own brand. But Husserl did not relent from his stance on phenomenological reductions, considering them crucial to phenomenology. Natural attitude can be metaphysical or epistemological. Husserl aims to suspend them all, since they constitute presuppositions. Elimination of presupposition does not mean that all presuppositions are abrogated or abolished, but instead rendered explicit, as best as possible. The non-acceptance of presuppositions is described as bracketing (or epoché), indicating Husserl's inclination towards mathematics, which was his doctoral discipline. But what is the reason for his insistence on suspension of natural attitude and bracketing? It strives to establish the primacy and pre-eminence of consciousness and its source, viz., the transcendental ego.

I am of the view that there are four reductions, eidetic, psychological, transcendental, and reduction by way of Life world. There are some commentators who describe eidetic as existential reduction, since existence is reduced in order to establish the priority of essence, for phenomenology after all, is an eidetic science, a science of essence. One point to be noted is that the word, 'reduction' is used in different senses in the context of reductions. While it refers to the suspension of existence and beliefs in eidetic and psychological reductions, it refers to the assigning of meaning, rather than reducing anything in transcendental reduction. In the context of reduction by Life world, it is used to expand individual meanings to a community, i.e., arriving at a communitarian meaning. There were also progressive additions to the number of reductions as Husserl advanced in his study and research in phenomenology. He spoke of just one reduction, the eidetic reduction in 1907, in *Idea of Phenomenology*, while in 1910, in *The Basic Problems of Phenomenology*, he discussed both eidetic and psychological reductions. In 1913, in *Ideas I*, he spoke of three, namely, eidetic, psychological and transcendental reductions. He went on to append a fourth reduction in 1936, in *Crisis of European Sciences*, namely reduction by way of Life world. But confusions seem to arise with regard to the number of reductions in the course of writing the *Crisis of European Sciences*, whence he spoke of eight reductions, some of them beyond the scope of phenomenology. In *Cartesian Meditations*, he spoke about transcendental-psychological reduction, which begs the question, are they two or just one reduction? In the end, Husserl's inconsistency cost him a lot of his followers, students and commentators. For example, amongst several others, Joseph Kochelmans, Iso Kern, Søren Overgaard, Sebastian Luft, Ronald Smith, Robert Walsh examined the notion of reductions, but none of them could agree on a final number of reductions, and even if they did, they differed with respect to the number and method of reductions. I am sure that there will be scholars who will disagree with me as well with regard to the number of reductions, though I have based myself exclusively on Husserl's well-established texts.

Husserl's Treatment of Noesis & Noema: *Conflict and Convergence* (Chapter 6) deals with how consciousness can be involved with an object. Brentano held that the relation between the physical and immanent object is casual, which Husserl was not prepared to accept. He contended that the directedness of consciousness or intentionality to an object is intrinsic to consciousness, and does not require a material, physical object. An intentional object is called *noema*, which is also the immanent object, the content, or the meaning of the object. This is illustrated by means of a chair as an example, which appears differently, depending on the situation. In other words, *noema* speaks of the specific way that the object appears to us; it is the object as…, it is the perceived object. While Husserl refers to *noema* as the so-called object-pole of consciousness in *Ideas I*, *noesis* is the subject-pole or the transcendental ego, which is that beyond which no phenomenological reduction can penetrate; it is the end of phenomenological analysis. Gurwitsch, with textual support from *Ideas I* and a few other of Husserl's writings, further developed the notion of *noema* as a perceived object. But Føllesdal proposed his theory of *noema* as an intentional entity through twelve theses based on *Ideas III* and further textual support from *Ideas I*, but with no reference to Gurwitsch's momentous contributions on the same. In my opinion, Føllesdal does not make much of an impact in the study of *noema*. While Gurwitsch's position is substantial and fully valid, Føllesdal's is just complimentary to the former, adding a logical dimension to the same, which was missing from the former's position. Other scholars such as Smith and McIntyre, McKenna, Langsdrof, Larabee have tried to further Husserl's understanding of *noema*, though their contributions are minor and negligible. In conclusion, Gurwitsch remains the towering figure in the interpretation and development of Husserl's notion of *noema*, while Føllesdal manages to lend a little logical support.

Husserl's Examination of Lived Body (Chapter 7) studies the human body, a subject not traditionally discussed in philosophy, since our body is considered mundane and a material thing of the empirical environment, a part of the transcendent realm over consciousness, according to Descartes. But Husserl's phenomenological approach considers that the human body has a very important role to play. He deals with the human body at three different levels, my subjectivity, the others' living body or his subjectivity, and finally, the material, empirical, physical body. Husserl began his examinations of body as early as 1907, in his lectures on *Thing and Space*. He distinguishes the lived human body, i.e., *Leib* and the material, physical body, i.e., *Körper*. While *Leib* is my living body, my life, my body with spirit, the ego, I, myself, *Körper* is the external, physical, material body, studied in naturalistic attitude and natural sciences such as medicine.

Spirit and spiritual unities are fundamental in personalistic attitude, making us members of social communities and organized institutions; thus, *Leib* is expressive of the person and personhood. The study of human body from a phenomenological attitude deals with the constitutional primacy of our living body, i.e., I can constitute the living body of others only when I have constituted my own. Our body belongs, not just to the constituted, transcendent, realm, but also to the constituting, transcendental realm. We can distance ourselves and move around all other objects except our body. Similarly, we can only sense our bodies internally, we are incapable of perceiving our bodies externally, which only others can, e.g., a physician. *Leib* has several characteristics. It is the organ of perception, domain of sensation, and the field of freedom. It is the zero point of orientation. Body has primacy in the case of touch. Husserl contends that my living body is an in-between, i.e., it is neither internal to my consciousness nor external to me in the environment, but a thing inserted in between the material world and the subjective sphere. Lived body also has a role in empathy or empathetic transfer, which is the key factor determining my relationship with the others' lived body, which is neither derived, deduced nor inferred from my body. Although my body is a self-enclosed entity, it is always open, revealing its incompleteness. My embodiment proves my bodily existence, that I live my body, yet with a certain degree of alienation from the same in the experience of illnesses and ailments. I conclude the chapter with a discussion of the different modes and layers of the lived body, revealed through its salient features.

Husserl on Life world: A Conceptual Overview (Chapter 8) and the notion of the other are based on genetic phenomenology. Husserl formulated his notion on Life world in *Crisis of European Sciences*, though his examination of the notion of the other can be found in *Cartesian Meditations* and in his post-*Crisis* writings. Husserl discusses the notion of the world from the beginning of his phenomenological career. He begins with empirical notions of the same in *Logical Investigations*, proceeding to describe both empirical and the subjective phenomenological world in *Ideas I*. His talk on the empirical world led him to examine the phenomenological, subjective world, insofar as phenomenology requires a transcendent reference for its theoretical enterprise. Though his examinations began with the empirical world in *Ideas I*, he progressively delved deeper into the transcendental, phenomenological, subjective world, no more mentioning the former, further into his career. Husserl compares and contrasts the subjective, phenomenological world, namely Life world, with Galileo's mathematical, objective world, pointing out the pitfalls of considering the world merely from the point of view of its primary and secondary qualities. He holds that everything in the world is given with its horizons constituting meaning; no object is given devoid of its horizon, and one needs to make genuine efforts to discover them. Husserl was initially hesitant to include science, scientists and scientific theories into the domain of Life world. But he modified his stance on further reflection, proceeding to include them under the cultural, constitutive component of the same, thus widening the scope and ambit of Life world, and in doing so, that which was once anathema, became its part and parcel. He also points out that objectivity, spoken about by scientists, is born in the very heart of subjectivity. Life world is the pre-given world, always and already given, the foundation of the yet to be constituted, and on which the scientific world is created. It is the *a priori*, necessary given world of science and scientific facts. It is also the pre-theoretical world, the centre stage for the unfolding of everyday, practical life, and the world of our immediate experience.

Husserl's Notion of the Other and Intersubjectivity (Chapter 9) is a phenomenological approach to social philosophy and Husserl treatment of intersubjectivity. We live amongst others in a society in a plurality of selves. Husserl deals with problems faced by a philosophy that insists on the primacy of consciousness, especially that of solipsism. He sorts out the issue in *Cartesian Meditations*, *Crisis of European Sciences* and Post-*Crisis* period writings. But he is not involved in the pursuit of proving or disproving anything that is best left to empirical sciences. He merely attempts to elucidate the question of intersubjectivity for purposes of better understanding. Solipsism claims that 'I' alone exist as a subject. But our experience lets us know that others exist too, each a subject of his own experience and object of my experiences. But the source of the other cannot be myself, yet is drawn from me, and made possible as I transfer my sense of myself to the other, by analogy, transcending my sphere of ownness. In other words, I analogically transfer my sense of ego from myself to the other, attributing my characteristics and qualities to the other. Since I am aware of myself as a *Leib* and not as a *Körper*, I cannot deny the same to the other, implying that the other is a *Leib* in himself. The basis for this analogical understanding of the other is reciprocity, i.e., since I am a subjectivity in myself, so too is the other. Husserl goes on to extend his reciprocity, speaking of an egological community, or a community of persons. This equalization by reciprocity not only abolishes the privileges of the single transcendental ego, but establishes equality of all members, dethroning my ego, and abolishing its exclusive rights. Husserl remarks that the potential to constitute intersubjectivity is *a priori* in me, since the other is present in my intentionality; this openness to the other is the condition for the possibility of my concrete experience of the other. Therefore, intersubjectivity is the *a priori* condition for the bodily experience of the other as well. Husserl's transitions from transcendental (singular) subjectivity in *Ideas I* to transcendental communitarian subjectivity is praiseworthy. This begs the question, is there any inconsistency in Husserl from 1913-1936? The answer should be in the negative, since he contends that apodictic transcendental subjectivity constitutes the world as intersubjective, with a co-equal other. Moreover, Husserl's position involves a transition from static to genetic phenomenology.

Husserl's Understanding of Lived Time (Chapter 10) is a summary of his enquiries on time, which began long before his elucidation of phenomenological concepts. Though he changed his stance several times with respect to other notions and ideas, he stood his ground, being absolutely sure about the validity of his initial insights into time. He holds that the question of time provides unity to all phenomenological notions, and that the phenomenological analysis of time consciousness can be undertaken only by the constitution of temporal objects. The perception of succession and change, unlike the perception of a temporal object like a chair, would have been impossible if consciousness was related exclusively to the present. But there are differences in the perception of static temporal objects and those involving succession and change. Time is the very basis of consciousness and all conscious experiences are temporal. How can one be conscious of the past and future while being conscious only of the present? Husserl answers this on the basis of his notion of *width of presence*, borrowed from William James, calling it the gnawing or extended present, in which he differs from Aristotle's notion of knife-edged present, considering it to be a duration block.

He explains this further using the notion of horizon, stating that the present phase or primal impression is given along with its horizons, namely, retention, or the consciousness of just having been, and protention or the consciousness of the immediate future, the expectation of something just about to occur. Primal impression never appears without its two horizons, retention and protention. It is not just a now-point or a pluck, but instead, the now phase presented along with its horizons. It has privileged status, being the point of origin or the moment of genesis; it is the point of reference of all temporal experiences. Retention and protention exist only with reference to the now phase. Retention was once prime impression, while protention will shortly become prime impression. Retention signifies the intentional relation of the just-past consciousness to the now phase. It is our attitude to the present as it slips into the past; it presupposes self-awareness, for it is the immediate awareness of the just-past as it sinks down. Husserl also speaks about the retention of retentions, double intentionality, including longitudinal and transverse intentionalities, making a strict distinction between retention and recollection.

Protention is the other horizon of primal impression. Intentionality gives us a sense of immanent future experiences, the yet-to-occur. It is not expectation in the usual sense, for it is the window to the yet-to-occur future, the opening to the new now. I fulfil my intuitions about the future by moving to the future phase through protention, since intuition extends beyond the present phase.

This is called the fulfilment of intentionality by Husserl. Husserl, being a 'transcendental idealist', was not satisfied with finding plurality as the source for the unity of primal impression, protention and retention. The source of unity, according to him is absolute consciousness, since time originates from temporalization, which in turn begins from the transcendental ego, i.e., the absolute consciousness, which temporalizes itself. Absolute consciousness consists of three components, namely, a) intentional consciousness or consciousness of the object; b) subjective consciousness or lived time, which is the domain of lived experiences, revealed by bracketing objective time and phenomenological reductions; it is the temporality of time within subjectivity; c) absolute time consciousness, constituting not merely subjective time, but itself temporally. It is the self-temporalization of temporality, unaffected by changes occurring in objective time. It does not arise or diminish like the temporality of intentionality, and is different from subjective time as well. In other words, absolute time is a-temporal or supra-temporal, distinguishing it from objective and subjective time. It is also called inner-time consciousness, one that occurs by self-temporalization of the transcendental ego, giving rise to primal impression, retention and protention. Therefore, primal impression, retention and protention in their unity, constitute primal impression, while absolute consciousness is their source. I am my experiences; there is an identity between myself and my experiences, cemented by the self-temporalization of the transcendental ego.

Inner-time consciousness involves three points, the first being self-awareness of the stream of consciousness, also called pre-reflective or absolute consciousness; it is the pre-reflective self-awareness of our experiences, implying that it is an intrinsic feature of our consciousness rather than an intentional act. The second point is the awareness of the temporal objects in one's own subjectivity, which is subjective reflective consciousness, while the third is objective time or the intentional consciousness of transcendent objects.

Chapter 10 also traces the journey and timeline of Husserl's understanding and development of time consciousness, in and through his lectures, edited and published by Heidegger entitled, *On the Phenomenology of the Consciousness of Internal Time, Bernau Manuscripts*, and finally the *C-Manuscripts* published under different volumes of *Husserliana*. Husserl's notion of time consciousness emanates a certain kind of mysticism, which I would call the transcendental mysticism of subjectivity.

The brief **Chapter 11** entitled, *On Presuppositionlessness in Phenomenology*, is an enquiry into Husserl's reasonings into presuppositionlessness in phenomenology, along with a summary of my personal quest for answers on the same. It might serve to remove misunderstandings into Husserl's said claim of phenomenology being a presuppositionless philosophy, aided by clarifications into which presuppositions were deleted from his phenomenology.

In the second part of the Conclusion, I wish to say the following. It is not my intention to blow my own trumpet. But I wish to call a spade a spade by an honest analysis of this book, and its differences from several other celebrated works of acclaimed authors. This book primarily deals with cardinal themes in Husserl's phenomenology from all his major phases. The question of meaning is one of the most important themes in his realist, static phenomenology, derived from my reflections and studies on *Logical Investigations*. Some may point out several other topics, equally important, that have not been included here. But this in no way minimizes their importance. Chapters 5 & 6 discuss Husserl's transcendental phase, derived from Ideas. Chapter 6 on *noema* and *noesis* also includes Føllesdal's analysis, derived from *Ideas III*. The examination of Lived body (Chapter 7) is from *Ideas II*, thus bringing all three *Ideas* into the purview of my study. Chapters 8 & 9 represent Husserl's genetic phase, gleaning thoughts from two books, *Cartesian Meditations* and *Crisis of European Sciences*, in addition to relevant material borrowed from writings from the post-*Crisis* period, which I consider his fourth phase. Chapter 10 also includes not just these four phases, but also traces back to Husserl's pre-phenomenological period, when he began writing about time consciousness as early as 1893, long before *Logical Investigations*, continuing to do so even in the post-*Crisis* period. I have no essays dealing exclusively with the latter period, as I am of the opinion that Husserl did not propose any new themes during that period; rather he continued to contribute materials and clarifications to append his previous phases. In this book, unlike several other notable and acclaimed survey books, I have dealt with all major, hardcore philosophical topics of Husserl's phenomenology.

Further reading materials furnished at the end of each chapter include books and materials that I used for my study and reflection. This book is aimed at doctoral and masters level scholars of Husserl's phenomenology and other allied disciplines, though it in no way constitutes a textbook. The treatment of topics is meant to equip them to read and study Husserl's original texts. Let me put it like this, I have not come across a single book with exhaustive analyses on all major themes of the four phases of Husserl's phenomenology, except this.

Chapter 12

Appendix

12.1 On Presuppositionlessness in Phenomenology

Ever since the beginning of my studies in phenomenology, as a student in the undergraduate courses, I have been listening to my teachers repeatedly stating that phenomenology is a presuppositionless science of philosophical reflections like Descartes's *cogito, ergo, sum*. It was also reiterated immediately thereafter, that the genesis of phenomenology is consciousness, intentionality and transcendental ego. With insufficient academic resources or intellectual acumen to question them, I left it at that at the time. But it continued to bother me, as I knew that Descartes, like Kant, refers to consciousness, and to (transcendental) ego. On one occasion, Professor Richard Sorabjee of the University of London told me that the notion of intentionality (of Husserl) originates from scholastic philosophy, which in turn is derived from Aristotle, through Avicenna (980-1037). This compounded to my problems of Husserl's presuppositionlessness of phenomenology. It made me feel that Husserl's contention regarding the latter meant something other than what is ordinarily spoken about. Its meaning must be sought elsewhere. I read books, talked to my teachers and friends. But I was left in the lurch without any satisfactory answers.

During my doctoral studies at the University of Delhi under the supervision of Professor Margaret Chatterjee, she pointed out that there are several kinds of presuppositions in the philosophical discourse, namely, a) material, b) cognitive and c) formal. Material presupposition consists in assuming that there is an external world, whose events are causally ordered, while cognitive presupposition expresses the belief that it is possible for us to know something, or that there is valid knowledge. Formal presupposition is the contention that the subject, copula, and the predicate scheme of judgement will lead us to substance. The fourth is the assumption regarding the validity of the central concept of predecessors. For example, Descartes' claim of *cogito, ergo, sum* is rooted in St. Augustine's contention regarding the credibility of his claim that, 'I doubt, therefore, I exist'. Karl Marx took it for granted that Hegel's dialects was valid for his own philosophy as well. Another presupposition is the claim that 'philosophy must be relevant to life, and a guide to human happiness'. Prof. Chatterjee pointed out that Husserl rejected all these presuppositions outrightly, including those of natural sciences.

Though it might be true, doubt continued to sow seeds in my mind with no satisfactory answers.

In February 2001, Professor Lester Embree, Chairman, Centre for Advanced Research in Phenomenology (CARP) visited Pondicherry to deliver lectures in the first workshop on phenomenology, conducted by Centre for Phenomenological Studies. During one of our discussions, I raised the question of presuppositionlessness in Husserl. He replied that in the early stages of the development of phenomenology, several scholars and commentators believed it to be Husserl's original insight. But now many Husserlian scholars are sure that the notion of presuppositionlessness is not just a philosophical or a phenomenological issue, as Husserl remarked so, when he rejected Catholic assertions regarding the infallibility of the Pope, immaculate birth of Mary, the mother of Jesus, the question of purgatory, etc. Hence it has very little to do with philosophy. Further questioning did not produce any more satisfactory answers. After a long wait of almost two decades, here is my explication for the same.

Centre for Phenomenological Studies conducted one of its programmes, a three-day workshop-cum-seminar on Time Consciousness in Husserl and Heidegger in Chennai in January 2019. Dr Thomas Kalary, a doctoral student of Professor Friedrich-Wilhelm von Herrmann at Freiburg im Breigau, delivered lectures on Heidegger's *Treatment of Time Consciousness*. It may be noted that Professor von Herrmann assisted Heidegger for a long time and was the chief editor of *Collected Works of Heidegger, Gesamtausgabe*. Dr Kalary is one of the translators of Heidegger's *Mindfulness*. Dr Kalary, during one of his lectures delivered on Heidegger's *Treatment of Time Consciousness*, remarked that after the first world war, paucity of funds forced several German universities to obtain financial support from the Catholic church, who in turn insisted that all professors take the 'Oath against Modernism and Affirmation to the Church' in order to obtain funds. The church's doctrines on the infallibility of the Pope, immaculate birth of Mary, purgatory, etc., formed part of the oath. And, the Church punished those who opposed, or criticised them. Husserl, who was born a Jew, converted to a Catholic much later under the persuasion and influence of his wife. Husserl's contention was that all such teachings and doctrines that do not require any philosophy were nothing but presuppositions for academic work. Husserl's claim that phenomenology is a presuppositionless science summarizes his strong criticism, stringent censure and vehement opposition to such doctrines hidden in the garb of the philosophical assertion of presuppositionlessness. It may also be noted that Husserl's teacher, Franz Brentano, a Catholic priest, a well-known philosopher and an eminent psychologist, was defrocked from priesthood, excommunicated from the church, and forced to resign his teaching position from the University of Vienna, as he vociferously criticized the Church's teachings on the infallibility of the Pope, a doctrine promulgated by the First Vatican Council (1869-1870). The church punished him very harshly. Unlike Brentano, Husserl was wise and kept himself away from open confrontations with the Church, and hence, managed to escape persecution from the same. He clothed his criticism of the Church's doctrines in philosophical attire, which is the historical background of Husserl's notion of presuppositionlessness in phenomenology. Hence any discussion on the same should be taken with a pinch of salt. As Professor Embree pointed out, it has very little to do with phenomenology. True, Husserl has not explicated his theory about his understanding of presuppositionlessness; had he done so, he would have gotten in trouble with the church. This is the meaning of the same to be understood from historical context. To put the entire discussion on a positive note, the 'Oath against Modernism and Affirmation to the Church' were just presuppositions for Husserl, ones that could be ignored in the context of phenomenology.

Unfortunately, without knowledge of the historical background of Husserl's claims on presuppositionlessness, many authors and commentators criticized Husserl very strongly. Among the several papers that I read, two stand out, one by Dr Robert W. Burch (Burch, 1975). I fail to understand why people write with such negativity. The second paper is by Philip Pettit (Pettit, 1972). It appears to me that Pettit is under the impression that Husserl uttered his last word in his phenomenological career in 1907 in *Idea of Phenomenology*. Hume's advice is very relevant and meaningful in this and several other contexts: "Understand the whole, do not criticise the parts." All that I can say about such authors is this, they are trying to shoot a black cat in a dark room where there is no cat at all.

12.2 References

Burch, R. W. (1975). Two Basic Claims of Phenomenology. *Rice University Studies, 61*(3), 13–19.

Pettit, P. (1972). On Phenomenology as a Methodology of Philosophy. In W. Mays & S. C. Brown (Eds.), *Linguistic Analysis and Phenomenology* (pp. 241–255). Palgrave Macmillan UK.

Bibliography

Ashworth, P., & Lucas, U. (1998). What is the 'World' of Phenomenography? *Scandinavian Journal of Educational Research, 42*(4), 415–431.

Atkinson, M. (1972). A Precise Phenomenology for the General Scholar. *The Journal of General Education, 23*(4), 261–297.

Baggini, J. (2005). *What's it all about? Philosophy and the Meaning of Life.* Oxford University Press.

Behnke, E. A. (1996). Edmund Husserl's Contribution to Phenomenology of the Body in Ideas II. In *Issues in Husserl's ideas II* (pp. 135–160). Springer.

Bernet, R. (2009). Husserl's Early Time-Analysis in Historical Context. *Journal of the British Society for Phenomenology, 40*(2), 117–154.

Bernet, R. (2010). Husserl's new Phenomenology of Time Consciousness in the Bernau Manuscripts. In D. Lohmar & Y. Ichiro (Eds.), *On Time-New Contributions to the Husserlian Phenomenology of Time: Phaenomenologica 197* (pp. 1–19). Springer.

Bernet, R., & Brown, W. (1982). Is the Present Ever Present? Phenomenology and the Metaphysics of Presence. *Research in Phenomenology, 12*, 85–112.

Berrios, G. E. (1989). What is Phenomenology? A Review. *Journal of the Royal Society of Medicine, 82*(7), 425–428.

Brough, J. (1972). The Emergence of an Absolute Consciousness in Husserl's Early Writings on Time-Consciousness. *Man and World, 5*(3), 298–326.

Brough, J. B. (1987). Temporality and the Presence of Language. *Third Annual Symposium of Simon Silverman Phenomenology Center: Phenomenology of Temporality, Time and Language*, 1–32.

Brough, J. B. (1993). Husserl and the Deconstruction of Time. *Review of Metaphysics, 46*(3), 503–536.

Brough, J. B. (2010). Notes on the Absolute Time-Constituting Flow of Consciousness. In D. Lohmar & Y. Ichiro (Eds.), *On Time-New Contributions to the Husserlian Phenomenology of Time: Phaenomenologica 197* (pp. 21–49). Springer.

Buttimer, A. (1976). Grasping the Dynamism of Life world. *Annals of the Association of American Geographers, 66*(2), 277–292.

Cairns, D. (1976). *Conversations with Husserl and Fink: Phaenomenologica 66.* The Hague: Martinus Nijhoff.

Carman, T. (1999). The Body in Husserl and Merleau-Ponty. *Philosophical Topics, 27*(2), 205–226.

Carr, D. (1970). Husserl's Problematic Concept of the Life world. *American Philosophical Quarterly, 7*(4), 331–339.

Carr, D. (1973). The 'Fifth Meditation' and Husserl's Cartesianism. *Philosophy and Phenomenological Research, 34*(1), 14–35.

Chapman, H. M. (1966). Realism and Phenomenology. In M. Natanson (Ed.), *Essays in Phenomenology* (pp. 79–115). Springer, Dordrecht.

Chatterjee, M. (1973). *The Existential Outlook.* The Orient Longman, Delhi.

Chattopadhyaya, D. P., Mohanty, J. N., & Embree, L. E. (Eds.). (1992). *Phenomenology and Indian Philosophy.* Indian Council of Philosophical Research in association with Motilal Banarsidass Publishers, New Delhi.

Chernyakov, A. (2002). *The Ontology of Time: Being and Time in the Philosophies of Aristotle, Husserl and Heidegger.* Springer-Science+Business Media, B.V.

Cooper, D. E. (2003). *Meaning (Central Problems of Philosophy).* McGill-Queen's University Press.

Cunningham, S. (1976). Language and the Phenomenological Reduction. In *Language and the Phenomenological Reductions of Edmund Husserl: Phaenomenologica 70* (pp. 14–34). Springer Science & Business Media.

de Beauvoir, S. (1948). Personal Freedom and Others. In B. Frechtman (Trans.), *The Ethics of Ambiguity* (pp. 35–73). Citadel Press, N.J.

De Preester, H. (2008). From Ego to Alter Ego: Husserl, Merleau-Ponty and a Layered Approach to Intersubjectivity. *Phenomenology and the Cognitive Sciences, 7*(1), 133.

De Warren, N. (2009). *Husserl and the Promise of Time: Subjectivity in Transcendental Phenomenology.* Cambridge University Press.

De Warren, N. (2014). Time. In S. Luft & S. Overgaard (Eds.), *The Routledge Companion to Phenomenology* (pp. 190–201). Routledge (Taylor & Francis), London and New York.

Dreyfus, H. L. (1993). Heidegger's Critique of the Husserl/Searle Account of Intentionality. *Social Research, 60*(1), 17–38.

Drummond, J. J. (1975). Husserl on the Ways to the Performance of the Reduction. *Man and World, 8*(1), 47–69.

Drummond, J. J. (1996). The 'Spiritual' World: The Personal, the Social, and the Communal. In T. Nenon & L. Embree (Eds.), *Issues in Husserl's Ideas II* (pp. 237–254). Springer-Science+Business Media, B.V.

Drummond, J. J. (2003). The Structure of Intentionality. In D. Welton (Ed.), *The New Husserl: A Critical Reader* (pp. 65–92). Indiana University Press.

Drummond, J. J. (2007). *Historical Dictionary of Husserl's Philosophy.* Scarecrow Press.

Drummond, J. J. (2012). Intentionality. In S. Luft (Ed.), *The Routledge Companion to Phenomenology* (pp. 125–134). Routledge.

Duranti, A. (2010). Husserl, Intersubjectivity and Anthropology. *Anthropological Theory, 10*(1–2), 16–35.

Durfee, H. A., & Rodier, D. F. T. (1989). *Phenomenology and Beyond: The Self and its Language.* Kluwer Academic Publishers, Dordrecht, The Netherlands; Boston.

Edie, J. M. (1965). *An Invitation to Phenomenology: Studies in the Philosophy of Experience.* Quadrangle Books, Chicago.

Edie, J. M. (1976). *Speaking and Meaning: The Phenomenology of Language.* Bloomington: Indiana University Press.

Ehrich, L. C. (2003). Phenomenology: The Quest for Meaning. In *Qualitative Educational Research in Action: Doing and Reflecting* (pp. 52–79).

Elliston, F. A. (1977). Husserl's Phenomenology of Empathy. In F. A. Elliston & P. McCormick (Eds.), *Husserl: Expositions and Appraisals* (pp. 213–236). University of Notre Dame Press.

Elliston, F. A., & McCormick, P. (1977). *Husserl: Expositions and Appraisals* (F. A. Elliston & P. McCormick, Eds.). Univ of Notre Dame Press.

Embree, L. (1997). *Encyclopedia of Phenomenology Contributions to Phenomenology* (E. A. Behnke, D. Carr, C. J. Evans, J. Huertas-Jourda, J. J. Kockelmans, W. R. McKenna, A. Mickunas, J. N. Mohanty, T. M. Seebohm, & R. M. Zaner, Eds.; Vol. 18). Springer-Science+Business Media, B.V.

Embree, L. E. (2012). *Can the Doing of Phenomenology be Learned?* Florida Atlantic University.

Evans, C. J. (1996). Where is the Life world? In T. Nenon & L. Embree (Eds.), *Issues in Husserl's Ideas II* (pp. 57–65). Springer-Science+Business Media, B.V.

Farber, M. (1943). *The Foundations of Phenomenology, Edmund Husserl and the Quest for a Rigorous Science of Philosophy*. Harvard University Press.

Fink, E. (1995). *Sixth Cartesian Meditation. The Idea of a Transcendental Theory of Method* (R. Bruzina, Trans.). Bloomington: Indiana University Press.

Finlay, L. (2009). Debating Phenomenological Research Methods. *Phenomenology & Practice, 3*(1), 6–25.

Flores-González, L. M. (2008). Phenomenological Views on intersubjectivity: Towards a Reinterpretation of Consciousness. *Integrative Psychological and Behavioral Science, 42*(2), 187–193.

Franck, D. (2014). *Flesh and Body: On the Phenomenology of Husserl* (J. Riviera & S. Davidson, Trans.). Bloomsbury Publishing.

Gallagher, S. (2001). Dimensions of Embodiment: Body Image and Body Schema in Medical Contexts. In S. K. Toombs (Ed.), *Handbook of Phenomenology and Medicine* (pp. 147–175). Springer Netherlands.

Gallagher, S. (2009). Two Problems of Intersubjectivity. *Journal of Consciousness Studies, 16*(6–7), 289–308.

Gallagher, S. (2012). *Phenomenology*. Palgrave Macmillan UK.

Geniusas, S. (2012). *The Origins of the Horizon in Husserl's Phenomenology*. Springer Netherlands.

Gurwitsch, A. (1973). On the Intentionality of Consciousness. In R. M. Zaner & D. Ihde (Eds.), *Phenomenology and Existentialism* (pp. 102–119). Capricorn Books.

Hall, D. E. (2004). *Subjectivity*. Routledge (Taylor & Francis), London and New York.

Hart, J. (1992). *The Person and the Common Life*. Springer Netherlands.

Heelan, P. A. (2001). The Life world and Scientific Interpretation. In S. K. Toombs (Ed.), *Handbook of Phenomenology and Medicine* (pp. 47–66). Springer-Science+Business Media, B.V.

Heidegger, M. (1978). The Concept of Time in the Science of History. *Journal of the British Society for Phenomenology, 9*(1), 3–10.

Heinämaa, S. (2011). The Body. In S. Luft & S. Overgaard (Eds.), *The Routledge Companion to Phenomenology* (pp. 222–232). Routledge (Taylor & Francis), London and New York.

Held, K. (2003a). Husserl's Phenomenological Method. In D. Welton (Ed.), *The New Husserl: A Critical Reader* (pp. 3–31). Indiana University Press.

Held, K. (2003b). Husserl's Phenomenology of the Life-World. In D. Welton (Ed.), *The New Husserl: A Critical Reader* (pp. 32–64). Indiana University Press.

Held, K. (2010). Phenomenology of "Authentic Time" in Husserl and Heidegger. In D. Lohmar & Y. Ichiro (Eds.), *On Time-New Contributions to the Husserlian Phenomenology of Time: Phaenomenologica 197* (pp. 21–49). Springer.

Husserl, E. (1960). *Cartesian Meditations* (D. Cairns, Trans.). Springer-Science+Business Media, B.V.

Husserl, E. (1965). *Phenomenology and the Crisis of Philosophy* (Q. Lauer, Trans.). Harper & Row, Publishers, New York.

Husserl, E. (1975a). *Experience and Judgment: Studies in Phenomenology and Existential Philosophy* (J. S. Churchill & K. Ameriks, Trans.). Northwestern University Press.

Husserl, E. (1975b). *Introduction to the Logical Investigations* (E. Fink, Ed.; C. H. Peters & P. J. Bossert, Trans.). Martinus Nijhoff, The Hague, Netherlands.

Husserl, E. (1976). *Ideas: General Introduction to Pure Phenomenology and to a Phenomenological Philosophy* (W. R. B. Gibson, Trans.). Humanities Press.

Husserl, E. (1977a). *Logical Investigations, Volume 1* (J. N. Findlay, Trans.). Routledge & Kegan Paul.

Husserl, E. (1977b). *Logical Investigations, Volume 2* (J. N. Findlay, Trans.). Routledge & Kegan Paul.

Husserl, E. (1977c). *Phenomenological Psychology, Lectures, Summer Semester, 1925* (J. Scanlon, Trans.). Springer Netherlands.

Husserl, E. (1980). *Phenomenology and the Foundations of the Sciences: Third book, Ideas Pertaining to a Pure Phenomenology and to a Phenomenological Philosophy* (T. E. Klein & W. E. Pohl, Trans.). Martinus Nijhoff Publishers, The Hague.

Husserl, E. (1981a). *Husserl: Shorter Works*. University of Notre Dame Press.

Husserl, E. (1981b). Husserl's inaugural lecture delivered at the University of Freiburg in Breisgau on May 3 1917. In P. McCormick & F. A. Elliston (Eds.), *Husserl: Shorter Works* (pp. 9–17). University of Notre Dame Press.

Husserl, E. (1981c). Pure Phenomenology, its Method, and its Field of Investigation. In P. McCormick & F. A. Elliston (Eds.), *Husserl: Shorter Works*. University of Notre Dame Press.

Husserl, E. (1989). *Ideas Pertaining to a Pure Phenomenology and to a Phenomenological Philosophy: Second Book: Studies in the Phenomenology of Constitution (Husserliana: Edmund Husserl-Collected Works, Vol. 3)* (R. Rojcewicz & A. Schuwer, Trans.). Martinus Nijhoff Publishers.

Husserl, E. (1991). *On the Phenomenology of the Consciousness of Internal Time (1893-1917): Husserliana: Edmund Husserl-Collected Works, Volume 4* (J. B. Brough, Trans.). Springer Netherlands.

Husserl, E. (1999). *The Idea of Phenomenology: Husserliana: Edmund Husserl-Collected Works, Volume 8* (L. Hardy & R. Bernet, Trans.). Kluwer Academic Publishers.

Husserl, E. (2001). *The Shorter Logical Investigations* (J. N. Findlay, Trans.). Routledge (Taylor & Francis), London and New York.

Husserl, E. (2006). *The Basic Problems of Phenomenology* (F. Ingo & G. H. James, Trans.). Springer Netherlands.

Hutcheson, P. (1980). Husserl's Problem of Intersubjectivity. *Journal of the British Society for Phenomenology, 11*(2), 144–162.

Iyer, A. (2010). Transcendental Subjectivity, Embodied Subjectivity and Intersubjectivity in Husserl's Transcendental Idealism. *Epistemology, Archaeology, Ethics Current Investigations of Husserl's Corpus,* 66–76.

Kern, I. (1977). The Three Ways to the Transcendental Phenomenological Reduction of the Philosophy of Edmund Husserl. In F. A. Elliston & P. McCormick (Eds.), *Husserl: Expositions and Appraisals* (pp. 126–149). University of Notre Dame Press.

Kersten, F. (1989). *Phenomenological Method: Theory and Practice.* Springer Netherlands.

Kircher, T., & David, A. (Eds.). (2003). *The Self in Neuroscience and Psychiatry.* Cambridge University Press.

Kockelmans, J. J. (1967). *A First Introduction to Husserl's Phenomenology.* Duquesne University Press.

Kockelmans, J. J. (1994a). *Edmund Husserl's Phenomenology.* Purdue University Press.

Kockelmans, J. J. (1994b). Intentionality in Logical Investigations. In *Edmund Husserl's Phenomenology* (p. 92). Purdue University Press.

Kortooms, T. (1993). Following Edmund Husserl on one of the Paths Leading to the Transcendental Reduction. *Husserl Studies, 10*(3), 163–180.

Küng, G. (1977). Phenomenological Reduction as Epoché and Explication. In F. Elliston & P. McCormick (Eds.), *Husserl: Expositions and Appraisals* (pp. 338–349). University of Notre Dame Press.

Lauer, Q. (1978). *The Triumph of Subjectivity: An Introduction to Transcendental Phenomenology.* Fordham University Press.

Lee, N.-I. (2006). Problems of Intersubjectivity in Husserl and Buber. *Husserl Studies, 22*(2), 137–160.

Liangkang, N. (2010). Horizontal-Intention: Time, Genesis, History-Husserl's Understanding of Their Immanent Relationship. In D. Lohmar & Y. Ichiro (Eds.), *On Time-New Contributions to the Husserlian Phenomenology of Time: Phaenomenologica 197* (pp. 187–211). Springer.

Lohmar, D. (2010). On the Constitution of the Time of the World: The Emergence of Objective Time on the Ground of Subjective Time. In D. Lohmar & Y. Ichiro (Eds.), *On Time-New Contributions to the Husserlian Phenomenology of Time: Phaenomenologica 197* (pp. 115–136). Springer.

Luft, S. (1998). Husserl's Phenomenological Discovery of the Natural Attitude. *Continental Philosophy Review, 31*(2), 153–170.

Luft, S. (2002). Husserl's Notion of the Natural Attitude and the Shift to Transcendental Phenomenology. In *Phenomenology World-Wide* (pp. 114–119). Springer.

Luft, S. (2004). Husserl's Theory of the Phenomenological Reduction: Between Life world and Cartesianism. *Research in Phenomenology, 34*(1), 198–234.

Luft, S. (2012a). Husserl's Method of Reduction. In S. Luft & S. Overgaard (Eds.), *The Routledge Companion to Phenomenology* (pp. 243–253). Routledge.

Luft, S. (2012b). Husserl's method of reduction. In S. Overgaard & S. Luft (Eds.), *The Routledge Companion to Phenomenology* (pp. 243–253). Routledge (Taylor & Francis), London and New York.

Luijpen, W. A. (1965). *Phenomenology and Metaphysics.* Pittsburgh: Duquesne University Press.

Luis, N. (2010). Temporality, Stream of Consciousness and the I in The Bernau Manuscripts. In D. Lohmar & I. Yamaguchi (Eds.), *On Time-New Contributions to the Husserlian Phenomenology of Time: Phaenomenologica 197* (pp. 213–230). Springer Netherlands.

Mall, R. A. (1993). Phenomenology-Essentialistic or Descriptive? *Husserl Studies, 1*(10), 13–30.

McIntyre, R. (1986). Husserl and the Representational Theory of Mind. *Topoi, 5*(2), 101–113.

McIntyre, R. (1987). Husserl and Frege. *Journal of Philosophy, 84*, 528–535.

McIntyre, R., & Smith, D. W. (1989). Theory of Intentionality. In J. N. Mohanty & McKenna William R (Eds.), *Husserl's Phenomenology: A Textbook* (pp. 147–179). Washington: D.C.: Center for Advanced Research in Phenomenology: University Press of America.

McKenna, W. R., Harlan, R. M., & Winters, L. E. (Eds.). (1981). *Apriori and World: European Contributions to Husserlian Phenomenology.* Springer Netherlands.

McNamara, M. S. (2005). Knowing and Doing Phenomenology: The Implications of the Critique of 'Nursing Phenomenology' for a Phenomenological Inquiry: A Discussion Paper. *International Journal of Nursing Studies, 42*(6), 695–704.

Melnick, A. (2011). *Phenomenology and the Physical Reality of Consciousness.* John Benjamins Publishing Company.

Mensch, J. (2010). Retention and the Schema. In D. Lohmar & Y. Ichiro (Eds.), *On Time-New Contributions to the Husserlian Phenomenology of Time: Phaenomenologica 197* (pp. 153–168). Springer.

Mensch, J. R. (1988). *Intersubjectivity and Transcendental Idealism.* SUNY Press.

Mensch, J. R. (1999). Husserl's Concept of the Future. *Husserl Studies, 16*(1), 41–64.

Merleau-Ponty, M. (1973). What is Phenomenology? Preface. In R. M. Zaner & D. Ihde (Eds.), *Phenomenology of Perception* (pp. vii–xxiv). Capricorn Books.

Mohanty, J. N. (1970). Phenomenology and Ontology. In *Phenomenology and Ontology: Phaenomenologica 37* (pp. 92–106). Springer Netherlands.

Mohanty, J. N. (1971). Husserl's Concept of Intentionality. In A.-T. Tymieniecka (Ed.), *Analecta Husserliana: The Yearbook of Phenomenological Research, Volume 1* (pp. 100–132). Reidel Publishing Company, Dordercht-Holland.

Mohanty, J. N. (1976). *Edmund Husserl's Theory of Meaning: Phaenomenologica 14.* Martinus Nijhoff Publishers, The Hague.

Mohanty, J. N. (1977a). Edmund Husserl's Theory of Meaning. In F. A. Elliston & P. McCormick (Eds.), *Husserl: Expositions and Appraisals* (pp. 18–37). University of Notre Dame Press.

Mohanty, J. N. (1977b). Husserl's Thesis of the Ideality of Meanings. In J. N. Mohanty (Ed.), *Readings on Husserl's Logical Investigations* (pp. 76–82). Martinus Nijhoff, The Hague.

Mohanty, J. N. (Ed.). (1977c). *Readings on Husserl's Logical Investigations.* Martinus Nijhoff Publishers, The Hague.

Mohanty, J. N. (1989). *Husserl's Phenomenology: A Textbook.* Washington: D. C.: Center for Advanced Research in Phenomenology: University Press of America, 1989.

Mohanty, J. N. (2002). On Husserl's Theory of Meaning. In B. Gupta (Ed.), *Explorations in Philosophy: Essays by J N Mohanty* (pp. 44–60). Oxford University Press.

Moran, D. (2000). *Introduction to Phenomenology.* Routledge (Taylor & Francis), London and New York.

Moran, D., & Embree, L. E. (Eds.). (2004). *Phenomenology: Critical Concepts in Philosophy, Volumes 1-5.* Routledge (Taylor & Francis), London and New York.

Moran, D., & Mooney, T. (Eds.). (2002). *The Phenomenology Reader* (1st ed.). Routledge.

Morrison, R. P. (1978). Kant, Husserl, and Heidegger on Time and the Unity of 'Consciousness'. *Philosophy and Phenomenological Research, 39*(2), 182–198.

Murphy, R. T. (1980). *Hume and Husserl: Towards Radical Subjectivism: Phaenomenologica 79.* Springer Netherlands.

Natanson, M. (Ed.). (1966). *Essays in Phenomenology.* Martinus Nijhoff, The Hague.

Nenon, T., & Embree, L. E. (Eds.). (1996). *Issues in Husserl's Ideas II: 24 (Contributions to Phenomenology).* Springer Netherlands.

Nota, J. (1967). *Phenomenology and History.* Loyola University Press, Chicago, IL.

Pol, V., & Luft, S. (Eds.). (2010). *Epistemology, Archaeology, Ethics Current Investigations of Husserl's Corpus.* Continuum International Publishing Group.

Poulet, G. (1956). *Studies in Human Time* (E. Coleman, Trans.). John Hopkins Press.

Rabanaque, L. R. (2010). The Body as Noematic Bridge between Nature and Culture. In P. Vandevelde & S. Luft (Eds.), *Epistemology, Archaeology, Ethics Current Investigations of Husserl's Corpus* (pp. 41–52). Continuum International Publishing Group.

Rajan, S. P. (1987). *Towards a Critique of Cultural Reason.* Oxford University Press.

Rajan, S. P. (1991). *Studies in Phenomenology, Hermeneutics, and Deconstruction.* Allied Publishers.

Rajan, S. P. (1998). *Beyond the Crisis of the European Sciences.* Indian Institute of Advanced Studies, Shimla.

Ricœur, P. (1967). *Husserl: An Analysis of his Phenomenology.* Northwestern University Press.

Ricœur, P. (1973). Existential Phenomenology. In R. Zaner & D. Ihde (Eds.), *Phenomenology and Existentialism* (pp. 87–98). Capricorn Books.

Rodemeyer, L. (2003). Developments in the Theory of Time-Consciousness: An Analysis of Protention. In D. Welton (Ed.), *The New Husserl: A Critical Reader* (pp. 125–156). Indiana University Press.

Rodemeyer, L. M. (2010). A Return to Retention and Recollection: An Analysis of the Possible Mutual Influence of Consciousness and its Content. In D. Lohmar & Y. Ichiro (Eds.), *On Time-New Contributions to the Husserlian Phenomenology of Time: Phaenomenologica 197* (pp. 231–249). Springer.

Saha, D., & Laxmikanta, P. (Eds.). (2014). *Phenomenological Meaning*. Northern Book Centre, New Delhi.

Sakakibara, T. (2010). Reflection Upon the Living Present and the Primal Consciousness in Husserl's Phenomenology. In D. Lohmar & Y. Ichiro (Eds.), *On Time-New Contributions to the Husserlian Phenomenology of Time: Phaenomenologica 197* (pp. 251–271). Springer.

Sartre, J.-P. (1970). Intentionality: A Fundamental Idea of Husserl's Phenomenology. *Journal of the British Society for Phenomenology, 1*(2), 4–5.

Scanlon, J. (1996). Objectivity and Introjection in Ideas II. In T. Nenon & L. Embree (Eds.), *Issues in Husserl's Ideas II* (pp. 213–222). Springer-Science+Business Media, B.V.

Scarry, E. (1985). *The Body in Pain: The Making and Unmaking of the World*. Oxford University Press, New York.

Schütz, A. (1966). Some Leading Concepts of Phenomenology. In M. Natanson (Ed.), *Essays in Phenomenology* (pp. 23–39). Springer Netherlands.

Silverman, H. J., & Ihde, D. (Eds.). (1985). *Hermeneutics and Deconstruction*. SUNY Press.

Smith, D. A. (2003). *Husserl and the Cartesian Meditations*. Routledge (Taylor & Francis), London and New York.

Smith, D. W. (2007). *Husserl*. Routledge.

Smith, D. W., & Thomasson, A. L. (Eds.). (2005). *Phenomenology and Philosophy of Mind*. Oxford University Press.

Smith, F. J. (1970). *Phenomenology in Perspective*. Springer Netherlands.

Sokolowski, R. (1964). *The Formation of Husserl's Concept of Constitution: Phaenomenologica 18*. Martinus Nijhoff, The Hague.

Sokolowski, R. (1974). *Husserlian Meditations* (J. M. Edie, Ed.). Northwestern University Press.

Sokolowski, R. (1988). *Edmund Husserl and the Phenomenological Tradition: Essays in Phenomenology*. Catholic University of Amer Press, 1988.

Spiegelberg, H. (1971). *The Phenomenological Movement: A Historical Introduction: Phaenomenologica 5*. Martinus Nijhoff Publishers, The Hague.

Stefano, M. (2010). The Temporalizations of the Absolute Flow of Time-Consciousness. In D. Lohmar & I. Yamaguchi (Eds.), *On Time-New Contributions to the Husserlian Phenomenology of Time: Phaenomenologica 197* (pp. 169–185). Springer Netherlands.

Ströker, E. (1993). *Husserl's Transcendental Phenomenology* (L. Hardy, Trans.). Stanford University Press, Stanford (CA).

Sukale, M. (1976). *Comparative Studies in Phenomenology*. Springer Netherlands.

Taipale, J. (2014). A Priori Intersubjectivity. In *Phenomenology and Embodiment: Husserl and the Constitution of Subjectivity* (pp. 69–86). Northwestern University Press, Illinois.

TeHennepe, E. (1965a). Expressive Meanings. In J. M. Edie (Ed.), *An Invitation to Phenomenology: Studies in the Philosophy of Experience* (pp. 240–251). Quadrangle Books, Chicago.

TeHennepe, E. (1965b). The Life world and the World of Ordinary Language. In J. M. Edie (Ed.), *An Invitation to Phenomenology* (pp. 132–146). Quadrangle Books, Chicago.

Theunissen, M. (1984). *The Other: Studies in the Social Ontology of Husserl, Heidegger, Sartre, and Buber* (C. Macann, Trans.). MIT Press.

Thomas, V. C. (1990). The Development of Time Consciousness from Husserl to Heidegger. In A.-T. Tymieniecka (Ed.), *The Moral Sense and Its Foundational Significance: Self, Person, Historicity, Community: Analecta Husserliana* (pp. 347–360). Springer, Dordrecht.

Thomas, V. C. (1997). Lived Time: Some Reflections. In S. J. Kozhamthadam (Ed.), *Interrelations and Interpretations* (pp. 246–264). Intercultural Publications, New Delhi.

Thomas, V. C. (2014). Phenomenological Concern for the Meaning of Existence. In D. Saha & P. Laxmikanta (Eds.), *Phenomenological Meaning* (pp. 1–14). Northern Book Centre, New Delhi.

Thompson, E. (2001). Empathy and Consciousness. *Journal of Consciousness Studies, 8*(5–6), 1–32.

Thompson, M. G. (2005). Phenomenology of Intersubjectivity: An Historical Overview of the Concept and Its Clinical Implications. In J. Mills (Ed.), *Intersubjectivity and Relational Theory in Psychoanalysis* (pp. 35–70). Hillsdale, NJ & London.

Toombs, S. K. (2001). Reflections on Bodily Change: The Lived Experience of Disability. In S. K. Toombs (Ed.), *Handbook of Phenomenology and Medicine* (pp. 247–261). Springer Netherlands.

Tripathy, L. K. (1989). *Husserl's Theory of Intentionality* [Master's Thesis]. University of Poona.

Tymieniecka, A.-T. (Ed.). (1991). *Husserl's Legacy in Phenomenological Philosophies: New Approaches to Reason, Language, Hermeneutics, the Human Condition. Book 3: Phenomenology in the World Fifty Years after the Death of Edmund Husserl.* Springer-Science+Business Media, B.V.

Weigelt, K. (2008). *The Signified World: The Problem of Occasionality in Husserl's Phenomenology of Meaning* [Doctoral Thesis]. Stockholm University, Sweden.

Welton, D. (1983). *The Origins of Meaning: A Critical Study of the Thresholds of Husserlian Phenomenology.* Martinus Nijhoff Publishers.

Welton, D. (1997). World. In L. E. Embree, E. A. Behnke, D. Carr, J. C. Evans, J. Huertas-Jourda, J. J. Kockelmans, W. R. McKenna, A. Mickunas, J. N. Mohanty, T. M. Seebohm, & R. M. Zaner (Eds.), *Encyclopedia of Phenomenology* (pp. 736–743). Springer-Science+Business Media, B.V.

Welton, D. (2003a). *The New Husserl: A Critical Reader.* Indiana University Press.

Welton, D. (2003b). World as Horizon. In D. Welton (Ed.), *The New Husserl: A Critical Reader* (pp. 223–232). Indiana University Press.

Wojnar, D. M., & Swanson, K. M. (2007). Phenomenology: An Exploration. *Journal of Holistic Nursing, 25*(3), 172–180.

Yoshimi, J. (2016). *Husserlian Phenomenology: A Unifying Interpretation.* Springer.

Zahavi, D. (1997). Horizontal Intentionality and Transcendental Intersubjectivity. *Tijdschrift Voor Filosofie, 59*(2), 304–321.

Zahavi, D. (1999). *Self-Awareness and Alterity: A Phenomenological Investigation.* Northwestern University Press.

Zahavi, D. (2001). *Husserl and Transcendental Intersubjectivity: A Response to the Linguistic-Pragmatic Critique* (E. A. Behnke, Trans.). Ohio University Press.

Zahavi, D. (2003a). Husserl's Intersubjective Transformation of Transcendental Philosophy. In D. Welton (Ed.), *The New Husserl: A Critical Reader* (pp. 233–254). Indiana University Press.

Zahavi, D. (2003b). *Husserl's Phenomenology.* Stanford University Press.

Zahavi, D. (2004). Husserl's Noema and the Internalism-Externalism Debate. *Inquiry, 47*(1), 42–66.

Zahavi, D. (2010). Empathy, Embodiment and Interpersonal Understanding: From Lipps to Schutz. *Inquiry, 53*(3), 285–306.

Zaner, R. M., & Ihde, D. (Eds.). (1973). *Phenomenology and Existentialism.* Capricorn Books, G.P. Putnam's Sons, NY.

Index

A

a posteriori level, 142, 143
act of perception, 83, 84, 173
aesthological, 106
apodicity of existence, 140
apperception, 6, 114, 115, 135, 138, 139, 140, 144, 149, 150
apprehension, 42, 59, 116, 131, 138, 148, 150, 154, 173, 178

B

Bedeutung, 44, 51, 52, 54, 85, 86, 87, 93, 98
being qua experience, 111, 112
being-qua-being, 111
bracketing, 17, 29, 65, 66, 68, 112, 171, 184, 189

C

cogitatum, 35
communicative speech, 2, 46, 47, 50
conceptual dualism, 112
confirmative speech, 2, 46, 47, 69, 183
constitutive awareness, 116,
constitutive intentionality, 36
corporeal body, 104

D

Dasein, 19, 20, 88, 176, 181
degrees of intentionality, 35

descriptive phenomenology, 10, 41, 182
descriptive psychology, 14, 15
descriptive science, 10
double intentionality, 120, 164, 165, 189

E

eidetic reduction, 46, 47, 57, 69, 71, 73, 137, 183, 185
empathetic transfer, 5, 116, 186
empirical realism, 140
empiricists' reduction, 68
epistemological reduction, 68

F

field of localization, 36, 108,

G

genetic constitution, 34
genetic phase, 6, 18, 181, 190
genetic phenomenology, xiii, 3, 5, 19, 20, 59, 104, 112, 158, 159, 187, 188
givenness, 10, 17, 30, 32, 82, 91, 107, 108, 117, 130, 136, 154

H

hermeneutic phenomenology, 10, 20, 41, 44, 181
horizon intentionality, 34, 35
horizontal intentionality, 6, 135, 144, 204

horizontal notion of
  intersubjectivity, 142
hyle, 35, 36, 100, 119, 158
hypostasizing, 54

I

ideal entity, 30, 41, 42, 79, 82, 183
ideality thesis, 46
I-monads, 6
inner-time consciousness, 155,
  171, 172, 189
instinctual level, 142, 146
intending acts of expressions, 52
intentional consciousness, 7, 32,
  55, 170, 172, 189
intentional correlate, 34, 43, 44,
  52, 53
intentional noema, 95, 98
intentionality of emotion, 35
intentionality of retention, 165

K

kinaesthetic characteristics, 108
Körper, 4, 35, 103, 104, 105, 106,
  111, 113, 138, 139, 140, 185, 187

L

Lebenswelt, 17
Leib, 4, 35, 104, 105, 108, 138, 139,
  140, 185, 186, 187
linguistic expressions, 45, 46, 49,
  50, 52, 94, 183
longitudinal intentionality, 164

M

mathesis univerlais, 17
meaning-conferring acts, 49
medium of reference, 52, 56

N

naturalistic attitude, 32, 35, 81,
  106, 107
noematic reflection, 55
noematic Sinne, 31, 89
noetico-noematic, 34, 53
Nunc stans, 159, 169, 175

O

object of perception, 83, 111, 112,
  114, 145
object of reference, 52, 56
objective space, 104, 106, 107, 109,
  148
objectivism, 126, 133
object-oriented attitude, 82
object-pole of consciousness, 185
ontological divide, 50
ontological neutrality, 112
ontological reduction, 68
open intersubjectivity, 135, 142,
  144, 145
open subjectivity, 6
operative intentionality, 34
organ and field of freedom, 4, 108,
  109
organ of movements, 106
organ of perception, 4, 83, 108,
  109, 110, 114, 186

P

passive synthesis, 35
perception by way of sense
  organs, 84
perception of reality, 109
perceptual noema, 5, 83, 84, 91,
  93, 94, 95, 96, 98, 100
personalistic attitude, 107, 108,
  186

Phainomena, 1
phenomenological attitude, 48,
   68, 79, 104, 107, 108, 138, 186
phenomenological reflection, 31,
   81, 90, 92
phenomenology of double
   sensation, 113
Platonism, 54, 60
plurality of subjects, 114, 145
pre-reflective consciousness, 55
presumptive ideality, 49
presuppositionlessness, 7, 189,
   191, 192, 193
primacy of touch, 5, 110, 111
psychic constitution, 142
psychic phenomenon, 28
psychological reduction, 69, 70,
   71, 72, 73, 184
psychologism, 13, 47, 51, 72, 183

R

realistic empiricism, 14
reciprocity of consciousness, 142
Rede, 46
reduction by critique of positive
   sciences, 70
reduction by intentional
   psychology, 70
reduction by the Cartesian Way, 70
reduction by the ontological way,
   70
reduction via Life world, 70
referent, 31, 44, 45, 50, 138
reflective capacity, 116
reflective consciousness, 55, 66,
   172, 189
retentional modification, 162, 163,
   168

S

self-temporalisation, 7, 171
sense perception, 4, 82, 84, 98
sense-field, 104
sensibility, 105
solipsism, 136, 138, 143, 150, 187
spatio-temporal horizon, 123
sphere of consciousness, 4, 111,
   112
sphere of ownness, 136, 137, 138,
   149, 150, 187
static phenomenology, 5, 112, 151,
   190
subjective attitude, 107
subjective experience(s), 11, 113,
   115, 145, 158
subject-pole, 185
synthesis of association, 142
synthesis of association and
   identity, 142

T

temporality of meanings, 91
transcendent reference, 84, 94, 98,
   186
transcendental attitude, 65, 67
transcendental idealism, 11, 14,
   140
transcendental intersubjectivity,
   10, 136, 146, 150, 151
transcendental phase, xiii, 6, 17,
   190
transcendental sphere, 19, 73, 138
transcendental subjectivity, 10, 11,
   17, 113, 146, 187
transcendental-psychological
   reduction, 69, 184
transfer of sense, 115
trans-phenomenality, 33, 127
transverse intentionality, 164

W

Weltanschauung, 11
we-relationships, 148
world as horizon, 127
world of immediate experience,
    126, 129, 130, 131, 132
world of things and subjects, 106

Z

zero point of orientation, 4, 109,
    110, 186

Authors

A

Adolf Boehm, 75
Aristotle, 14, 28, 35, 48, 81, 95, 154,
    155, 188, 191
Atkins, 70
Avicenna, 28, 191

B

Brentano, 1, 2, 15, 27, 28, 29, 30,
    54, 77, 87, 95, 161, 182, 185, 192,
    193

C

Cairns, 146

D

de Bore, 28, 93

E

Edith Stein, 6, 74, 86, 156
Ehrlich, 70

Euclid, 1, 14

F

Farber, 51, 69
Frege, 3, 31, 49, 50, 51, 52, 53, 75,
    82, 93, 100, 183

H

Hegel, 1, 15, 57, 64, 191
Hume, 18, 77

I

Iso Kern, 69, 70, 73, 75, 184

J

James, 26, 33, 154, 174, 188

K

Kochelmans, 4, 91, 184

L

Lambert, 1, 14, 15
Langsdrof, 4, 70, 91, 92, 185
Larabee, 4, 91, 92, 185
Lotze, 50, 51, 54, 183
Luft, 70, 73, 75, 185

M

Mach, 1
MacIntyre, 4
McKenna, 4, 91, 92, 185
Merleau-Ponty, xiii, 9, 19, 41, 68,
    181, 182
Mohanty, 2, 29, 36, 37, 38, 51, 54,
    57, 58, 89, 182, 183

N

Natanson, 69

O

Oetinger, 1, 14, 15

R

Ricœur, 19

S

Sartre, 9, 10, 19, 33, 41, 55, 56, 68, 88, 91, 127, 147, 149, 181, 182
Scheler, 105
Schröder, 3, 50, 51, 183
Schütz, 4, 75, 91, 148, 149, 150
Smith, 4, 70, 91
Søren Overgaard, 71, 184
Spiegelberg, 105

W

Walsh, 70, 184

Books

A

Algebra der Logik, 51, 61
An Introduction to Metaphysics, 44
Analyses Concerning Passive and Active Synthesis, 120, 167, 178

B

Basic Problems of Phenomenology, 1, 6, 8, 69, 76, 104, 105, 108, 121, 123, 133, 136, 152, 184, 199
Being and Nothingness, 19, 91, 147, 152, 182
Bernau Manuscripts, xiv, 6, 156, 157, 158, 159, 178, 179, 189, 191, 195, 200

C

C-Manuscripts, xiv, 6, 9, 157, 158, 159, 175
Confessions by St. Augustine, 10
Conversations with Husserl and Fink, 146, 151, 195
Critique of Pure Reason, 15, 17, 21

F

Field of Consciousness, Theme, Thematic Field and Margin, 86
From Hegel to Existentialism, 57, 61

M

My Experiments with Truth, 10

N

Nature and Spirit, 4, 105, 106, 112, 114
Noema und Sinn, 85, 93, 94,

O

On the Phenomenology of the Consciousness and Internal Time, 6

P

Phenomenological Psychology, 4,
20, 35, 105, 119, 120, 159, 176,
198
Phenomenology of Perception, 19,
21, 200
Philosophy of Arithmetic, 3, 8, 50,
183
Problems of Intersubjectivity, 105,
197, 199
Psycholog from an Empirical
Standpoint, 15, 20, 29

T

The Crisis of European Sciences
and Transcendental
Phenomenology, xiii, 3, 5, 6, 7,
60, 118, 132, 178
The Development of Husserl, 28,
60, 100
The Idea of Phenomenology, 3, 8,
46, 60, 69, 71, 73, 74, 76, 178, 198
Thing and Space, 4, 103, 104, 107,
185
Time and Individuation, 74, 156,
157

www.ingramcontent.com/pod-product-compliance
Lightning Source LLC
Chambersburg PA
CBHW050433280326
41932CB00013BA/2098